301.44
T85s

84130

DATE DUE			
Feb 4 '76			
Nov 27 ?8			

The Social Context of Ambition

CHANDLER PUBLICATIONS IN
ANTHROPOLOGY AND SOCIOLOGY

Leonard Broom, *Editor*

THE SOCIAL

CONTEXT OF AMBITION

A Study of High-School Seniors in Los Angeles

By Ralph H. Turner
University of California
Los Angeles

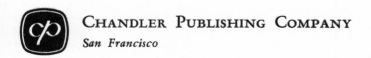

CHANDLER PUBLISHING COMPANY
San Francisco

16939

June 12, 1969

301.44
T85s
84130
aug 1973

To

HERBERT TURNER

and the memory of

HILDA TURNER

Contents

Tables

ix

Foreword

BEHIND MOST RESEARCH in the social sciences is the hope that light may be shed on some issue in human values. The day when the choice of values could be the exclusive province of philosophers and religionists is long past. The assertion of values is of little consequence when divorced from an adequate understanding of how the values will work out in practice. Without the meticulous research of the social scientist, the philosopher cannot say what value systems will work as intended, and what systems will produce unsought and destructive by-products.

Liberal democratic values have inspired a major portion of sociological research and have already been affected by its conclusions. The goal of a totally equalitarian society has suffered because of the social scientists' conclusions regarding the inevitability and social utility of some system of stratification. Hence, democratic values are increasingly translated to mean an open-class system, in which each individual is free to establish his own station in society within the limits of his inherited capacities, without help or hindrance from the socioeconomic level of his parents. Much effort has accordingly been devoted to measuring rates of mobility, as indicators of functioning democracy, and to uncovering conditions which facilitate or impede mobility.

But a popular suspicion that mobility leaves scars on the personalities of the successful and the unsuccessful alike, given impetus by the pronouncements of psychiatrists, poses a dilemma for the open-class interpretation of democratic values. If a high rate of mobility necessarily means a society whose direction is in the hands of a cadre of Molière's *bourgeois gentilshommes,* the very realization of democracy may lead to its negation, or to the destruction of other values of equal importance. Careful study of the effects of mobility is required to ascertain how serious is this dilemma, to suggest courses of action which will minimize it, and to aid in the definition of a goal of optimal mobility.

But mobility may be achieved in many ways and through diverse channels. If mobility does leave its impress on the personalities of the successful, that impress will certainly vary according to the nature of the mobility experience. Hence, a detailed examination of the social settings within which mobility is pursued and achieved is important to the ultimate interpretation of democratic values. It is to this objective that we hope this research will contribute.

The steps from empirical research to values are many and tortuous. A single research project is unlikely to supply conclusive implications for the realm of values. At best the project can supply a few new observations or perspectives which show the application of democratic values in a somewhat different light. It is our hope that certain ideas incorporated in this research, such as the stratification of destination, intrastratum ambition, value relevancy, and the value differentiation between male and female forms of ambition will make a small contribution of this character. We have generally avoided the direct discussion of value implications from our findings, in the conviction that scientific results are most useful when the investigator does not mix his roles. But the ultimate measure of this and related researches will be their contribution to the practical realization of democratic values.

An investigation of this character could not have been conducted without the assistance of many people. Financial support came from the Social Science Research Council and the U.C.L.A. Research Committee. Important initial encouragement came from Leonard Broom, now of the University of Texas, and the late Harold Jones, formerly West Coast representative of the S.S.R.C. Numerous colleagues gave advice and assistance at various stages in the investigation. Ruth Riemer, William S. Robinson, and Richard J. Hill patiently answered my statistical questions. Many discussions with Richard T. Morris supplemented my understanding of social-stratification research. He, William A. Lessa, and Richard Centers read critically an earlier version of the monograph. Matilda White Riley kindly sent me the questionnaire from her study of youth culture in advance of publication. Andrew Comrey generously supplied and helped me use his computer program for factor analysis. Among the student assistants who contributed some of their own thinking to the project were Milton Bloombaum, Judith Fairston Ellis, Will Kennedy, Sheldon Messinger, George Saunders, and Fred Thalheimer. The dedicated work of Robert Freeman had much to do with the successful administration of the questionnaires. And the critical work of Dorothy Fabian was crucial in the initial classification of questionnaire responses and devising the occupational scheme used in the study. Facilities of the U.C.L.A. Institute of Numerical Analysis and the Western Data Processing Center were extensively used in the statistical treatment of data.

Securing the data required the cooperation of many officials in the Los Angeles and Beverly Hills School Systems. The active help of Robert E. Kelly, Associate Superintendent of Schools, was the key to securing cooperation from principals and teachers in the Los Angeles system. Howard Bowman, Supervisor of Measurement, supplied much helpful advice toward revising the questionnaire and helped in many ways to work out detailed procedures for securing the data. All of the following principals smoothed the way for the use of their schools as subjects for the main investigation or pretests: D. Raymond Brothers, William W. Brown, George C. Dirkx, Thomas C. Dyer, John C. Holt, Malcolm MacDonald, Lowell McGinnis, Gerwin C. Neher, Richard Nida, Kenneth L. Peters, George J. Smith, Charles E. Sutcliffe. The help of teachers in the 97 classes in which the questionnaires were administered was uniformly generous, and their own interest in the problems of the investigation supplied many of the insights which have been reflected in the interpretation of the data.

Three papers which make use of these data have already been published. The first is an effort to characterize the mobility ideology of the men students and to relate it to changing social currents. The second relates ambition to certain family variables not discussed in the present report. The third compares 67 boys whose mobility orientations are extreme with nonmobile control groups with high and low socioeconomic backgrounds. The references are:

"The Changing Ideology of Success: A Study of the Aspirations of High School Men in Los Angeles," *Transactions of the Third World Congress of Sociology,* Vol. V (London: International Sociological Association, 1956), pp. 35–44; "Some Family Determinants of Ambition," *Sociology and Social Research,* 46 (July, 1962), pp. 397–412; "Upward Mobility and Class Values," *Social Problems,* 11 (Spring, 1964), pp. 359–371.

The Social Context of Ambition

CHAPTER ONE

The Nature and Background of the Investigation

To MANY a nineteenth-century American ambition was a simple matter. One either had it, or did not. If he had it, success was largely a foregone conclusion. Ambition was an uncomplicated personal trait, associated with strength of character. In pursuit of his goals, the ambitious man underwent a series of trials. As his ambition enabled him to pass each test, he became steadily more self-assured in his knowledge that he possessed the qualities all men envied.

The development of psychology and the social sciences in the twentieth century started a search for naturalistic causes of ambition. In many instances, investigators read the biographies of great men and tabulated their qualities so as to locate the personal traits and experiences most frequently associated with prominence.[1] A theory of level of aspiration, elaborated through experimental study, started with the simple assumption that present aspiration reflects prior experiences of success and failure.[2] Many social scientists looked for the clue to ambition in a family setting which taught the value of deferring present gratification for the sake of a greater reward in the future, and which taught the child to want the way of life and prestige which were most readily available to occupants of high stations in society.[3] In a comprehensive theory, David McClelland attributed ambition to a

[1] Cf., for example, Emory S. Bogardus, *Leaders and Leadership* (New York: D. Appleton-Century, 1934).

[2] Kurt Lewin, Tamar Bembo, Leon Festinger, and Pauline S. Sears, "Level of Aspiration," in J. McVeigh Hunt, ed., *Personality and the Behavioral Disorders* (New York: Ronald Press, 1944), I, pp. 333–378.

[3] Joseph Kahl, "Educational and Occupational Aspirations of 'Common Man' Boys," *Harvard Educational Review*, 23 (Summer, 1953), pp. 186–203; David J. Bordua, "Educational Aspirations and Parental Stress on College," *Social Forces*, 38 (March, 1960), pp. 262–269.

measurable personality characteristic known as the achievement motive, which in turn is produced in a family which expects early self-reliant mastery by the child, but does not practice generalized restrictiveness, authoritarianism, or rejection.[4]

The emerging scientific interest in ambition also turned attention toward its consequences for the individual, and led quickly to a less sanguine view of ambition. Anthropologists, psychiatrists, educators, and others became worried about the consequences of pervasive competitiveness, fearing that interpersonal hostility and uncertain self-esteem were the by-products.[5] Some investigators noted the stress involved in pursuing high ambitions, and found ambition a contributing factor in the production of neuroses and other personality disturbances.[6] Warner and Abegglen examined the personalities of successful men from modest backgrounds, suggesting that the practice of seeking friendships only for their usefulness and dropping them when they were no longer serviceable deprived ambitious people of the ability to establish genuine and intimate friendships.[7] Robert Stone noted that a greater concern for the good opinions of one's superiors and a lesser concern for the good opinions of one's peers is part of the complex of attitudes associated with ambition.[8]

While interest in ambition was taking these and other directions, the application of sociological thinking supplied a somewhat different perspective toward the subject. Neither the creation nor the pursuit of ambition takes place in a social vacuum. Complex societies generally seem to be divided into somewhat identifiable groups of people, and these classes or *strata* are ranked from the point of view of prestige and the possession of goods and power. Systems of stratification differ in the amount of movement they allow between strata. This movement is called vertical mobility—"mobility" because it is movement from one social location to another, and "vertical" because it represents either an improvement of or a loss of standing. In any open-class society—one which allows vertical mobility—ambition is likely to

4 David C. McClelland, *The Achievement Motive* (New York: Appleton-Century-Crofts, 1953), pp. 276–288; *The Achieving Society* (Princeton: Van Nostrand, 1961).

5 For example, cf. Karen Horney, *The Neurotic Personality of Our Time* (New York: W. W. Norton, 1937); Margaret Mead, ed., *Cooperation and Competition among Primitive Societies* (New York: McGraw-Hill, 1937).

6 August B. Hollingshead, Robert Ellis, and E. Kirby, "Social Mobility and Mental Illness," *American Sociological Review,* 19 (Oct., 1954), pp. 577–584.

7 W. Lloyd Warner and James C. Abegglen, *Big Business Leaders in America* (New York: Harper, 1955).

8 Robert C. Stone, "Mobility Factors as They Affect Workers' Attitudes and Conduct toward Incentive Systems," *American Sociological Review,* 17 (Feb., 1952), pp. 58–64.

find expression in the pursuit of upward mobility. Ambition, then, becomes a desire to abandon one social position and attain another. Its character and effects will depend largely upon the nature of the system of stratification and of the channels through which mobility occurs. When ambition is viewed as mobility-orientation, attention is redirected toward the social setting and the mobile person's relationship to that setting.

The present investigation is an effort to shed light on the social setting in which ambition is nurtured and in which it is translated into concrete steps in mobility. A complete examination of the social setting for mobility would require that different stages in the life cycle be explored. In childhood the individual's relationship with his peers and family, who constitute the stratum he will seek to leave, is crucial. In secondary school social contacts become more heterogeneous, the influence of parents loses its pervasiveness, and the individual is forced to make choices which will affect his future status. During young adulthood the practical side of implementing mobility is uppermost. Later still there is the endless process of working out the modus vivendi between one's present and past.

The study we report here is concerned with a single period, the conclusion of high school. Students are culminating a period of involvement in the adolescent peer group, they are preparing to go separate ways which will in many instances predetermine their future choice of careers, and they are beginning to assume adult status in society, with all that is entailed. This period is a major transition point in the individual's life cycle, in which the boy or girl is confronted by choices whose consequences are real, lasting, and relatively inescapable.

For our inspection of the social setting we draw mainly from two bodies of theory. (1) It is the sociological theory of social stratification that points our attention to the general characteristics of social strata, the relations between strata, the transportation of stratification into special settings such as the school, and leads us to look at ambition as an orientation toward mobility. (2) Limitation of the investigation to a particular time span leads us to draw upon a more recent, but rapidly growing, body of theory about the social organization and culture of youth groups in American society. The existence of a pervasive and influential social unit which is not fully integrated with the larger society, and which is anchored to the school setting, complicates any effort to explore mobility. Within youth society the larger scheme of stratification, the criteria for judging personal success and failure, and many other important facets of the social order undergo diffraction or are displaced by distinctively youthful systems. It is the manner in which the youth society comes to terms with the stratification system of the larger society which constitutes the major point of emphasis in this study.

However, a third type of theory is required to focus the use of concepts about stratification and youth society. Our purpose is to uncover aspects of the social setting which will determine what the effect of the mobility experience on the mobile person will be. Hence, some theory of the possible effects of upward mobility must serve as a guide, telling us what aspects of stratification and youth society to examine. Of the possible theories we have chosen that of the marginal man. As an approach it probably incorporates better than others the distinctively sociological way of thinking about mobility, and it has the added advantage of affording a more comprehensive perspective on the experience of mobility than many other theories.

In the discussion to follow, the theory of the marginal man will be our point of departure, leading us quickly into an effort to relate the alternative systems of organization suggested by stratification theory to the key dimensions of marginality theory. Except for a brief introduction, the extended discussion of the theory of youth society will be delayed until Chapter Six.

Although Chapter Two deals with the sample and method of the investigation, we can note briefly here that the findings are based on a sample questionnaire investigation involving 2,793 high-school seniors in Los Angeles and Beverly Hills, California. The questionnaire contained principally four kinds of items. One group of items was directed toward the student's ambitions. A second group was intended to identify his socioeconomic background. The third and longest group provided for choices involving a fairly wide range of hypothetically class-related values. A final group contained sociometric questions.

In general, the first two groups of items supplied the independent or causal variables and the other groups the dependent or effect variables. These in turn could be interrelated in two ways, to describe the general organization of the student community and to identify the place and characteristics of the upwardly mobile person.

THE MARGINAL MAN

The concept of the marginal man has had considerable currency since it was first introduced by Robert E. Park and elaborated by Everett Stonequist.[9] The term was first applied to the European Jew who

9 Robert E. Park, "Human Migration and the Marginal Man," *American Journal of Sociology*, 33 (May, 1928), pp. 881–893; Everett Stonequist, *The Marginal Man* (New York: Charles Scribner's, 1937).

sought to leave the ghetto, then, finding himself rebuffed, could no longer find satisfaction in the ghetto way of life. The conception seemed also to fit other minority groups and to describe the situation of many persons who belonged to no distinguishable racial or ethnic group. In the most general sense, the marginal man is an individual who lives on the border of two societies which make incompatible demands upon him. But before the term can be useful for present purposes a somewhat more precise conception must be developed.

Objective, Experiential, and Symptomatic Marginality

In practice, marginality has been identified in three distinct ways, which we can label *objective, experiential,* and *symptomatic. Objectively* a person is identified as marginal by the position he occupies. A marginal position is one which makes the occupant a member of two different groups or societies which place contradictory demands upon him. More technically, a marginal position is one whose role is legitimately defined by each of two societies or subsocieties in a contradictory manner. Reference to the foreman as the "marginal man of industry," meant initially that the position of foreman is not clearly located by consensus in either the labor or the management stratum. In some respects the foreman is expected to act as a laborer, and in other respects he is supposed to behave as a member of management.[10]

The *experientially* marginal man is one who experiences the conflicting demands which converge upon those in his marginal position. A person in a marginal position may be confused about his proper identification and torn by the conflicting demands, or he may regard himself unequivocally as a member of one group and not of the other. Thus objective marginality tends to induce experiential marginality, but does not invariably do so.

Those who occupy marginal positions and who experience them as such are hypothesized to develop certain characteristic personality traits which set them off from most of the nonmarginals. These characteristics are the consequence of an extended period of experiential marginality and represent long-term modifications in the individual's outlook. The individual's subjective marginality may be a private thing, an experience concealed from outsiders and only incompletely recognized by the individual himself. But the resultant personality characteristics show in the marginal man's interaction with others. Thus, in a legitimate sense it is appropriate to speak of them as the

[10] Donald E. Wray, "Marginal Men of Industry: The Foreman," *American Journal of Sociology,* 54 (January, 1949), pp. 298–301.

symptoms of marginality—the observable characteristics which point to the existence of experiential marginality. When the marginal man is identified by his possession of these characteristics, we shall say that the investigator has used the *symptomatic* rather than the objective or experiential criteria of marginality.

The personality characteristics or symptoms of marginality are of two general sorts. The first is the possession of a novel perspective from which to view events. The thoroughgoing involvement in two ways of thought allows escape from the limitations of the ordinary culture-bound individual. The marginal man is able to see each society with its system of values through the eyes of the other society. Thus what is absolute to the ordinary person is seen relativistically by the marginal man, who questions and criticizes the cultural axioms. He may also be able to conceive new ideas not available to the culture-bound. The great questioners and the great innovators in any era are likely to be marginal men.

While the foregoing qualities are those stressed by Robert Park in his exposition of the marginal-man concept, a second set of characteristics has received considerably more attention. These characteristics are the qualities which stem from the rootlessness, the isolation from intimate relationships, and the absence of clear standards to guide behavior, which plague the marginal person. Inability to make decisions, hypersensitiveness, irritability, lack of ease in interpersonal relations, inconsistency in behavior, are among the characteristics noted. Melvin Seeman has suggested that the creativity qualities of the marginal man appear when the individual solves his marginality problems so as to overcome this second set of characteristics.[11] In the original statements by Robert Park, however, case illustrations were cited of noted persons who continued to exhibit these qualities simultaneously with the inventiveness that won them fame.[12]

In research directed toward discovering whether the upwardly mobile person is a marginal man, the objective and experiential criteria of marginality should be pivotal. We cannot begin with the symptomatic criteria since many of them can be attributed to other circumstances than marginality. Thus either existence or absence of most of the symptomatic qualities could not of itself demonstate that marginality was present or lacking. The essential procedure is rather to determine first, whether the individual under study occupies a marginal position and experiences it as such and second, if he is subjectively marginal,

---

[11] Melvin Seeman, "Intellectual Perspective and Adjustment to Minority Status," *Social Problems*, 3 (January, 1956), pp. 142–153.

[12] Park, *op. cit.*

to test for the presence of the various hypothesized symptomatic characteristics of marginality.

The Marginality Experience

The marginal man is intensively involved in two groups or societies. These groups represent two things to him: on the one hand they are ways of life—cultures with their values and rituals; on the other hand they are groups in which he may find an identity and establish strong social ties. They consist of sets of values to guide his conduct and serve as the criteria by which to assess his personal worth. And they consist of people with whom to identify himself.

The assumed interdependence of these two phases of group membership was perhaps the most critical theoretical contribution of the marginal-man concept, an idea which has gained revived currency in recent discussions of compliant behavior [13] and reference-group behavior.[14]

In the classic illustration, the Jew who became fully absorbed in the outside and despised the ghetto culture was rebuffed in his attempts to be accepted as a member of the gentile world. Once he had rejected the value system of the ghetto, he could no longer be comfortable associating primarily with the people of the ghetto. Since he no longer shared their values he could no longer enjoy informal conversation with them, and he could not acknowledge their evaluations as criteria for his own self-estimate. Consequently, he sought like-minded persons for satisfying communication and peers through whose eyes he could establish his own identity. But when he was unable to establish social ties among gentiles, it became difficult for him to continue to accept their culture. Values exist not merely in abstraction but as the possession of a group of people. The resentments the rejected man felt after experiencing discrimination now made it difficult for him to continue to think highly of the gentile way of life.[15] His attitude toward either group's values affected his ability to establish close interpersonal relationships with its members, and his experience in interpersonal relationships affected his attitude toward the values held by that group.

Even when no group disapproval has been registered, the individual who has been an active member can hardly escape the feeling that he

[13] Leon Festinger, "An Analysis of Compliant Behavior," in Muzafer Sherif and M. O. Wilson, eds., *Group Relations at the Crossroads* (New York: Harper, 1953), pp. 232–256.
[14] Robert K. Merton, *Social Theory and Social Structure* (Glencoe, Ill.: Free Press, 1957), pp. 225–386.
[15] Louis Wirth, *The Ghetto* (Chicago: Univ. of Chicago Press, 1928), pp. 263 ff.

is personally disloyal to the members of the group when he no longer accepts their system of values. If the ties are strong, as are those to parents and intimate friends, the marginal man will wish to be able once again to accept his earlier set of values in order to overcome the sense of disloyalty.

The foregoing shows clearly that the involvement in the two groups must be intensive and not merely superficial. It is not enough simply to learn about another culture, or to visit in another society in the manner of a tourist or tradesman. Through his family and childhood associations, the marginal man has deeply internalized one way of life and been deeply involved as a group member. He has accepted the values of an outside group to such an extent that he thinks more like members of the outside group than of his original membership group. Accordingly, he is driven to think of himself as a member of the second group and to seek associations which will validate this conception of himself.

Finally, marginality hinges upon the inability to choose between the two groups. If a person is confronted with a choice but makes his selection and abides by it without regret, the essential condition for marginality is absent. The potential qualities of innovation and incisive criticism arise because the marginal man's involvement in the other culture prevents his ever accepting one culture uncritically, and because each culture provides an external perspective from which the other may be viewed.[16]

In the classic instance of the marginal man, the obstacle to a clear choice is the refusal of members of the outside group to accept the newcomer. However, there seems no valid reason why other sources of inability to choose should not be included.

UPWARD MOBILITY AS MARGINALITY

The justification for viewing the upwardly mobile person as a marginal man lies in the assumptions that there are distinct classes [17] in American society and that the mobile person is ambivalent toward these classes. Mobility is movement from one class to another and must be distinguished from mere improvement of standing within the same class. In order to supply the essential context for the marginality experience, these classes must be characterized by (a) somewhat distinct

---

[16] Everett Stonequist, *op. cit.*, pp. 218 ff.

[17] Although earlier writers had spoken of classes in American society, the serious argument for empirically verifiable classes was made by W. Lloyd Warner and Paul S. Lunt, in *The Social Life of a Modern Community* (New Haven: Yale University Press, 1941).

and contradictory systems of values and (b) some degree of class consciousness and ingroup loyalty which render strong ties across class lines untenable.

Subculture versus Culture Variation

To test for marginality we must first determine whether the students from various class backgrounds endorse different values or not. A variety of evidence from prior investigations makes it almost a foregone conclusion that some such correlation between class background and values will emerge. Indeed, if we failed to discover such a correlation, we might more readily suppose that our methods were at fault than to accept the finding at face value. What is more important, then, is to consider the extent and character of the class-value correlations.

High correlations between class background and values will make the experience of marginality relatively inescapable for the upwardly mobile person. Low correlations, while they do not rule out the marginality experience, mean more opportunity for a person to shift class membership without having to undergo a change in the values he endorses. Likewise, the range or variety of values which are class-linked will indicate whether the marginality experience is likely to incorporate a rather comprehensive crisis in the realm of values or whether the crisis is likely to be segmental. Finally, identification of the particular kinds of value differences between classes will enable us to speculate more intelligently about the nature and significance of the choices which an upwardly mobile person must make.

One issue will take precedence over all others in our exploration of class-value linkages. This is the choice between two contending hypotheses which we shall label the *culture-variation* hypothesis and the *subculture* hypothesis of class values. For clarity these hypotheses are stated as mutually exclusive explanations for the existence of correlation between class and values. In practice they need not be mutually exclusive, but may operate in some measurable combination to produce the observed correlations.

The subculture approach assumes that each class is to some degree a self-contained universe, developing a distinctive set of values which guides its members' way of life. While these class subcultures are constrained by the necessity to maintain working relations with other classes within a general national framework, the subcultures of different classes are in important respects mutually contradictory. Objects which are positively valued in one class subculture may be negatively valued in another. If it is true that the man who will fight to protect his honor against any slight, however minor, is highly esteemed in some lower-class groups and is despised as humorless and a trouble-maker in middle-class groups, we have an illustration of such value contradictions. According to this view, the classes have different conceptions of what objectives are worthy of pursuit and what qualities entitle a person to the esteem of his fellows.

Those who base their thinking overwhelmingly upon the subculture approach are likely to explain the presence of any nationally accepted values which crosscut class lines by the ascendance of one class within the nation. Thus we may be told that the transition to modern times in Europe witnessed a shift in dominant values away from those of the feudal aristocracy and toward those of the mercantile middle class. The relation between so-called national values and class values, then, remains an uneasy one, the dominated classes *accommodating* to the national values rather than accepting them as their own. National values play a small part in such a system since the apparent national values are in reality largely the imposed values of the ascendant class. Such an approach makes subculture rather than culture the key concept in the study of modern society, since class subcultures incorporate the systems of values which are most deeply rooted in the people's life situation.[18] Adherence to culture values, on the other hand, should be a fairly superficial matter because such values are imposed, rather than being a product of a life situation.

An extreme version of the subculture position depicts class differences in value as differences in kind rather than in degree. Objects positively valued in one class would either be neutral in value or negative in other classes. However, the essentials of the position can be maintained while asserting relative differences between classes. If two classes adopt the same values but assign different degrees of value to them, the value systems are in effect contradictory. If we assume that important courses of action usually require some choice among contending values, the relative importance assigned to different values is all-important. If, for example, both oratorical excellence and athletic prowess are positively valued, the relative importance assigned to each may still differ crucially. The result is that in one class athletic prowess is always the favored choice, and in another class oratorical excellence will be preferred.

The concept of the marginal man derives from such a view as this. The marginal man is confronted with the necessity of being disloyal to

18 Ruth Benedict many years ago suggested that the integrated cultures of modern society are class cultures rather than national cultures. Cf. *Patterns of Culture* (Boston: Houghton Mifflin Company, 1934), p. 230.

his earlier values as he adopts the values of the class into which he is moving. What is good by the criteria of one subculture is bad by the standards of the other. Such a conception was derived from the examination of ethnic subcultures which contain a core of values which are not indigenous to the larger society within which the subcultures are now found. Thus there is every reason to expect such contradictory subcultures when ethnic groups are involved. The issue when studying upward mobility is whether the same phenomenon may develop between subcultures which are indigenous to the same larger society.

The culture-variation approach, by contrast, begins by assuming a generally uniform system of values throughout a society and treats class differences as variations on a society-wide theme. Culture takes priority in analysis over subculture. The observed differences in values between classes arise because the characteristic life situation in each class makes any given value relatively attainable or unattainable, or relatively comprehensible or incomprehensible.

A distinction can be made between values and goals. Value is the more inclusive term, and not all objects of value become goals of endeavor to an individual. Discovering a rich uranium deposit would undoubtedly rank high as a value to most Americans, but to most people it remains too unattainable and remote to be translated into a goal. The difference does not render value in the broad sense meaningless or irrelevant.Most of us would regard the discoverer of such a rich uranium deposit with some awe and respect. At any moment when circumstances made the value appear more attainable and less remote we might readily adopt it as a goal.

Applied to class values, such a distinction points our search in the direction of class differences in the translation of society-wide values into goals rather than in the direction of contradictory values. Classes differ, then, not so much in generating distinctive value systems, but more in the relative emphasis and the embodiment of their society's values, which derive from their distinctive life situations.

Such an approach finds its simplest rationale in the psychological theory of level of aspiration.[19] The members of different classes differ in the ease with which many of society's values can be attained. Extrapolating beyond the experimentally verified aspects of level of aspiration theory, we suggest that the experience of success and failure in pursuing a given value, in pursuing related values, or in the observed experiences of one's immediate associates determines the relative emphasis placed upon that value within the total value hierarchy. If,

---

[19] Kurt Lewin *et al., loc. cit.*

for example, it is relatively more difficult for the lower-class child than for the middle-class child to satisfy his wants without stealing, theft need not cease to be a negative value, but may be regarded as a less severely negative value among working-class than among middle-class children. Attainment of worldly success and community prestige may not cease to be a value but may be less salient in the value system of the lower classes, to whom the prospects are less promising.

In order to distinguish the pattern of class-value differences which should prevail under this hypothesis from that which should prevail under the subculture hypothesis (in its moderate form allowing for relative differences in values), it is necessary to distinguish the acceptance of values as guides to one's own immediate behavior from their uses in other ways. If the culture-variation hypothesis is correct, we should expect to find class-value differences clustered in the realm of self-evaluation and find them less marked in other applications. Our concrete hypothesis, then, is that correlations between class and values vary directly with the proximity of their application to the individual's own behavior.

The situation of the upwardly mobile person in such a case is different from what it would be under the subculture condition. Under culture variation, the individual will have to make some alteration in his value system, but the alterations are in a direction comprehensible to him and to the friends and family in his class of origin. Raising one's sights is likely to be accompanied by adjustment pains, and there is bound to be an uncertain base for self-evaluation during the transition and perhaps permanently. But these pains do not incorporate the same element of moral conflict experienced in a change between groups with contradictory values. Some of the elements of marginality may be present because of the lack of well-established standards, but the whole classic pattern will not be there.

Class Consciousness versus Prestige Identification

A comparable distinction is important in the realm of social relations within and between classes. We shall call these contending hypotheses *class consciousness* and *prestige identification*. The former hypothesis assumes, in its extreme form, that the dominant interpersonal attitude among the classes is a highly developed ingroup-outgroup attitude. Ingroup superiority is assumed, and members of outgroups are viewed with resentment, contempt, suspicion, or fear, all tending toward hostility when any very active interclass relations are established. The class as ingroup demands loyalty first to its own members. Loyalties to the larger society are tolerated only to the extent to which they can be reconciled with class loyalties. Paralleling the assumptions of subculture theory, such an approach treats within-class loyalty as causally prior to society-wide loyalty, and explains the latter in terms of the former. Society-wide loyalties are strong in those classes whose interests are served by the existing relations among classes. Thus the present-day upper-middle class does not appear to have such provincial or ingroup loyalties because promoting the idea of classless loyalty serves their class purposes. Class consciousness should be present in a much more active and conspicuous fashion among the working classes for whom society-wide loyalties interfere with the exercise of intraclass obligations.

In such a setting, the upwardly mobile person is necessarily viewed by his own class as a traitor and by the class into which he moves as an unwelcome intruder. Even if the latter attitude is the lesser one, the attitudes of family and friends from his class of origin must be acknowledged. In attempting the shift, the mobile person must decide to accept antagonism and resentment from members of his class of origin which will make his return, in case he cannot establish himself satisfactorily at the high level, extremely awkward. Thus upward mobility is a process involving double risk: alienation from erstwhile friends and family and rejection by ingroup members at the higher level. Under such circumstances the most extreme sort of marginality crisis would be very likely to occur.

The *prestige-identification* thesis assumes that within-class loyalties, while they exist, are a small variation from a general pattern of establishing loyalties on the basis of other than class membership. Insofar as attitudes between classes are concerned, the ingrouping tendency is more than offset by gratification that comes from identifying with prestige figures. There is considerable satisfaction from merely being a member of the same society as a famous and successful man. Any claims whatever to closeness bring greater satisfaction. The young person imagines the day when he will achieve comparable standing, while the older person identifies in fantasy, imagining what he could have done had he really tried.

While it would run manifestly contrary to all knowledge to suggest that there is no greater social distance between classes than within classes, social distance can be of diverse sorts. Interclass social distance under the thesis of class consciousness is dominated by negative attitudes of fear, hostility, and contempt. The social distance between classes under the prestige-identification principle is the discomfort of association with the unfamiliar and awe of too closely intruding on the superior. The relationship is one of a genuine ambivalence. Persons at the lower levels would like to have the gratification obtainable from associating with persons of higher prestige than themselves. But the principal circumstance keeping the classes apart is the greater ease in associating with the familiar and the predictable.

In this type of setting, the upwardly mobile person augments the social distance between himself and the friends from his class of origin. There is likely to be mutual disappointment over the reduction of intimacy. But what the upwardly mobile person loses in intimacy he gains in the esteem in which he is held by his former fellows. Rather than despising him as a traitor, his early associates and family take personal pride through identifying with him in his successes. They are proud to claim him as one of their own who succeeded and are pleased to have him back among them whenever possible.

A term which best describes the social distance which thus exists between the mobile person and his former peers and family is *prestige isolation*. It is a common plaint of popular heroes and successful men that they do not have the close relations they would like with a few people. To some extent the admiration and respect accorded a superior being appears to be incompatible with a completely uninhibited and intimate relation.[20] The upwardly mobile individual, under this conception of interclass relations, experiences prestige isolation rather than hostility isolation in his relations with members of his class of origin.

The character of the marginality crisis brought about by prestige isolation will certainly be different from that brought on by hostile social distance. It will be much easier to aspire to mobility; personal maladjustment to one's class peers will be a less important variable in selecting the upwardly mobile, and the mobile person will seem to be risking less. However, the likelihood of continuing to maintain ties to the class of origin, which in turn prevent full consolidation of position in the class of aspiration, is greater because of the absence of hostility. The probable situation of the would-be upwardly mobile person who is not fully successful in a highly class-conscious society is almost complete isolation from effective ties to any class, making his position that of the declassé rather than of the strictly marginal person. Such an isolation is marked by hostility and resentment and, we might suppose, would characteristically lead to the attitude of the critic and the cynic. In a system marked by prestige identification, the upwardly mobile person is more likely to experience con-

---

20 Such an observation formed the basis for W. I. Thomas' distinction between the "wish for response" and the "wish for recognition." Cf. *The Unadjusted Girl* (Boston: Little, Brown, and Co., 1925), pp. 1–40.

tinuing ties so that his situation is one of divided loyalties rather than rejection of all ties. His situation is more correctly marginal since he retains effective membership in two classes. It is in such a person that we might expect to find the unusual breadth of understanding which comes from the ability to see events from alternate perspectives.

Anticipatory Socialization

Two further complications must be noted and taken into account in exploring these distinctions, however. One version of reference-group theory holds that people adopt the attitudes and values of groups to which they hope to belong or in which they are striving to achieve membership. They "anticipate" their future membership by learning in advance the attitudes which will be appropriate when they achieve the desired membership. This process has been dubbed *anticipatory socialization* by Robert Merton.[21] Needless to say, the learning cannot be altogether complete and accurate because the group attitudes are seen from outside. But the fewer the barriers to casual relations across established group lines, the greater the possibilities for such anticipatory socialization to take place.

Anticipatory socialization suggests the premarginality phase of the marginal-man sequence under another name. However, it conveys a process of considerably more generality, potentially affecting many more people. If a large share of persons had ambitions different from their parents' social strata, destination might be equally important as or more important than origin as a determinant of value cleavages among the students. If this were true, like-mindedness in values would lose much of its force in holding students to their strata of origin, but would gain force in bringing students together according to destination.

The most pertinent information about the probable situation in which the mobility-oriented student will find himself should be supplied by comparing the evidence of anticipatory socialization with the lines of cleavage in peer-friendship preference. If friendship cleavages remain strong along lines of family background in the face of considerable anticipatory socialization, the stage is set for a great deal of marginality. Many students would be prepared for mobility but unable

[21] Robert K. Merton and Alice Kitt, "Contributions to the Theory of Reference Group Behavior," in Robert K. Merton and Paul Lazarsfeld, eds., *Studies in the Scope and Method of the American Soldier* (Glencoe, Ill.: Free Press, 1950), pp. 40–105. It had been suggested earlier that class-atypical attitudes heralded preparation for mobility. Cf. Margherita MacDonald, Carson McGuire, and Robert J. Havighurst, "Leisure Activities and the Socioeconomic Status of Children," *American Journal of Sociology*, 54 (May, 1949), pp. 505–519.

to gain personal acceptance. If cleavages in friendship preference also take as much or more account of destination as of origin, then the transitions of mobility are considerably eased. If marginality were to characterize the upwardly mobile students, it would be in spite of the school situation rather than because of it.

Conventional analyses of social stratification often overlook the possibility that there may be a future-oriented system as well as one organized about each individual's past. But to the extent to which the entire orientation of a group of persons, such as those in a high school, is toward the future, there is good reason to consider the possibility of such a stratification system. Some foreign educational systems are specifically designed to institutionalize such stratification by early segregation of students according to probable destination. The possibility that some such organization may develop on a more informal basis under the American system deserves exploration.

Youth Subculture

The other complication is introduced by the concept of *youth subculture*. The idea of a somewhat special youth subculture in our society has been widely used since the term's introduction in a very brief statement by Talcott Parsons.[22] Youth culture is generally assumed to cut across class boundaries, to reject adult-imposed responsibilities, and to exalt qualities such as athletic prowess, glamor, and intense peer-group loyalty. If the youth culture enters deeply into the attitudes of the students in our investigation, there should be two important effects. First, the differentiation of values and discrimination of social ties along lines of either stratum of origin or stratum of aspiration will be obscured. Second, an intense and widely effective youth culture will constitute a serious obstacle to all ambitious students, forcing them to accept disparagement and social isolation as the cost of pursuing high academic success.[23]

The existence of a conspicuous youth subculture can hardly be seriously doubted. But the systematic study of the adolescent individual's relation to the subculture has yet to be conducted. There are questions to be asked about the proportion of adolescents who are affected by the subculture to an important degree: to what degree

22 "Age and Sex in the Social Structure of the United States," *American Sociological Review*, 7 (October, 1942), pp. 604–616.
23 The effects of different kinds of youth climates have been impressively documented by James S. Coleman, in *The Adolescent Society* (Glencoe, Ill.: The Free Press, 1961). Cf. also, Ernest A. Smith, *American Youth Culture: Group Life in Teenage Society* (New York: Free Press of Glencoe, 1962).

is the subculture a deeply internalized system of values or a playful ritual; to what degree is it participated in for enjoyment or from compulsion; to what degree is it a spontaneous phenomenon of youth or a commercial product "sold" by adult promoters; to what degree does it constitute a serious anti-adult and anti-parent coalition; and to what degree does it genuinely obscure social-class divisions?

The apparent overlap between what are often designated as class values and some of the elements of youth culture makes it essential that we deal explicitly with the latter in the investigation. Some facets of individualism, for example, have been labeled both middle-class values and anti-youth-culture values. But the further fact that we shall be studying students who are near the peak of their involvement in youth subculture requires that we consider the relation of ambition to acceptance of youth values. We shall look for evidence that there are some youth values which have an appeal which cuts across stratum boundaries, which are related to personal friendship desirability, and which are negatively related to ambition. To the extent to which we find each of these conditions, we would be justified in believing that the pattern of marginality is altered but not eliminated. The ambitious student encounters resistance, not from the higher group into which he seeks entry, but from the spokesmen for his peers. We shall also look for some evidence regarding the seriousness with which youth-culture values are internalized. If youth culture is merely a set of superficial rituals for many of its apparent adherents, its total impact will be significantly lessened, except on the student whose social isolation makes him insensitive to the distinction between the ritual and personal feelings.

Ambition Emphases

In our discussion of marginality we were forced to note that mobility has more than one facet, and that it is possible to be mobile in one respect and not in another. The conditions of marginality are best satisfied when mobility is total rather than merely segmental. But when mobility is segmental, the experience of the mobile person will vary according to the facet of mobility which he emphasizes. Perhaps the simplest such distinction that can be made is between acquisition of the material benefits of mobility and participation in a culturally superior way of life. An individual may be ambitious to achieve the greater luxury and security afforded by a higher income and appreciated by those from all walks of life, without looking toward any change in values. Such ambition is directed toward continuing in the same way of life with more of its advantages and fewer of its disadvantages. The mobility-orientation is segmental with an emphasis on material improvement.

The contrasting emphasis is upon participation in a way of life which involves activities popularly referred to as "cultural." A person with this sort of mobility-orientation seeks an environment more congenial to his interests in the arts, in intellectual subjects, in a "gentler" mode of social intercourse, than is the class into which he was born. Unlike people of the first type of segmental mobility-orientation, such an individual is likely to be interested in education for its own sake, for its content apart from strictly practical utility.

The person whose segmental mobility-orientation is toward material improvement is likely to eschew any but the strictly practical courses. Consequently, in our study of the mobile person's values and social position in relation to peer organization, we shall attempt to identify persons who represent these divergent kinds of segmental interest. We shall attempt to discover whether there are such instances, whether the persons' backgrounds are distinctive in any respects, and whether they endorse distinctive values and occupy special positions in the peer group. If, as we suppose, those who are segmentally mobile differ according to the main emphasis in their ambition, we shall seek such indications as will tell us about the probable relation of their experience to marginality. Ultimately there may be more gain from differentiating types of mobile persons in this fashion than in uncovering the characteristics of an undifferentiated mobile type.

PLAN OF THE BOOK

Chapter Two describes the sample and the collection of data. The extent of ambition and its relation to socioeconomic background is examined in Chapter Three. Chapter Four concerns the relationship between values and stratification, with major stress on the problem of value contradiction versus discrepancy and anticipatory socialization. The issue of class consciousness or prestige identification is treated in Chapter Five, on the basis of sociometric data. The applicability of the concept of youth subculture and its relation to the mobility experience is the subject of Chapter Six. In Chapter Seven we note some alternative emphases which may dominate mobility striving. And Chapter Eight offers conclusions and suggests some possible implications from the study.

CHAPTER TWO

The Nature of the Population and Sample

BEFORE REPORTING FINDINGS we must describe the characteristics of the sample and the procedures employed in securing the data. These topics are briefly reviewed in this chapter.

THE SAMPLE

The sample for the investigation consists of 1,352 boys and 1,441 girls from the senior classes (twelfth grade) of ten high schools in Los Angeles and Beverly Hills. It was clearly not practical, either financially or in the handling of sociometric data, to administer the questionnaire to a simple random sample of all students in the Los Angeles city or metropolitan area. Hence the sampling unit had to be at least whole classes and, most practically, whole schools. With this limitation, however, it was essential to sample as well as possible the range of socioeconomic backgrounds and ambitions to be found in the larger community.

Sampling Procedure

The high schools in these two systems offered a course entitled "Senior Problems" for all students in their last year. In the majority of schools this course is required, and a near-complete sampling of senior students from a given school can conveniently be secured by using these classes. The limitation was imposed on our sample, however, that we use only schools in which "Senior Problems" was a required course. Policies in this matter did not have any apparent relationship with socioeconomic characteristics of the areas in which schools were located.

In order to locate ten schools which would be representative of the socioeconomic range in Los Angeles, we employed the *index of social rank*, which had been devised by Eshref Shevky and Marilyn Williams specifically for the classification of social areas in Los Angeles, and subsequently modified in collaboration with Wendell Bell.[1] The index is formed by translating the proportion of the population in manual labor and the proportion with eight years of education or less into standard scores and averaging them. On the basis of 1950 census data the Laboratory in Urban Culture at Occidental College had already computed index values for each census tract in the city of Los Angeles, and these computations were made available to us by Scott Greer.

In order to select schools, we divided the census tracts into quartiles and noted schools which drew upon fairly homogeneous areas. We further noted the proportions of Negro and Mexican population and ruled out schools with very large proportions of nonwhite, non-Anglo populations. A few schools in the extreme southern portion of the city were eliminated because of inaccessibility, and, at the request of school officials, we excluded two schools which carried a heavy burden of student teaching and student research for the major universities in Los Angeles. Apparently suitable schools from each of the social-rank quartiles were investigated informally through school officials to determine whether census data gave a correct impression of the student bodies and whether notable shifts in population had occurred during the five years since the decennial census. In the final selection, we further attempted to use schools which were physically dispersed, particularly within each of the social-area-rank quartiles. Taking into account size of enrollment, we then settled upon two schools each from the two top quartiles and three each from the two bottom quartiles. A last-minute substitution was made for one top-level school in which the principal refused cooperation.

Although the social rank of adjacent census tracts was the basis for selecting the sample of schools, the socioeconomic level assigned to each school for correlational purposes was based on information supplied by the students in the questionnaire. Each student was assigned a *background-index* value ranging from zero to seven on the basis of the family breadwinner's occupation, education, and independent-employee status. Points were assigned for occupation as follows: unskilled, semiskilled labor, 0; skilled labor, clerical work, 1; small business, semiprofessional, business agents-managers, 2; professional, large-business owner-official, 3. Points were assigned for schooling as follows: no schooling, grade school, other, 0; high school, 1; business or trade school, junior college, 2; college graduate, postgraduate, 3. An addi-

[1] Eshref Shevky and Marilyn Williams, *Social Areas of Los Angeles* (Berkeley and Los Angeles: Univ. of California Press, 1949), pp. 37–40; Eshref Shevky and Wendell Bell, *Social Area Analysis* (Stanford: Stanford University Press, 1955), pp. 23–24, 54–55.

Table 1. Socioeconomic Characteristic of Schools

School level	Social-area rank	Mean background index		
		All students	Nonethnic students	
			Male	Female
High:				
A	1	5.30	5.13	5.52
B	2	3.74	3.89	3.73
Middle:				
C	3	3.50	3.52	3.51
D	4	3.22	3.23	3.21
E	7	2.72	2.72	2.91
F	6	2.59	2.82	2.69
G	5	2.47	2.53	2.37
Low:				
H	8	1.97	1.82	2.07
I	9	1.86	2.22	2.32
J	10	1.49	1.50	1.71

tional point was assigned if the breadwinner were self-employed or sometimes self-employed. The mean background-index value for all students who filled out questionnaires in a given school was computed and used as the school's socioeconomic rating.

Since the socioeconomic level of the senior class is probably higher than that of the whole school because of differential drop-out, the absolute index is an overestimate. However, as indicated in Table 1, there is very little discrepancy between the rank orders based on social area and mean background index. In no case is the grouping into high, middle, and low schools affected. There are two schools in which the rank is higher when Negro, Oriental, and Spanish-name students are eliminated. Schools "F" and "I" are both suburban centers of working-class Mexican population which the postwar building boom has surrounded with upper working-class and lower middle-class "Anglo" tract dwellings.

On the basis of the foregoing procedures we are relatively confident that the sample is representative of the twelfth-grade population of Los Angeles, though it is biased away from the most socioeconomically heterogeneous areas and the areas in which the majority population is Negro and Mexican. We do not, however, have a sample whose characteristics can be exactly specified, or which qualifies as a statistically random sample. The problem with samples of this sort is not that the findings derived from them are unrepresentative of the population from which they are drawn, but that it is not possible to tell exactly how large a relationship must be before we can be sure that it would apply to the relevant population.[2] In a statistically random sample and certain other special types of samples the standard measures of statistical significance answer the latter question for us.

It is still necessary, however, to set some kind of minimum beneath which any observed relationship should be discounted. This may be done arbitrarily, or by the cautious use of measures of significance. We have followed the latter course, with the following precautions: (a) Only two-tailed tests have been employed, even though most of our hypotheses are directional; (b) We have generally insisted on .01 or 02 levels of significance, noting .05 levels as borderline. Significance figures must accordingly be interpreted throughout the monograph as relative rather than absolute measures of the confidence which can be placed in any finding.

Sample Characteristics

Since we were primarily interested in the nonethnic population, an effort was made to secure schools with minimal minority populations. It was impossible in the lower socioeconomic levels, however, to avoid a sizable number of Negroes and Mexicans and some Orientals. Altogether, 12 percent had Spanish names, six percent were Negro, and another four percent were Oriental or foreign born. Only the 78 percent who fall into our classification of nonethnic are included in the investigation of relationships reported throughout most of the book. However, since ethnic and nonethnic students together constitute the effective peer environment within which the individual student forms or modifies his values, identifies his ambitions, and selects his friends,

2 Among recent cautionary articles regarding the inappropriate use of tests of statistical significance are the following: Leslie Kish, "Confidence Intervals for Clustered Samples," *American Sociological Review* 22 (April, 1957), pp. 154–165; Hannan C. Selvin, "A Critique of Tests of Significance in Survey Research," *American Socological Review* 22 (Oct., 1957), pp. 519–527.

all are included in certain of the general characterizations of peer society and subculture.

The age distribution is surprisingly homogeneous. Approximately 93 percent of the boys and 95 percent of the girls were either seventeen or eighteen years of age at their last birthdays.

Approximately half of the sample is drawn from manual-laboring backgrounds. The breadwinners for three fifths of the students have had no appreciable experience in self-employment, and only one quarter have had any exposure to collegiate-level schooling. When only the nonethnic students are included, the general level is somewhat higher by all three measures. Since most of the Negroes are concentrated in one of the bottom three schools and most of the Mexicans in three of the five lower schools, the difference is to be expected. The only grossly notable deficiency in the nonethnic sample is the minimal number of students from completely unskilled family backgrounds. Otherwise, there is a fair representation from all socioeconomic levels.

Ideally, we should compare the distribution with that of Los Angeles at large, as it is reported in the 1950 census. While we have made a crude effort to do so, there are a number of serious obstacles to any rigorous comparison. First, the occupational categories used in this study cannot be completely equated with those employed in the census. Second, the universe in which we are interested is the parents of boys and girls seventeen and eighteen years old rather than all adults. Furthermore, we should include such parents even though some are unemployed, some are retired, some are deceased, and some may no longer be working at the occupation which they have followed most of their children's lives. Most of the breadwinners in our sample are men, but a few are women, and it is not to be anticipated that they would be representative of the occupational distribution of all gainfully employed women. Since occupations are listed by age in the census reports, it is possible to omit those men who are too young to have children seventeen years of age, but this is only a crude adjustment.

In Table 2 we report a gross sort of comparison between the occupational distribution of employed males in the Los Angeles metropolitan district and the reported occupations of family breadwinners in our sample. The study categories have been condensed so that they may be equated with groups of census categories. The three business categories have been condensed into one, and the professional and semi-professional groups have been combined. The two sets of categories are still no more than very roughly equivalent.

The sample is high on craftsmen and business occupations and low

Table 2. Occupational Distribution for Sample
and 1950 U.S. Census

Occupational group[a]	Distribution		
	Family breadwinners in high-school sample	U.S. Census: employed males[b]	
		14 years and older	35 years and older
Unskilled workers	7%	15%	15%
Semiskilled workers	11	18	15
Skilled workers	31	22	23
Clerical workers	7	7	6
Business	31	25	29
Professionals and semi-professionals	<u>12</u>	<u>12</u>	<u>12</u>
Total	99%	99%	100%

a/ The occupational groups have been condensed in order to equate the census categories approximately with those employed in this study.

b/ Census data are taken from Census of Population: 1950. Vol II, Characteristics of the Population. Part 5, California (Washington: U.S. Government Printing Office, 1952), pp. 323-324.

on semiskilled and unskilled labor. When only the older population is examined, the business occupations appear to be less oversampled and semiskilled labor less undersampled. There is no change in the discrepancies involving unskilled and skilled labor. On the basis of the census listing of workers thirty-five years old and over, manual labor is undersampled by about four percentage points, though there is a further undersampling in the lower types of manual labor. If we note also that the census figures include only the employed, and that the unemployed are drawn disproportionately from low-ranking occupations, the bias is probably somewhat larger than these figures indicate.

Table 3 reports a similar comparison of educational attainment with all males twenty-five years of age and over and with males thirty-five and over. Here the principal discrepancy is not in the general distribution of schooling, which is surprisingly close, but in the division between high school and grade school. It is quite possible that a sizable number of students transferred to Los Angeles from Eastern systems in which grade school lasts eight years and high school four, rather than six and six as in Los Angeles and surrounding systems. Such students may have reported seventh and eight grades as grade school, thus inflating the one category at the expense of the other. Some error is accordingly introduced into the educational-background variable employed in this study. However, the over-all distribution of educational background seems to be less biased than the distribution of occupational background.

The Decision to Study High-School Seniors

The decision to study twelfth graders, normally seventeen to eighteen years of age, has further implications which should be noted. The students are just coming to a turning point which is crucial for mobility. They are confronted with the problem of making responsible decisions of far-reaching import. They are not yet institutionally segregated by ambition except according to program of study. The direct impact of class background on their forward progress is still less marked than it will be when employment and higher education are encountered. It is unlikely that mobility-oriented students will yet be fully into the marginality-crisis stage, though they may have begun to move out of the premarginal stage. At the same time, some mobility has taken place and some of the patterns of group separation and subcultural differentiation should have advanced sufficiently to be observable.

There is one major drawback to the study of high-school seniors. After the tenth grade substantial drop-outs from school begin, the rate increasing with each semester. As a result, a sizable minority of the people in the age range are excluded from the study. Since these undoubtedly contain a disproportion of nonmobiles and of persons from lower-level backgrounds, their omission biases the results in foreseeable directions. Barring resources sufficient to trace down and study

Table 3. Educational Attainment for Sample
and 1950 U.S. Census

| Educational attainment[a] | Distribution | | |
| | Education of breadwinners in high-school sample | U.S. Census[b] | |
		25 years and older	35 years and older
No schooling	1%	2%	2%
Grade school	23	12	14
High school	53	62	62
Attended college	10	13	11
College graduate	13	11	10
Total	100%	100%	99%

   a/ The educational categories have been condensed
in order to equate the census categories approximately with
those employed in this study.
   b/ Census data are from op. cit., in Table 2, p. 253.

these drop-outs, the damage done by their omission had to be weighed
against the advantages of using the twelfth-grade class. A study of
tenth graders would almost completely have eliminated the drop-out
bias. But we know that relatively few tenth graders are able to make
responsible statements about their vocational objectives. The security
of secondary schooling for many students serves as a shield against
having to subject their fantasy ambitions to the test of practicality
or even to set themselves clear goals. Under the circumstances, the
identification of those who were pointed toward mobility would be
quite precarious. The advantage of securing subjects, most of whom
would have been forced by the imminence of their graduation to think
realistically about the future, was judged to outweigh the drawback
of sample loss through drop-outs.
   It should be stressed that we are studying those who intend to be

mobile rather than persons who have achieved mobility. Some who indicate high ambitions at this stage will actually achieve no mobility, and others with low ambitions now may either develop them later or encounter chance good fortune and become mobile. We cannot, therefore, say that we are studying those who will become upwardly mobile, but merely that we are studying the *mobility-oriented*.

The Problem of Drop-Outs

In deciding to study twelfth graders, we were forced to accept the effects of eleventh- and twelfth-year drop-outs on the sample. Clearly it will not be possible to generalize from our sample to the complete population of seventeen- and eighteen-year-olds. Nor can we speak as if these students are the same group that entered senior high school three years earlier. We shall be discussing a special school culture shaped by the dual circumstances, that the students are at the point where they can no longer escape making decisions about their future and that they are a group selected by elimination of many other students.

A good deal has been written by educators regarding the "drop-out problem," though the available evidence deals more with its quantitative than with its qualitative aspects.[3] The findings of a study by Robert Thomas regarding drop-outs in a large Chicago high school are representative of the evidence regarding selectivity.[4] Drop-out rates are highest among students from low socioeconomic backgrounds and certain ethnic backgrounds, and drop-out is less related to I.Q. among students of high socieoeconomic level than among students from low backgrounds.

In order to estimate the extent of drop-out affecting our sample and to ascertain its socioeconomic bias, we have made use of a report of the Los Angeles School System giving drop-out rates for individual schools.[5] The report concerns a period of five years after our data were collected, and drop-out rates may have declined somewhat during the interval. However, because the reporting is more accurate in the

[3] Studies dealing with school drop-out are reviewed in the following works: Orville G. Brim, Jr., *Sociology and the Field of Education* (New York: Russell Sage Foundation, 1958), pp. 56–63; Robert J. Havighurst and Bernice L. Neugarten, *Society and Education* (Boston: Allyn and Bacon, 1957), pp. 222–228; Charles M. Allen, *Combating the Drop-out Problem* (Chicago: Science Research Associates, 1956).

[4] "An Empirical Study of High School Drop-outs in Regard to Ten Possibly Related Factors," *Journal of Educational Sociology*, 28 (Sept., 1954), pp. 11–18.

[5] Evaluation and Research Section, Los Angeles City School Districts, *Transfers, Entrants, and Drop-outs in Los Angeles City Secondary Schools*, 1959–1960, Research Report No. 233 (Los Angeles: Los Angeles City School Districts, 1961).

later study than in earlier investigations, and because rates for schools are available for the first time, we shall depend upon this report.

Drop-outs from junior and senior high schools were studied for a one-year period. In the three-year senior high schools the ratio of drop-outs to initial full enrollment was .105. By considering drop-outs in each grade level separately, the investigators estimated the drop-out rate in a typical class from its entry to its graduation as 29.1 percent for the three years of senior high school, and 31.8 percent for the six years of junior and senior high school. Since the rate drops to below one half of one percent in the seventh grade, we may well take 32 percent as approximating the total loss from grades one through twelve.

The drop-out rates for 1959–60 are reported in Table 4 for seven of the schools in our sample. The report does not deal with the one high school not in the Los Angeles system, and rates for the two schools which combine junior and senior high school are noncomparable. Since rates by grades are not available for individual schools, we can only estimate the three-year drop-out rate for a given class by assuming that this rate bears the same relationship to the one-year drop-out rate for each individual school that it does in all schools taken together. To provide such an estimate all one-year rates have been multiplied by 2.7. The resulting indication is that drop-out rates vary greatly among schools, and may approach 50 percent in at least one of the schools.

When drop-out rates are compared in relation to the mean background index of students in each school there is a marked negative correlation. The extent of correlation is underestimated because the background index could be computed only for students who remained in school. The larger the drop-out rate, the greater the overestimate of mean background level for the neighborhood from which the school draws its population.

The rate of drop-out at each socioeconomic level might have been estimated from these data, except that a linear regression produces negative drop-out rates at the higher socioeconomic levels—a logical impossibility.[6] Hence, we must be content to recognize that the drop-out rate of students from low-socioeconomic status is so great that

---

[6] An attempt was made to fit logarithmic or hyperbolic curves to the relationship, without an adequate solution. A plausible interpretation can be made for the fact that the predicted drop-out rate based on a linear regression produces drop-out rates which are less than zero as the background index rises from four to five. If the neighborhood or the individual school society accentuates the tendencies characteristic of the majority of its students, drop-out rates in high-level neighborhoods will be lower than can be attributed to the backgrounds of individuals making up the student body, and rates in low neighborhoods will be lower than can be attributed to the socioeconomic distribution of their students.

Table 4. Drop-out Rates and
Mean Background Index by Schools

School	Percentage of school enrollment		Mean background index
	Drop-out rate for one year	Estimated drop-out during three-year school career	
B	4.7%	12.7%	3.74
C	7.4	20.0	3.50
E	7.7	20.8	2.72
F	8.7	23.5	2.59
G	13.1	35.3	2.47
H	13.2	35.6	1.97
I	17.6	47.5	1.86

students in our low group are quite atypical of their status mates. Furthermore, during the three years of senior high school, the school classes in low status areas may undergo so radical a change in composition as to transform their atmosphere rather thoroughly. The present study must then be interpreted as an investigation of mobility in the setting of twelfth-grade student society and culture. Any extension to mobility in a more inclusive context will require a strong presumption that the relationships in question are unaffected by socioeconomic selectivity of drop-out.

Another possible kind of distortion through drop-out is suggested by the distribution of sibling position in the sample. The proportion of oldest children is strikingly larger than the proportion of youngest children among the nonethnic population, though not among the ethnics. There may be some tendency to invest psychic and tangible

Hence, the "true" regression between socioeconomic background and drop-out will show a less extreme slope than the regression between school rates and school mean background indexes. The more modest slope would then avoid the negative values which make it impossible to extrapolate from the relationship observed in our data. Such an interpretation is consistent with the finding that average ambition differs more greatly between high and low neighborhood schools than can be attributed to the population differences between schools, as reported in Chapter Three.

resources in the oldest child, which is negated in Negro and Mexican populations by the practice of sending the oldest son to work for the family. However, the disproportion of older children might also be a function of an increasing birth rate, or of movements of population of a given age.[7] The years 1937 and 1938, when most of these students were born, are too early to reflect the wartime birth increase. Evidence in support of the population-movement hypothesis was sought by a comparison of suburban and nonsuburban area schools, but no consistent relationship emerged. Either of the drop-out hypotheses should apply more clearly to males than to females. In the case of nonethnics this is not so. But the reverse hypothesis that the oldest son in Negro and Mexican families is withdrawn from school to work for the support of the family does correctly predict the difference between male and female rates.

Again we must be satisfied with uncertainty about the sample, though we are prepared to make the following guesses. The similar patterns for nonethnic men and women combine with subsequent negative findings regarding the relationship between ambition and family position [8] to call the drop-out hypothesis into question. On the other hand, there is some support for the hypothesis that the oldest son in Mexican and Negro families drops out. The mobility of Los Angeles as a whole and its failure to fit into classic zonal patterns probably accounts for failure of the ecological test of the spatial-mobility hypothesis, which still seems the most likely explanation for the finding.

ADMINISTRATION OF THE QUESTIONNAIRE

It is crucial in a questionnaire that asks for value judgments that the circumstances of administration be carefully controlled. The questionnaires were administered in "Senior Problems" classes, taken by students in their last semester of high school. In two schools, the Senior Problems classes were brought together into a large assembly room, where three and seven classes respectively took the questionnaire together. In the remaining schools, questionnaires were administered in the 87 classrooms separately. The investigator himself administered the questionnaires in the two schools where classes were brought together, and in approximately half of the remaining classes. A research assistant, Robert Freeman, administered the questionnaires in about another

---

[7] Richard J. Hill and George C. Meyers suggested some of the interpretations for the unequal incidence of older siblings in the sample.

[8] There is probably no correlation between ambition and sibling position when correction is made for family size. Cf. "Some Family Determinants of Ambition," *Sociology and Social Research*, 46 (July, 1962), p. 408.

quarter of the classes. Schedules in the two remaining schools required that the questionnaire be administered in several classes simultaneously. Here a group of sociology graduate students, after a careful briefing by the investigator, administered the questionnaires.

A set of detailed instructions for administering the questionnaire was followed to insure uniformity. Before the questionnaires were distributed the administrator attempted to set the appropriate atmosphere and to eliminate any anticipated sources of resistance. Administration was broken into three parts, the students being stopped until all had finished a section, and then given oral instructions for the next part. The administrator remained in the room and answered questions privately when they occurred.

Identifying the subject who filled out each questionnaire was necessary, while providing sufficient assurance of anonymity that answers would be given freely. When the investigator or his assistant administered questionnaires, identification was handled through seating charts prepared by the teacher in each classroom. Questionnaires were prenumbered and handed individually to each student by the administrator, so that numbers would be appropriately matched with the seating chart. When classes were combined for administration, or when graduate students administered the questionnaire, three-by-five slips of paper bearing the same number as the questionnaire were stapled to each questionnaire. Following a simple explanation that we needed to be able to match names and questionnaires for certain purposes, but wished to protect anonymity, we asked students to write their names on the slips, detach them, and hand them in separately. In both cases, the administrator identified the Negroes and Orientals by inspection or consultation with the teacher while the students were answering the questionnaire. Spanish names were later identified by consultation with two professors in the Spanish Department at U.C.L.A.

Several stages of pretesting the questionnaire preceded the preparation of the completed form. All questions were first tried out on available sociology classes at U.C.L.A., and a number of simple tabulations and cross-tabulations made. When items were assembled into a preliminary questionnaire, it was examined and discussed at length with the Chief of the Los Angeles City Schools Testing Division and the Assistant Superintendent of Schools for High Schools, both of whom were able to offer helpful advice. One high school (not in the sample) was then made available for final pretesting. Here, on each of three successive days, the questionnaire was administered to a different class of about thirty students. After each administration, a series of hurried tabulations was made, note was taken of responses and difficulties of the students, and the questionnaire was revised before the next day's administration. Both the investigator and his assistant were present at each administration, so that the routine for administering the questionnaire could also be tested and timed. With the benefit of this advance testing and revision, administration of the questionnaire ran very smoothly when work was begun on the sample itself.

There are critics and defenders of the questionnaire method. Charges are made that questionnaires are not answered honestly, that subjects do not understand their own attitudes well enough to make meaningful choices in response to direct question, and that meanings are insufficiently communicated in the queries and arbitrary alternatives supplied in the questionnaire. On the other hand, the questionnaire offers more anonymity than other methods of data gathering, and reduces the salience of the interaction between subject and investigator which is paramount in the individual-interview situation. The stimuli the questionnaire presents to the subjects are more uniform than interview questions, and the short queries afford less danger of the reassessment and reorganization of attitudes which are an inevitable part of the "deep" interview. Furthermore, there is much to be said for the view that, on matters not hedged about by guilt and shame, an individual knows his own attitude better than an investigator can gauge it from a brief sample of his conversation. Finally, the questionnaire method has the advantage that the data are fully placed before the reader so that he can check the investigator's interpretations against his own interpretations of the same data. With carefully controlled administration of carefully devised questionnaires, we are convinced that the merit of the method is considerable.

THE LOS ANGELES AREA

The only justification for studying people in one metropolitan area is the assumption that findings there may be in some respects generalizable to other areas. We cannot pretend to estimate just how much any of our results would differ if the investigation had been conducted elsewhere. But we can call attention to some features of Los Angeles which might make a difference.[9]

---

[9] Relevant characterizations of Los Angeles may be found in the following sources: Harry Carr, *Los Angeles: City of Dreams* (New York: D. Appleton-Century, 1935); Kathleen Doyle, *Californians: Who? Whence? Whither?* (Los Angeles: Haynes Foundation, 1956); Carey McWilliams, *Southern California Country: An Island on the Land* (New York: Duell, Sloan & Pearce, 1946); Mel Scott, *Metropolitan Los Angeles: One Community* (Los Angeles: Haynes Foundation, 1949); Eshref Shevky and Marilyn Williams, *op. cit.*

The Los Angeles Metropolitan District has the second largest population in the United States. It ranks third, after New York and Chicago, in a number of commercial indexes, but ranks fifth, after Detroit and Philadelphia, in manufacturing.[10] The basic structure of communities upon which the metropolis rests has existed less than a century, having been established largely between 1875 and 1888. An indigenous Mexican population, replenished constantly by migration from across the border, has been historically the principal minority group, though Negroes began entering the area in large numbers during World War II and have continued to do so. Most of the migrants to Southern California came from other parts of the United States. Unlike the large Eastern cities, Los Angeles has never had a sizable lower class composed of recent migrants from Europe. The stable community structure was chiefly the product of small-city and rural migrants from the Midwest. It is important for the community class structure that there was almost no homesteading, all the land being held by the descendants of Spanish land grantees. Whole ranchos were bought and subdivided for sale, so that a disproportionate number of the basic settlers were people with cash to purchase land. The growth of the entertainment industry, the discovery of oil, migration from the Dust Bowl, and the wartime development of industry all disturbed the stable structure of the community. The Depression freed Los Angeles from dominance of its social life by wealthy Easterners who had formerly wintered there. Rapid growth and the absence of clear ethnic lines of differentiation have contributed to what is probably a more amorphous and fluid class system than in other large metropolitan areas in the United States. Even San Francisco, half a century older as an effective city, has both a physical and symbolic centralization lacking in Los Angeles.

One of the important implications of the historical background of Los Angeles is that it provides an opportunity to study social stratification more independently of ethnic subculture than has been possible in Eastern cities. It still remains a moot question to what extent the characteristics ascribed to lower classes in most sociological studies of American cities are genuinely class characteristics and to what extent they are (a) characteristics of the peasant subcultures brought to this country during the "second" migration or (b) the consequences of minority-ethnic status. In the present sample we were at first surprised to discover that the proportion of foreign-born is greater among parents

[10] Los Angeles Chamber of Commerce, *The Researcher,* 22 (First quarter, 1954), p. 32.

with high socioeconomic status than among those with low status (disregarding Mexicans). The proportion of non-Mexican foreign-born is so low that the post-quota migration of relatively high-status persons from Europe could create this reversal of the usual relationships.

Another impression which is hard to verify by the methods of science is that Los Angeles has an "atmosphere" more favorable to mobility and less sensitive to traditional criteria of social rank than most metropolitan communities. If the impression is sound, evidence of amorphousness in the class system should be generalized to other communities only with great caution.

One further peculiarity of Los Angeles requires special note. An estimate of the Jewish population in Los Angeles as a whole and by eighteen major areas was prepared in 1953 for the Los Angeles Jewish Community Council. Drawing upon sample inquiries, the investigators estimated that 12.2 percent of the population were Jewish, and that the proportion in major areas ranged from 66.3 to 1.1 percent.[11] While the relationship was not made explicit in the report, anyone familiar with the areas of Los Angeles will recognize that there is considerable positive correlation between the socioeconomic rating of areas and the proportion of the population who are Jewish. This relationship is also reflected in our sample. The two top-ranking schools are from areas where the proportion of Jews is estimated as 37.1 and 28.7 percent, respectively, in the publication cited. The three bottom schools are in areas where the Jewish population is estimated as 6.4 and 1.7 percent.

Unfortunately, we have no way to estimate the effects of this correlation between socioeconomic standing and Jewishness upon findings. Policies of the school systems made it impossible to include any item which would differentiate Jews from gentiles. Nor can we say with any confidence whether Jews differ from gentiles of comparable socioeconomic status with respect to any of the variables under examination. Hence, we can do no more than note that an alternative interpretation for some of our findings may lie in the merging of high background with Jewishness.

11 Fred Massarick, *A Report on the Jewish Population of Los Angeles* (Los Angeles: Los Angeles Jewish Community Council, 1953), mimeographed.

CHAPTER THREE

The Extent of Mobility-Orientation

THE FIRST IMPORTANT evidence regarding the applicability of the marginal-man hypothesis to the upwardly mobile individual is the prevalence of mobility aspirations. If mobility is very common, the mobiles are likely to develop their own subculture, or at least to have a recognized place in the peer society. They then cease to be marginal.[1] A high degree of mobility aspiration further suggests that the relationship between classes is one of prestige identification rather than class consciousness. Knowledge of the extent and character of mobility striving will also supply a background for interpreting class distinctions in values and personal ties.

Ambition will be examined in three steps. First, we shall compare the ambitions of the students with their backgrounds. Second, we shall explore the relationship between an individual's ambitions and his background. Third, we shall consider the effect of neighborhood on ambition.

THE EXTENT OF AMBITION

Occupational Ambition: Men

Occupation was taken as the basic measure of ambition. In order to lessen fantasy and wishful responses, we asked the men students to name their "life work—what do you expect to be doing *ten* and *twenty* years from now?" Their responses were classified into nine occupational groups, which were intended to separate the entrepreneurial types of occupation from the bureaucratic types, as well as to make the usual differentiations of rank. (See Appendix B for the detailed classification.)

The responses are summarized in Table 5, and compared with the occupations indicated for parents. The prevalent pattern is clearly one of high ambition. Fully a third of the students name one of the professions as their goal. Combined with those who select semiprofessional occupations, they constitute more than half of the subjects. Yet only

---

[1] Milton M. Goldberg, "A Qualification of the Marginal Man Theory," *American Sociological Review*, 6 (Feb., 1941), pp. 52–58.

Table 5. Occupational Background and Ambition: Males

| Occupational category | Distribution | | | Ratio: ambition to back-ground |
	Back-ground	Ambition	Second choice	
Unskilled labor	5.9%	0.5%	0.7%	.08
Semiskilled labor	10.3	1.2	3.4	.12
Skilled labor	32.2	24.1	34.3	.75
Clerical workers, salesclerks	6.6	3.2	3.9	.48
Small-business owners-managers, salesmen	19.6	11.6	10.6	.60
Semiprofessionals	3.6	17.8	22.0	4.89
Business agents, managers	8.2	3.6	3.8	.44
Professionals	8.4	35.2	19.1	4.19
Large business owners, officials	5.2	2.9	2.2	.55
Total	100.0%	100.1%	100.0%	
Total number	1262	1262	1205	
No answer	90	90	147	

a/ To make the first two columns in the table exactly comparable, all cases in which either ambition or occupational background was unanswered or unclassifiable were removed in these tabulations. The actual numbers were 77 "no answer" on background and 16 on ambition, including three on both questions.

twelve percent of the parents fall into these two categories. Against nearly half of the students who come from manual-labor backgrounds, barely more than a quarter are aiming toward manual labor and nearly all of these have a skilled craft in mind. The prevalent pattern is upward mobility, and the upwardly mobile person in this community of students is the rule rather than the exception.

In addition to the generally high levels of aspiration indicated, three features of the aspiration patterns command special note. First is the overwhelming choice of the professions. It appears that high ambition is largely identified as professional aspiration among these boys. Even among those boys who come from large-business backgrounds there is a high degree of preference for the professions.

Second, skilled labor commands an important position, taking into account its general level in the occupational hierarchy. Skilled labor holds its own against any possible preference for white-collar over blue-collar work. The category of minor white-collar workers, including the clerical and salesclerk occupations, receives only a small number of choices. Plainly, the status of the craftsman as the top of the manual-laboring situs is generally preferred to the bottom of a perhaps generally higher set of white-collar occupations.[2]

Third, slightly more than one ninth of the students find their goal in the small-entrepreneur class. The choice is notable when compared with the weaker position of the two groups of large-business occupations, and when account is taken of evidence from recent studies of successful careers in American business indicating that the promotional hierarchy of the large-business organization is replacing small business as the route for upward mobility.[3]

Among the professions, the largest group of aspirants have set engineering as their goal. About a quarter have named professions in the education and science bracket, while just under a fifth each have selected a medical or legal profession. A small remaining group name religious occupations. Among the semiprofessional and public administrative aspirants, a majority have named the entertainment-artist-literary group of occupations, with nearly a sixth having named government administrative positions.

In response to a multiple-choice question, about half the men expressed themselves as just about positive regarding their occupational choices, while only ten percent were not at all sure. When the answers are cross-tabulated with occupational aspiration, there is a fairly notable positive association between confidence and the level of occupation selected. Another clue to the predominant mobility-orientation is perhaps supplied by this correlation. It appears that some students would have preferred to name a higher goal than they felt able to select.

2 For explanation of the concept of "situs," see Richard T. Morris and Raymond J. Murphy, "The Situs Dimension in Occupational Structure," *American Sociological Review*, 24 (April, 1959), pp. 213–239.

3 W. Lloyd Warner and James C. Abegglen, *Occupational Mobility in American Business and Industry* (Minneapolis: University of Minnesota Press, 1955).

The specific deviations from rank-order correlation between confidence and occupational ambition are worth further note. Less often confident than their rank would warrant are the lower white-collar aspirants and the large-business agents and managers. More often confident than their rank would suggest are the semiprofessional and the small-business and craft aspirants. The popularity of these occupations is also reflected in the confidence of those who choose them.

Students were also asked to name alternate occupational choices, and these choices were classified as consistent (falling into the same broad category as their first choice) or as inconsistent. When more than one occupation was listed, only the first was coded. Just over ten percent named no second choice, and about thirty-five percent of the remaining students named a second choice in the same socioeconomic category as their first choice. Consistency between first and second choice is significantly associated with the confidence expressed over the occupational choice, although the degree of association is modest.

Consistency is not a positive correlate of occupational ambition in the same fashion as confidence, but men aspiring to the most popular occupations—the professions, crafts, semiprofessions and small entrepreneurship—most frequently name a different occupation in the same group as their alternate choice. Consistency is greatest among craft aspirants, half of whom name a different craft as their alternate choice. In contrast, the large-business aspirants more often select a different kind of occupation as their alternative.

The most popular second choice occupation is one of the skilled crafts, with the semiprofessions and professions following (Table 5). When occupational categories are examined separately it appears that either the crafts or the semiprofessions are each group's most popular second choice. When first and second choice of occupation are treated as coordinates, with occupations placed in order according to socioeconomic level, one might have anticipated a clustering of second choices along the diagonal, each group's most popular second choice being adjacent to the first choice. But such is not the case. Aspirants to lower occupations (small business and below) consistently name a skilled craft as their second choice. Aspirants to higher occupations consistently name a semiprofessional occupation as their second choice, except that the craft aspirants name a profession and the professional aspirants name a craft as second choice.[4] The professions, the semiprofessions, and the crafts appear to have some common appeal.

---

[4] The table of cross-tabulations between first and second choice of occupation upon which these observations are based is not reproduced here.

Whether it is the fact that each indicates the mastery of a special competence achieved through specialized education or that each suggests a position of dignity and some independence, we cannot at present judge. But the observed interchangeability of crafts and professions in the occupational plans of many of these students would seem of considerable import in understanding the dimensions of ambition.

As a final question to clarify the nature of occupational aspiration we asked whether students expected to be employees or owners. Forty-four percent said they would be owners, and the remaining fifty-six percent said they would be "employed by someone." These percentages indicate rather little shift from the sixty percent of their parents who are employees. There is a small positive association between high occupational aspiration and ownership rather than employee aspiration, and ownership aspiration is also associated with expression of confidence in choice of occupation. However, 253 of the 594 would-be owners are in the two relatively modest brackets of skilled laborer and small entrepreneur. Far from reflecting the traditional independence and entrepreneurship, choice of the professions means employee status to fifty-six percent of the boys. While the highest ranking professions in popular evaluation are still those with an entrepreneurial emphasis (medicine and law), the largest numbers of professional aspirants are headed toward the two categories which convey overwhelmingly employee status (education and engineering).

Husband Occupation: Women

It can be safely assumed that the husband's occupation is the key status [5] for most women in American society. But it is not usually possible for women to select their husband's occupation in the direct and specific way that men choose their own occupations, and the romantic attitude requires disavowal of any desire to do so. Because of the latter considerations, we felt it best to ask women for minimum acceptable husband occupations, applicable to the whole life span. The lowest-ranking category marked acceptable on a check list was taken as the answer.[6]

[5] E. T. Hiller, *Social Relations and Structure* (New York: Harper & Brothers, 1947), pp. 339–343.

[6] The complete wording appears in Appendix A. Three of the groups referred to the single category, "small-business owner-manager and commission sales." The listing does not correspond exactly with the classification used elsewhere in the study in two respects. First, at the time the questionnaires were prepared the investigator was unaware of the importance of employing a special category of semi-professionals, so none was included. And second, professionals were classified above large-business executives. Since there was no need to differentiate between these two categories in analysis, the responses were not later recoded.

Table 6. Minimum and Desired
Husband Occupation and Background: Females

Occupational category	Distribution		
	Background	Minimum occupation	Desired occupation
Unskilled labor	8.2%	31.7%	1.4%
Semiskilled labor	12.2	24.1	1.3
Skilled labor	30.5	28.3	12.3
Clerical workers, salesclerks	6.9	2.5	1.3
Small-business owners- managers, salesmen	18.4	11.8	14.3
Semiprofessionals	3.4	--[a]	8.4
Business agents, managers	7.2	0.1	2.4
Professionals	8.4	0.3	47.7
Large-business owners, officials	4.8	1.1	10.8
Total	100.0%	99.9%	99.9%
Total number	1410	1437	990
No answer	31	4	451

a/ No example of semiprofessional occupations was
included in the questionnaire on minimum husband occupation.

Table 6 supplies an approximate comparison between the minimum
husband occupations named by the students and the occupations of
their parents. In a group of women of whom twenty percent come
from unskilled and semiskilled parental backgrounds, fifty-six percent
indicate that they would not even be a little disappointed to have their
husbands spend their whole lives in such occupations. Only one percent insist on a business executive or professional husband, while
thirteen percent come from families at this level. Even when the difference between stating an expectation (men) and setting a minimum
(women) is kept in mind, the discrepancy between the men's and

women's responses is surprising. The extremely low occupational minimums suggest that the specific reference to the husband in this question has maximized the romantic distortion. To the extent to which the latter is true, it would be dangerous to accept the absolute levels at face value, although the relative levels might still be valid in comparing the ambitions of different groups of women.

In order to balance the statement of a minimum occupation, we followed the preceding question with the direct query, "What kind of occupation would you *like* your future husband to have?" It was hoped that romantic resistance would have been lowered by the first question so that the girls would not resist suggesting a particular occupation. Approximately two thirds of the girls named a classifiable occupation, and these replies are also summarized in Table 6. The replies are of an entirely different character from the answers naming minimum occupation, falling much more disproportionately at the upper end of the continuum than even the men's statements of their own ambitions. The fifty-nine percent of the girls naming professions or large-business owners and officials compares with thirty-eight percent for men.

Anticipating the resistance and inability of girls to naming a desired husband occupation, we arranged to code all nonresponses under five headings. The headings and the number under each are as follows: "Don't know or don't care," 25; "Financial specifications," 63; "Romantic, altruistic considerations," 108; "Other specific conditions," 145; and "General preference for upper-level occupations," 80. In addition, there were thirty who simply left the question blank. If we add those in the first and third categories to "unskilled labor," distribute those in the second and fifth categories proportionately among the four top-occupational groups, and distribute those in the fourth category and those who left the question unanswered proportionately throughout the whole scale, we get a distribution of occupations with considerably higher frequencies at both the top and bottom of the scale than we have for men's ambitions, but with about the same average level.

At the present it seems probable that (1) women more than men are preparing themselves for nonmobility in the occupational sense and that (2) men view their occupational goals with somewhat more intrinsic value than women view their prospective husbands' occupations. But it is also clear that (3) women have some fairly definite ideal husband occupations in mind which are more often drawn from the highest categories than are the men students' expectations, and which are much higher than most of them can realistically expect to attain.

Educational Expectations

Educational expectations, like those for occupation, indicate very high ambitions and a considerable increase as compared with backgrounds (Table 7). Over two thirds of the men plan to attend college or junior college and forty-one percent expect at least to graduate from a college or a university. By contrast, less than a quarter of their parents attended a college or junior college.

In answer to the related question, "What do you expect to be doing the year after you graduate from high school?", sixty percent of the men said they would be attending college or junior college and eight percent said that they would be attending business school, trade school, or some other technical school. Even without allowing for the ten percent who expect to have to interrupt their long-range plans to serve in the armed forces immediately after graduation, the long-range goal of more education is reflected in the plans of most of the boys for the period immediately following graduation.

A very small clue to the seriousness, if not the realism, of these students' stated occupational ambitions is supplied by comparing educational and occupational ambitions. Considerably more students named a professional ambition than expected to attend graduate school. Even after making an allowance for the engineers, who do not require graduate training to assume their profession, the percent naming graduate work is too small. Or we might compare the fifty-nine and one-half percent naming the four top occupational categories with forty-one percent who expect to graduate from college. While college education is not absolutely essential for all of these occupations, it is required in most and is a marked asset in the others. Allowing for a fair number of small-business aspirants who plan to graduate from college, we gain the impression that the distribution of educational ambition is a little low for the corresponding occupational goals. The difference might suggest that some of the occupational goals are sheer fantasy, though it is equally plausible to assume that many of the boys are not fully apprised of the recent increase in educational standards in most occupations. Many may still suppose they can be teachers directly upon college graduation or feel that lack of a college degree will be only a minor drawback in the world of business.

The educational goals of women students are somewhat lower than those of the men. Ten percent more men than women plan to take graduate or professional training after college, while ten percent more women than men plan to terminate their schooling with high school. The general level of educational expectation is still high in an absolute

Table 7. Educational Background and Ambition

Educational level	Men		Women		
	Background	Ambition	Background	Ambition	Minimum for husband
No schooling	1.4%	--	1.1%	--	2.4%
Grade school	23.2	--	22.7	--	18.2
High school	45.3	15.1%	41.8	25.2%	34.2
Business, trade or technical school	6.8	14.8	9.9	17.4	30.0
Junior college	10.0	27.8	10.5	30.2	4.9
Four-year-college graduation	6.1	22.5	6.5	17.7	8.8
Postgraduate or professional school	6.2	18.3	6.6	7.6	1.5
Other	1.0	1.6	0.9	1.8	--
Total	100.0%	100.1%	100.0%	99.9%	100.0%
Total number	1316	1351	1425	1439	1435
No answer	36	1	16	2	6

sense, however. Three fourths of the women plan to have some further education, and fifty-six percent expect to have at least some college or junior-college training. For women, as for men, junior college is the anticipated modal stopping point. The three fourths who plan schooling beyond high school compares strikingly with the one third of their fathers (or breadwinners) who had further education. The rate of graduate- and professional-school planning, however, is about the same as the actual rate for their fathers. The rate of high educational ambition for women is like that for men, apparently inadequate for the level of occupational ambition. Many girls are apparently unaware of the educational requirements for teaching, nursing, and some of the other professional and semiprofessional occupations they have named as careers.

Women were also asked for the minimum education which would be acceptable in their husbands. The answers run somewhat lower than the parental education of the girls and considerably lower than the educational goals the girls have set for themselves. However, the distribution of minimum education is higher than is absolutely essential for entry into the occupations listed in response to the parallel question.

Material Aspiration

Probably the most ticklish variable to measure is the level of monetary ambition. People from different backgrounds have quite different understandings of what a given sum of money will purchase. Since it seems reasonable to assume that individuals aspire more to a scale of living than to a specific dollar income and that people are satisfied or dissatisfied with their income according to what it enables them to buy rather than according to a preconceived dollar scale, material aspiration must reflect a scale of living if it is to constitute a scale in any usable sense. In order to escape the problem of the uncertain value of the dollar, we sought to locate two or three items of consumption which were part of nearly everyone's plans for his own scale of living and which might be described in increments which would mean nearly the same thing to everyone. We tried to avoid items like swimming pools, which many people would not want even if they could easily afford them.

Eventually we settled upon house and automobile as the most nearly consensual items. Size of house could be presented in simple quantitative terms, and it was felt that among the age group we were studying the greater desirability of a large than of a small house would be generally accepted. The automobile could also be described in well-

Table 8. Material Ambition

Material level	Men	Women
One-room house, fifteen-year-old car	5.3%	3.2%
Three-room house, used low-priced car	9.8	11.8
Five-room house, used middle-priced car	22.9	37.8
Seven-room house, new middle-priced car	35.4	36.9
Nine-room house, new top-priced car	16.7	8.1
Twelve-room house, two new top-priced cars	6.6	1.7
Two large houses, several new top-priced cars	1.6	0.2
Several large houses, several new top-priced cars	1.6	0.2
Total	99.9%	99.9%
Total number	1334	1433
No answer	18	8

recognized terms according to known price-classes (high-priced, middle-priced, and low-priced), and is thought to be an essential part of the Southern California scale of living. In some sections of the United States people avoid ownership of an automobile by choice, but it was judged that in Los Angeles such individuals would be trivial in number among the younger generation. In order that the question should be equally applicable to men and women, an acceptable minimum rather than a goal was asked for.

The median ambition for men falls between the five- and seven-room house and just short of the new middle-priced car (Table 8). This scale of living corresponds well with what seems to characterize those "tract" residence areas in Los Angeles that appeal to families who want to move up from the strictly working-class tracts with their four-

and five-room houses. These "better" tract areas are likely to feature three-bedroom-and-den houses with a "bath and a half," and the expectation is that residents will have cars in the middle-price range or the more expensive models of cars in the low-price range.

There is a clear and positive relationship between occupational and material aspiration, the rank order of median material aspiration corresponding exactly to the order we have assigned to the occupational groups with the exception of a reversal between skilled and other labor. Each higher level of educational aspiration also carries a higher median material aspiration. However, those who aspire to be owners do not have significantly higher material aspirations than those aiming toward employee status. Thus there is considerable commonality among the three principal measures of ambition—the occupational, educational, and material scales—but the concern to be independent rather than an employee represents a rather different kind of objective.

The material ambition of women is a little lower on the average than that of the men. Only ten percent set more than a seven-room house and a middle-priced car as their minimum standard, as compared with thirty-eight percent of the men. Their median ambition falls in the five-room house range as compared with the seven-room house for men.

Ambition Index

In order to obtain general measures of ambition, responses to the several types of ambition were assigned arbitrary weights and combined. For men, occupation, education, and material ambition were each assigned values from zero to three, and a value of one was assigned for independent rather than employee status. For women, material ambition and minimum husband occupation were assigned values from zero to three and educational ambition and minimum husband education were valued from zero to two. Both resulting indexes range from zero to ten; their distributions approximate the normal curve. These two indexes have been used throughout the remainder of the report.

AMBITION AND BACKGROUND

From the preceding discussion it is abundantly clear that the youth aggregate represented in our sample is mobility oriented. It remains to be determined how the class origin of the subject affects his ambition.

In the introductory statement we called attention to two polar views of the relations between classes in a formally open-class society. When *class consciousness* is thought to be the governing relation between classes, active antagonism and disparagement of higher classes is cultivated, and the social network in which the lower-class boy is caught places mobility-orientation in an unfavorable light. Thus the incidence of mobility-orientation should be low in the manual classes, and only the social isolates and misfits should exhibit such ambition. When *prestige identification* is the crucial relation between classes, the lower-class boy would experience encouragement and admiration for mobility aspiration. The reduction of intimacy with peers would be offset by augmented admiration and respect and a tendency to assign leadership to the ambitious in many areas of life.

Race and Ladder as Models of Mobility

What we expect to find in the relation of ambition to family background will reflect a further choice between two ideal models of the open-class system. Employing simplifying metaphors, we can speak of generational upward mobility as a *race* or as movement up a *ladder*. In the race the important consideration is that everyone starts at the same place and must cover the same ground to reach a given goal. The race institutionalizes the goal of equal opportunity, and the public school systems of modern democratic countries are all geared toward approximating such a model. The ladder, on the other hand, consists of a series of steps, each of which must be traversed to reach the next higher step. Each individual starts from a given rung, and the unskilled laborer has as far to climb in moving up two rungs to the skilled-labor category as the small-business owner has in moving up to a managerial position in large business. On the other hand, the son of a large-business owner or official has nothing more to do than to "stay put" in order to remain in the same category, and requires no more ambition to do so than the semiskilled laborer's son who becomes a semiskilled laborer himself.

Since most studies have indicated that the absolute level of ambition is less among children of lower-level parents, the results are often interpreted on the basis of the race model as indicating that ambition is something of a "middle-class value." Viewed against the ladder model, however, the absolute level of aspiration is irrelevant as a measure of ambition since it assigns the same value to the son of a professional who is downwardly mobile two rungs and the son of a clerk who is upwardly mobile two rungs. If we employ the ladder model we can only acknowledge measures of ambition which relate the level of aspiration to the point of departure. The latter point of view is adopted by LaMar Empey, who stresses the importance of distinguishing between *absolute* and *relative* measures of ambition.

In a study of high-school seniors in Washington State, Empey found that students from lower-class backgrounds had relative ambitions as great or greater than students from higher strata, in spite of their lower absolute ambition.[7]

The precedent of sociological writings strongly favors the ladder model and the view that the school does not effectively supply all students with an equivalent starting point. But while sociologists have abundantly noted the faults in the naive "race" model, they have not adequately directed their critical attention toward the ladder model. Several contemporary conditions weaken the tenability of the ladder model. First, the impact of the public school system cannot be discounted, and while it has not succeeded in obliterating family background as an advantage or disadvantage, neither has it failed completely. Second, the model depicts mobility as movement requiring that each intervening rung be crossed. But one does not necessarily have to become a skilled craftsman en route from semiskilled labor to a profession; small-business ownership may be an intermediate stop on the way to large-business ownership, but need not be; and acquisition of a profession such as law may be a step toward large-business officialdom, but is not indispensable.

Third, the very assumption that the son of a high-level family starts his career automatically at the level his parents have attained is increasingly untenable under contemporary conditions. The traditional assumption has been that family status can be transmitted rather easily from father to son through any one or a combination of (1) property, (2) skill, and (3) opportunity. But the rise of modern stock corporations and the increasing importance of management rather than ownership per se has lessened the significance of property as a means of status transmission by way of business. The rise of the professions which depend more upon education and skill than on capital assets further lessens the general impact of such transmission. While there is undoubtedly still a great deal of informal skill transmission, the burden of training for higher-level occupations has increasingly been shifted to formal educational institutions. The top-flight physician cannot guarantee the status of doctor to his son unless the son can successfully complete medical school. The third variable, opportunity, has probably retained its importance more fully than the others.

The ability of a father to transmit his status intact to his son varies

---

[7] LaMar T. Empey, "Social Class and Occupational Aspiration: A Comparison of Absolute and Relative Measurement," *American Sociological Review*, 21 (December, 1956), pp. 703–9.

according to the type of occupation in which he is employed. Business ownership and even officialdom and high-level management are intrinsically more transmissible than the professions, which depend more fully upon education. To the extent to which the students or those who advise them are sensitive to these differences, we should anticipate some preference on the part of students from lower backgrounds for mobility through channels which free them most effectively from the disadvantages of transmitted position. Accordingly, we should anticipate that the professions, which exemplify more fully the model of the race, would be preferred by lower-background boys with high ambition.

Occupational Ambition and Background

The product-moment correlation between the composite ambition and background indexes is .38 for males and .42 for females. Both relationships are significant beyond the one percent level. The moderate size of the relationship indicates that many students' aspirations are not strictly limited by the occupations of their fathers. But, unless differential capacity can account for the observed relationship, the model of the race does not find complete confirmation. Since coefficients of partial correlation between the ambition and background indexes with I.Q. held constant are .29 and .35 for males and females, respectively, the relationship cannot be entirely attributed to capacity. A similar, but grouped, tabulation of occupational ambition against occupational background, presented as a set of ratios between observed and expected ambition frequencies,[8] underlines the higher aspiration level of students from higher backgrounds. There is an almost perfect ordering of ratios according to background level.

Without an absolute measure of the distance between steps, applicability of the ladder model can only be tested by treating ordinal values as cardinal numbers.

The complete cross-tabulation of occupational background with occupational aspiration was used in the following way (Table 9). First, the median level of occupational aspiration was determined separately for students from each of the nine groups of occupational background. The median was used in preference to the mean because it is less subject to distortion by the fact that the continuum has absolute upper and lower limits. Second, the assumed median (midpoint) of each background group was subtracted from the median ambition level

[8] The table appears in Ralph H. Turner, "The Changing Ideology of Success," *Transactions of the Third World Congress of Sociology, 1956*, V, p. 41.

Table 9. Median Occupational Ambition
by Background for Males

Occupational background	Median[a] aspiration	Aspiration increment
1. Unskilled labor	4.5	+3.0
2. Semiskilled labor	5.4	+2.9
3. Skilled labor	6.1	+2.6
4. Clerical workers, sales-clerks	6.3	+1.8
5. Small-business owners-managers	6.8	+1.3
6. Semiprofessionals	6.8	+ .3
7. Business agents, managers	8.0	+ .5
8. Professionals	8.2	- .3
9. Large-business owners, officials	8.5	-1.0

a/ Each occupational category was assumed to consist of the range of values such as: 1.0 to 1.9', 2.0 to 2.9'. The aspiration increment is the difference between median aspiration and the occupational background midpoint (that is, 1.5, 2.5, . . . 9.5).

for that group. If the ladder model were a correct representation of the relationships, the resulting *ambition increments* should be the same for each background category except for the top two or three whose ambition is arbitrarily limited by the upper end of the continuum. To the extent to which the race model impinges on the situation, there should be a steady decline in the ambition increment as we move from the lower-background groups to the upper. The latter is clearly the case, with only one small reversal in the eight steps. The average boy at the lower levels does aspire to move up more steps than does the average boy at the middle levels in the scale, though the previously noted correlation between ambition and background shows that he is not entirely free from the impact of his starting position.

Another way in which the ladder system might make itself felt is in the confidence and consistency of occupational choice. The high ambitions of students from lower backgrounds might be somewhat offset by uncertainty and by a tendency to name different kinds of occupations as their second choice. Herman Case has noted that in a sample of about 160 undergraduate men and women students at Washington State College there was a lower degree of "true crystallization of choice" among the students from low backgrounds than among those with high backgrounds.[9] True crystallization was judged on the basis of certainty and satisfaction with college major and amount of information secured about the chosen occupation.

The evidence generally fails to indicate any such relationship in the present data. There appears to be no relationship between confidence and background, and a positive relationship (phi = .07) between consistency and occupational background reaches only the level of borderline significance (P < .05). Students from lower backgrounds who have lasted out high school to the final semester seem to be as clear about their occupational goals as those from high backgrounds.

The Problem of Intelligence

We have noted that the correlations between ambition and background are surprisingly little reduced by partialing out I.Q. Like Sewell, Haller, and Straus,[10] we find no substantial support for the view that it is difference in native intelligence which accounts for the higher ambition of students from high family backgrounds. A precarious further step in the interpretation of the place of I.Q. can be taken if we are prepared to make certain assumptions.

In any causal chain we must assume that influences which are extraneous for our purposes play upon each link. The effect of the extraneous influences is to reduce the observed correlations. So long as the causation with which we are concerned follows a simple chain pattern, the effects of these extraneous variables will become relatively greater as the number of intervening links in the chain increases. Consequently, so long as the extraneous factors are constant, the correlations between variables which are separated by one or more intervening variables will be less than the correlations between variables which operate directly upon one another. When this logic is applied, the hypothesis that background determines ambition indirectly through

[9] Herman M. Case, "Two Kinds of Crystallized Occupational Choice Behavior: A Problem in Delineation and Relationship," *American Sociological Review,* 19 (February, 1954), pp. 85–87.

[10] William H. Sewell, Archie O. Haller, and Murray A. Straus, "Social Status and Educational and Occupational Aspiration," *American Sociological Review,* 22 (February, 1957), pp. 67–73.

the intervening variable of intelligence leads to the prediction that correlations of both ambition and background with I.Q. should be larger than the correlation between ambition and background. The relevant coefficients are as follows for males and females, respectively:

$$r_{BI \cdot AI} = .38, .42; \qquad r_{BI \cdot IQ} = .31, .30; \qquad r_{AI \cdot IQ} = .46, .39.$$

The prediction is not borne out by the evidence, although differences in the sizes of coefficients are not great enough to warrant confident comparison. The position is even less tenable for women, with both coefficients smaller than the background-ambition correlation.

On the other hand, the assumption that ambition is the intervening variable by which background determines I.Q. is nicely fitted by the coefficients both for men and for women. In each case the correlation between background and I.Q. is the smallest of the three. The students who have the motivations and attitudes which lead to high ambition may be those who are accordingly motivated to learn the tasks which are measured by intelligence tests and motivated to make their best performance in the tests.

NEIGHBORHOOD BACKGROUND

The background variables of occupation, education, and independent-employee status with which we have concerned ourselves are properly attached to the family as such. While they largely determine the kind of neighborhood in which a family may live and the class of peers with whom the child may find himself associated, there is not always a perfect correspondence between family and neighborhood influences upon the child. Furthermore, the school itself creates an effective neighborhood for the child which need not correspond to the boundaries of the neighborhood with which the parents identify themselves. The wealthy neighborhood may be within the same school boundaries as more modest neighborhoods, and the high-school student's effective peer group may be as much determined by this fact as by residential contiguity. Hence, even while the parents live socially and physically entirely within a neighborhood consonant with their family attributes, the children may live socially in a neighborhood dominated by another stratum.

Because of the fact that neighborhood can be at variance with other stratification attributes of a family, W. Lloyd Warner has adopted the expedient of treating it as one of the components in his Index of Status Characteristics.[11] For the purposes of exploring the determinants of

---

[11] W. Lloyd Warner, Marchia Meeker, and Kenneth Eels, *Social Class in America* (Chicago: Science Research Associates, Inc., 1949).

mobility ambitions and the nature of the mobility experience, however, such an approach obscures distinctions which may be of considerable importance. If peers have any independent influence on ambitions, the influence should be revealed most clearly in cases where the
family and neighborhood influences are not consonant. Including
neighborhood rating in a general index of background would group
together students who are associated primarily with peers from a somewhat lower family background than their own and students from a
little lower background who are associated chiefly with peers from a
higher background. If both groups of students have upward mobility
ambitions, the latter will have the opportunity to achieve some effective
social mobility within the neighborhood environment itself while the
former will more likely be forced to delay actual mobility experience
and perhaps isolate themselves from their peers as a means of preparing
for upward movement.

The criterion of neighborhood which we have at our disposal is
simply which one of the ten high schools the student attends. An
initial ranking is provided by the socioeconomic characteristics of the
census tracts servicing each school. A further basis for ranking is provided by the average background index of the students from each
school. The two rankings are identical except for a reversal between the
fifth- and seventh-ranked schools, whose ratings by either criterion are
extremely close together. School neighborhoods have been handled in
two ways for our purposes. First, the schools have sometimes been
grouped into either two or three ranked sets. Separating the top five
schools from the bottom five schools provides large and nearly equal
numbers for comparison. But division into the top two, the middle five,
and the bottom three schools places the dividing lines where there are
fairly sizable differences between schools and corresponds better to
the investigator's impressions of the recognized distinctions which function in the Los Angeles community.

The second procedure is an expedient to allow neighborhood to be
employed as a variable in correlation analysis. The problem of whether
neighborhood has influence independent of family background suggests the technique of partial correlation, which in turn requires that
some numerical rating be assigned each school. The procedure followed
is to assign to each student the mean background-index value characterizing all the students, both male and female and ethnic and nonethnic, at his school. Computationally the procedure is quite simple
when correlations are computed from grouped data and these values
are treated as the midpoints for each school. The effect of this
procedure, in comparison with the use of simple rank order, is to skew
the distribution, creating somewhat larger gaps between schools at the

upper than at the lower end. The crudeness of the simple grouping of schools into high, middle, and low, and the artifact of school ratings and slightly skewed distribution affecting the correlation analysis have led us to employ each procedure whenever practicable as a check upon the correctness of the other.

Neighborhood may enter into the constellation under investigation in two distinct ways. First, it may be simply another factor determining ambition. In a more radical fashion, however, neighborhoods may constitute distinctive causal universes within which a set of variables assumes different interrelationships. The determinants of ambition may not be entirely the same in a low area and a high area in the same community. We shall take up these two approaches to neighborhood separately.

School as Determinant of Ambition

An initial impression of which ambition variables are related to the school that boys attend can be secured from simple four-fold cross tabulations between school and a series of measures for the sample. Ownership ambition, consistency, and confidence of choice are all unrelated to school. Occupational, educational, and material ambition are all related significantly (P < .001), with phi = coefficients of .23, .28, and .15, respectively. For a more complete summary of these latter relationships we present percentage summaries in Table 10. In order to reflect faithfully the character of the school as locus of the effective peer neighborhood, we have included both ethnic and nonethnic students in the tabulation.

Relatively few boys in any of the schools aspire only to unskilled or semiskilled labor or to the top bracket of large-business owners and officials, though the students who do name this latter occupation are almost all in the top two schools. A more dramatic indication of the different patterns in high- and low-level schools can be secured by comparing skilled labor, the top of the manual-labor ladder, with the professions, the top of the higher-education ladder. Forty percent of boys in the three lowest-area schools name skilled labor as their ambition, while only nine percent of boys in the two top-area schools do likewise. In the three lowest schools, twenty percent of the boys speak for the professions, while fifty-four percent do so in the top schools. The comparison appears to suggest two different observations. On the one hand, a marked difference in the atmosphere in schools which are located in different neighborhoods is plainly visible. But on the other hand, there are no schools in which the student who chooses the professions is without company. The extent of ambition and of mobility-orientation

Table 10a. Occupational Ambition as Related to Neighborhood

Degree of ambition: occupation	Male			Female[a]		
	High schools	Middle schools	Low schools	High schools	Middle schools	Low schools
Unskilled, semiskilled labor	1%	2%	4%	--	2%	6%
Skilled labor	9	24	40	5	13	16
Clerical worker, salesclerk	2	3	3	1	1	3
Small-business owner-manager, salesman	8	14	12	9	14	20
Semiprofessional	15	18	18	9	10	4
Business agent, manager	4	4	3	3	3	2
Professional	54	33	20	59	47	41
Large-business owner, official	7	2	--	14	11	9
Total	100%	100%	100%	100%	101%	101%
Total number	235	762	337	273	795	373
No answer	--	8	8	92	237	122

a/ For women, answers under occupational ambition are answers to the question, "What kind of occupation would you like your future husband to have?"

is reflected in the fact that fully one fifth of the boys from the lowest schools say that they expect eventually to find their niches in one of the professions.

The differences between high and low schools in educational ambition are more striking and may be more realistic prognosticators than occupational ambition. Just over six times as many boys in the bottom schools as in the top schools do not plan to take further schooling after high school, while just over six times as many boys in the top schools

Table 10b. Educational Ambition as Related to Neighborhood

Degree of ambition: education	Male			Female		
	High schools	Middle schools	Low schools	High schools	Middle schools	Low schools
No schooling beyond high school	4%	15%	25%	9%	27%	33%
Business, technical school, and "other"	9	16	24	14	20	22
Junior college	17	30	31	36	28	29
Graduate four-year college	33	23	15	30	16	12
Postgraduate college	38	17	6	11	8	3
Total	101%	101%	101%	100%	99%	99%
Total number	235	762	337	273	795	373
No answer	--	--	1	--	1	1

as in the low schools do plan to continue their education beyond college graduation. Again there remain about a fifth of the boys even in the lowest schools who intend to complete a four-year-college program, and about half of the boys in these schools intend to secure some college or junior-college training. Whatever atmosphere prevails in the low-area high schools does not preclude a sizeable number of students aspiring to levels of education and occupation which will most probably carry them into higher-rated areas if they are successful.

Inspection suggests that the relationship of level of school with material ambition may be somewhat less than the relationship with educational ambition (for men), and that the educational ambitions of girls are less strongly related to the school they attend than are those of boys. The former observation is consistent with the interpretation that a material standard of living is more nearly equally understandable and similarly valued from level to level than are the goals of education and occupation.

Table 10c. Material Ambition as Related to Neighborhood

Degree of ambition: material goods	Male			Female		
	High schools	Middle schools	Low schools	High schools	Middle schools	Low schools
One-room house, fifteen-year-old car	4%	5%	7%	3%	3%	4%
Three-room house, used low-priced car	6	9	15	8	11	17
Five-room house, used middle-priced car	13	23	29	29	38	45
Seven-room house, new middle-priced car	38	36	32	45	38	29
Nine-room house, new top-priced car	22	17	11	10	9	4
Twelve-room house, two new top-priced cars	13	6	4	5	1	1
Two or more large houses, several top-priced cars	4	3	2	--	--	1
Total	100%	99%	100%	100%	100%	101%
Total number	253	762	337	273	795	373
No answer	1	6	11	--	4	4

A final remark should be made about the women students' choices of desirable occupations for husbands. The responses are necessarily high-level occupations because of the wording of the question and because the nearly one third who could not name an occupation are omitted from the percentages. But the figures are useful in showing whether the atmosphere in the lowest schools is one which deprecates higher occupations, or one in which considerable temerity is required to aspire so high. If the stratification system is dominated by class consciousness, the "highest" occupations will actually be disparaged by the students

Table 11a. Correlations of Ambition Index
with Background Index and School

Variables correlated	Variables constant	Male	Female
Ambition index with background index	---	.38	.42
Ambition index with school	---	.36	.34
Background index with school	---	.46	.48
Ambition index with background index	School	.29	.31
Ambition index with school	Background index	.21	.18
Ambition index with background index and school	---	.44	.45

in low-area schools. If prestige identification is the dominant relationship, students will continue to hold the highest occupations in high repute while lacking the self-assurance to set their own sights on them. The fact that fifty percent of the girls from the lowest schools who gave an answer named the professions or large-business ownership-officialdom as their preference in a husband's occupation reveals that there is no lack of high regard for these occupations in even the lowest-area schools. Even when the nonrespondents are added to the percentage base, there are thirty-four percent of the girls in the lowest schools who name these two groups of occupations, a percentage more than fifty percent larger than the proportion of boys who selected them as their goals.

This review of the differences in ambition between high-, middle-, and low-level schools does not in itself tell us anything about the influence of school neighborhood apart from individual family background. In a recent investigation in the San Francisco Bay region, Alan B. Wilson has shown that students from comparable family backgrounds vary in ambition according to the school they attend.[12]

---

[12] Alan B. Wilson, "Residential Segregation of Social Classes and Aspirations of High School Boys," *American Sociological Review*, 24 (December, 1959), pp. 836–845.

Table 11b. Correlations of Ambition Index
with Background Index, School, and I.Q.

Variables correlated	Variables constant	Male	Female
School with I.Q.	---	.31	.34
School with I.Q.	Background index	.20	.23
Ambition index with school	Background index and I.Q.	.16	.12
Ambition index with I.Q.	Background index and school	.36	.27
Ambition index with background index and school	I.Q.	.33	.36
Ambition index with background index, school, and I.Q.	---	.54	.51

Students from schools where the average background is high exhibit higher ambitions than students from comparable families in schools that are less well situated. Table 11 contains a correlation analysis which is intended to show whether the same thing is true among our ten schools.

In light of the derivation of school weights from the background index, it is not surprising that the zero order correlations of ambition with background and school are similar. Correlations are also quite similar for males and females. The important observation, however, is that there is sufficient independence between the two measures so that each retains an appreciable and significant relationship with ambition after the influence of the other has been removed through partial correlation. Although the partial correlations are a little higher for background than for school, the independent impact of neighborhood is measured by the clearly significant correlations of the latter. Students' ambitions are higher or lower than would be predicted from their family backgrounds in accordance with the general level of the school which they attend. The coefficients of multiple correlation show the small increment which school adds to background in predicting ambition.

When we examine these relationships with the inclusion of the intelligence quotient, we observe that I.Q., too, is boosted by attending a school which draws its student body from high-level backgrounds. The correlation of school with I.Q. remains significant and appreciable for both men and women students after the influence of background has been partialed out. While partial coefficients of .20 and .23 are not indications of large relationships in their own right, the fact that the very measures of supposed intellectual capacity are related not only to family background but also to the school attended is of much interest. Whether through "test-wiseness," motivation, learned intellectual ability, or exposure to better teachers, attendance at a school in a socioeconomically superior neighborhood is associated with superior performance on the type of test which is widely used for counseling and selection related to occupational and educational goals.

Ambition and the intelligence quotient continue to show considerable interrelationship when the impact of both background and school are partialed out. Thus, the possible importance of the I.Q. in singling out those from similar family and neighborhood backgrounds who will develop mobility aspirations is underlined. The independent association of I.Q. with ambition is quite similar in magnitude to the combined association of ambition with background and school when the influence of I.Q. is removed.

The correlation of ambition with school is further reduced when I.Q. is held constant in addition to background. However, the small but significant coefficients of .16 and .12 (men and women, respectively) are conservative measures of the impact of school. Unless we are prepared to assume that I.Q. differences between schools are chiefly true reflections of inherited superiority, we must acknowledge that the measures holding only background constant (.21 and .18) may be as close or closer to a correct estimate of the importance of neighborhood.

The multiple correlation coefficients of .54 and .51 reveal the extent of predictability for ambition which can be secured by combining family background, school, and I.Q.

In case the linearity assumptions of correlational analysis had been a source of error, we re-examined the impact of neighborhood for men by the use of the expected-cases technique.[13] About 47 percent of the difference in occupational ambition between the high and low neighborhood schools remains after the influence of individual backgrounds has been removed by standardization. Fifty percent of the difference in educational ambition and sixty percent of the difference

[13] Ralph H. Turner, "The Expected Cases Method Applied to the Nonwhite Male Labor Force," *American Journal of Sociology*, 55 (September, 1949), pp. 146–156.

in material ambition can likewise not be accounted for by the differences in family background. When I.Q. is introduced it accounts for roughly another quarter of the difference in each type of ambition, leaving 23 percent of occupational and educational ambition and 36 percent of material ambition assignable to the neighborhood itself.

If we disregard I.Q. entirely, combining the joint influence of I.Q. and background with the net influence of background, we secure about equal division of influence between family background and school neighborhood, except in case of material ambition where neighborhood is more important. The measure of neighborhood impact is still conservative, since all the joint influence of family background and neighborhood is assigned to family background when we measure neighborhood as residual variation.

The correlation and the expected-cases analyses tell much the same story, that neighborhood serves to accentuate whatever differences in the major forms of ambition are already related to family background. Upward-mobility ambitions appear to be most common among students who find themselves in school neighborhoods where the prevalent family background is higher than their own.

While we consider the foregoing interpretation to be the most likely, there are other plausible interpretations of the findings. First, our measures of family background are imperfect, and the apparently equivalent backgrounds in different neighborhoods may not be fully equivalent. By introducing neighborhood, we may be only measuring family background more precisely. However, high-school districts are large, and examination of census tract data and direct observations of the areas show that there is some socioeconomic heterogeneity in nearly all of them. The development of the Los Angeles community around multiple nuclei and the irregular topography (desirable hilltop locations adjacent to less attractive areas) are among the circumstances fostering the heterogeneity. Furthermore, whether we use merely occupational background or the background index including educational and ownership status, we get about the same results. If neighborhood were but one more index of family background, we should expect its importance to be rather less when we employ the composite index than when we use only occupational background.

Second, families may choose their place of residence in accordance with their own mobility aspirations and the ambitions they hold for their children. The lower-background boys who attend high schools where the general level is higher than their own may have parents who have trained them to mobility ambitions. Thus, the crucial influence may still be from the family rather than from the peers or the school

Table 12. Correlations with Background Index and Ambition Index by Type of Neighborhood

| Sex | Variables correlated | Nonethnic students, by school level | | | All students, low schools |
		High	Middle	Low	
Male	Ambition index with background index	.35	.30	.16	.08
	Background index with I.Q.	.04	.18	.02	- - -
	Ambition index with I.Q.	.43	.43	.23	.33
	Number of cases	236	692	129	337
Female	Ambition index with background index	.41	.32	.33	.29
	Background index with I.Q.	.33	.16	.24	.16
	Ambition index with I.Q.	.37	.30	.35	.33
	Number of cases	255	727	136	373

itself.[14] It is more difficult to dispose of this line of interpretation, since it returns to the moot area of direction of causation.

Neighborhood as Causal Universe

The radical possibility that neighborhood may be more than an additional factor in a homogeneous causal complex, that it may be a setting within which the causal interrelation of variables itself is different, requires that we examine neighborhoods separately. To this end, we have repeated some of the general cross-tabulations involving ambition and background within the three separate groups of schools designated low, middle, and high.

The only finding which appears justified by Table 12 is that ambition is a more loosely determined or fortuitous matter for men in the low neighborhoods than elsewhere. Neither family background nor the kind of conceptual skills measured by the standard group intelligence tests is so powerful a predictor of ambition here. Linear multiple coefficients of correlation for ambition with background and I.Q. together are .54 and .51 in high- and middle-area schools, but are only .28 for nonethnic and .34 for all boys in the low-area schools.

SUMMARY

The objective of this chapter has been to determine the general extent of ambition and mobility aspiration among the students in this study and the degree to which their ambitions are limited by their backgrounds. Other investigations have found that high-school students in the United States characteristically have ambitions above what many of them are likely to attain.[15] Hence, we are hardly surprised to observe that high ambition is the rule, that the boys set higher occupational goals than their fathers have achieved, and that both boys and

[14] Joseph A. Kahl presents a strong case for parental determination of high ambition below the middle class. Cf. "Educational and Occupational Aspirations of 'Common Man' Boys," *Harvard Educational Review*, 23 (Summer, 1953), pp. 186–203. Cf. also David J. Bordua, "Educational Aspirations and Parental Stress on College," *Social Forces*, 38 (March, 1960), pp. 262–269.

[15] William E. Myers, "High School Graduates Choose Vocations Unrealistically," *Occupations*, 25 (March, 1947), pp. 332–333; Richard L. Simpson, David R. Norsworthy, and H. Max Miller, *Occupational Choice and Mobility in the Urbanizing Piedmont of North Carolina* (Chapel Hill: Institute for Research in Social Science, Univ. of North Carolina, 1960), p. 146; Burton R. Clark, "The 'Cooling-out' Function in Higher Education," *American Journal of Sociology*, 65 (May, 1960), pp. 569–576. Sanderson suggests that an unrealistic positive outlook regarding vocational future is an adjustment mechanism for the adolescent, but notes that "there does not seem to be much agreement among the investigators who conduct research in vocational aspirations among adolescents." Cf. Herbert Sanderson, *Basic Concepts in Vocational Guidance* (New York: McGraw-Hill, 1954), pp. 245–246.

girls have educational goals higher than their parents' attainments.

Not only are the occupational ambitions high among the boys; the great majority of the boys express considerable confidence that their choices are what they really want. Though the level of ambition is high, the preference is overwhelmingly for the professions and semi-professions rather than for the standard high-level managerial and sales posts in large businesses. Small-business entrepreneurship and the skilled crafts are the other popular categories. Educational ambition is also high relative to family background, most of the boys planning to have additional education beyond high school. However, educational ambitions are in many instances not sufficient for the stated occupational ambition. By contrast, there is no general tendency to aspire toward independent or ownership status, and there is no over-all correlation between ownership and other forms of ambition. The level of ambition toward a material standard of living is probably more within reason than either occupational or educational ambition, the median corresponding fairly well with the scale common in those Los Angeles tract neighborhoods designed for the "second stage" of home ownership.

The evidence suggests that the routes to high standing best understood by these boys are through higher education and special skill or through cultivation of a popular following (as in some of the semi-professions). Entrepreneurship is more associated with limited ambition than with personal advancement. The newer pattern of success by movement up a large-business bureaucracy is likewise little represented, the students generally expecting to start in the category to which they aspire ultimately rather than to "work up." [16] The popular professions, semiprofessions, and crafts all suggest this pattern, and small-business entrepreneurship also takes on this character when it ceases to be regarded as a step toward larger-scale entrepreneurship.

Women's educational and material ambitions are a little lower than those of the men, though they still indicate some advancement beyond parental education. When asked to select a minimum occupation for their future husbands, the girls generally set quite low standards, considerably beneath the level of their own parents. The minimum husband-educational level is similarly low. But when asked to name the occupation they would like in a husband, the two thirds of the girls who supply definitive answers name an exceptionally high group of

[16] Cf. W. Lloyd Warner and James C. Abegglen, *Occupational Mobility in American Business and Industry* (Minneapolis: Univ. of Minnesota Press, 1955), p. 31 *et passim.*

occupations, appreciably above those to which the men in the sample aspire.

These apparent inconsistencies lend themselves to the interpretation that a girl is interested in her future husband's occupation in a different way than he is. She is perhaps less concerned about the occupational level per se, but not necessarily less interested in the material and other benefits with respect to which there is much overlap between major occupational categories.

Discussions of mobility often employ a polar contrast between immobility and the absence of relationship between origin and destination. Deviations from the latter must be understood, however, in relation to an alternative model of mobility as movement up the rungs of a ladder. Ambitions among these students fall clearly between the pattern in which all start the *race* to success from a common starting point and that in which all climb the *ladder* of success, starting from the rung on which their parents are located. Although the ladder principle is effective to the extent of creating a moderate correlation between background and ambition, the race principle is required to account for the absence of correlation between confidence and background independently of the relationship with ambition. Relationships are not impressively reduced by correcting for I.Q. by partial correlation, and the relative sizes of correlation coefficients lend more support to the view that background causes ambition, which in turn causes I.Q., than to the view that background causes I.Q., which causes ambition.

The differences in level of ambition between schools in high and low neighborhoods are considerably greater than can be attributed to the differences in individual family background levels. The average level of the neighborhood probably has about as much effect as the level of individual family background in determining how high the child's ambition will be. The I.Q. also varies by neighborhood to a greater degree than is attributable to family backgrounds.

There is also a suggestion that the determinants of ambition are not the same in all kinds of neighborhoods. While the pattern of relationships among background, ambition, and I.Q. is similar in the high and low neighborhoods, all the relationships are smaller for men in the low neighborhoods. Ambition is less closely determined by either background or I.Q., and I.Q. is less closely linked with background in the low neighborhoods.

CHAPTER FOUR

Values and Social Stratification

THE MARGINAL-MAN THEORY anchors the mobile person's distinctive experience in the difference between value systems and the incompatibility of social ties in the strata of origin and destination. In this chapter we shall focus on class-value differences, asking especially whether there are value contradictions or merely discrepancies and whether anticipatory socialization pervades the system.

THE VALUES AND THEIR SELECTION

The values with which we are concerned are those which can be translated into goals for the individual's behavior and those which the researches of others have suggested are linked to socioeconomic status. We have assumed that the important differences would lie in choices between values rather than in the simple acceptance or rejection of values. We have also assumed that the compartmentalization and situationalization of value choices is such that specific choices rather than logically conceived general values should be the basic unit of analysis.

Thirty-one items were included in the questionnaire, each employing the same introductory query, "Which kind of person would you rather be?" Following each choice between two alternatives, the student was also asked how sure of his choice he was. The two responses were coded as one on a four-point continuum. There was a heavy preponderance of answers indicating that students felt quite sure of their choices on most items.

Items were selected with a few broad value alternatives in mind. Two steps were taken to determine whether a more parsimonious and powerful analysis might be achieved by the use of the broad value groupings rather than the individual items. First, indexes were computed for each of the value groupings and were included in all major cross-tabulations. No relationships with ambition or background emerged, though item relationships were found. Second, a factor-analysis of the thirty-one items, employing phi coefficients, was conducted.[1] Since none of the item intercorrelations exceeded .25, no usable factors were uncovered.

The value groupings and the items in each are listed below. It should be noted that some items were felt to belong in more than one grouping. In order to facilitate interpretation, items were deliberately chosen which varied in the directness with which they posed the broad antitheses. Items placed in brackets are those which are only tangentially related to the grouping in question.

> Secular success versus tender values: 9, 13, 17, 21, 34, 36, 37, [32].
> Self-reliance versus mutual aid: 22, 23, 28, 36.
> Individuality versus "fitting in": 8, 14, 18, 24, 25, 26.
> Independence and freedom versus authority and tradition: 10, 17, 19, 20.
> Deferred gratification versus *carpe diem*: 11, 12, 17, 33, 35, 37.
> Strict integrity versus moral opportunism: 15, 21, 30, 36, 38, [31].

The items classified under the additional heading of youth subculture will be discussed in Chapter Six.

The Values Items and Groups

In order to provide some check on the investigator's choice and classification of items, statements of each general value and its principal antithesis were prepared and presented with the thirty-one items to three graduate students in sociology. Each student independently classified the items, and their classifications were compared with each other's and with the investigator's. The investigator then made alterations in his own classification when appropriate, and in some cases clarified the statement of a general value to reduce confusion. Since the general value statements are available to the reader, along with the list of value items assigned to each, the investigator employed considerable discretion in the final assignment of items. The procedure here is in contrast to a reliability check in content analysis where the reader cannot see the material which has been classified in order to determine for himself whether he agrees with the investigator's decisions.

The first broad category is the value of *secular success,* and opposed to *tender values.*

---

[1] Centroid factors were sought from a systematic random sample of 1152 questionnaires, employing a program for SWAC prepared by Andrew Comrey.

Secular success. The important thing is to get ahead in the world, to succeed. Success is measured by such criteria as material possession, power, and position of influence and prestige. A certain amount of ruthlessness and risk is required to achieve these goals, but one must not allow himself to be deflected from them by lesser goals.

Tender values. The principal aim of everyone should be kindness, compassion, and tenderness. It is within the intimate circle of the family that these values find their highest and most constant expression. The capacity for sympathy and love is man's highest quality.

The idea that "success" is a "middle-class" value has been widespread in sociological writings. A great deal of the literature geared to educational problems has been concerned with explaining why working-class children do not place the same high value on success as middle-class children.[2] Two decades ago, Allison Davis asserted that lower-class children in schools are induced to seek goals for which they are not rewarded in practice.[3] Genevieve Knupfer suggested that members of higher classes have more opportunity to cultivate the habit of ignoring obstacles in the path of success than members of lower classes.[4] More recently Donald N. Michael interpreted findings from the comparison of small numbers of upper-middle-class and lower-lower-class persons as showing that the former have a greater sense of potency, or feeling that the individual's own powers make a difference.[5] When a group of high-school juniors and seniors were asked to assign ratings to a list of personal traits, the adjective *shrewd* was more favorably rated by middle-class students than by working-class students, and the word *lazy* was less favorably rated.[6] Leonard Reissman observed that higher-level respondents offered a more realistic pattern of sacrifices which they were willing to make for the sake of success than lower-level respondents among a small group of white adult males.[7] Recent discussions of social-class subcultures have frequently treated success as

[2] Cf., for example, Allison Davis, *Social Class Influences upon Learning* (Cambridge: Harvard University Press, 1958).

[3] Allison Davis, "American Status Systems and Socialization of the Child," *American Sociological Review*, 6 (June, 1941), pp. 345–354.

[4] Genevieve Knupfer, *Indices of Socio-Economic Status: A Study of Some Problems of Measurement* (New York: private publication, 1946), p. 134.

[5] Donald N. Michael, "The Use of Culture Concepts in the Functional Analysis of Public Opinion," *International Journal of Opinion and Attitude Research*, 5 (Fall, 1951), pp. 407–15.

[6] Ivan D. Steiner, "Some Social Values Associated with Objectively and Subjectively Defined Social Class Memberships," *Social Forces*, 31 (May, 1953), pp. 327–332.

[7] Leonard Reissman, "Class, Leisure, and Social Participation," *American Sociological Review*, 19 (February, 1954), pp. 76–84.

more salient in the value systems of the middle class than of lower groups.[8]

Secular success could have been opposed by several kinds of values. Most frequently the lesser emphasis upon success is attributed to the perception of obstacles at the lower levels. But if there is a genuine value differentiation it should be expressed in a pattern of alternate preference. Impressionistic accounts of working-class values, like that of Richard Hoggart, stress the importance of the family circle and the tender sentiments that are part of the enlarged primary-group relationship.[9] The items selected for use in this investigation include some which do not oppose success to tender values, so that it is possible to determine whether this choice is critical.

We have attempted to devise each item so that it supplies somewhat different information from any other item. Different kinds of "tender values" are opposed to success in questions 9 (aesthetic-literary), 13 (family), 21 (kindness), and 36 (rewarding effort). In addition, success is opposed to security in question 34, to the acceptance of orders from a superior in question 17, and enjoyment of what one has in question 37. An eighth item was not included in the general index of success values, but bears a tangential relationship to this group. Item 32 is an effort to reflect the nineteenth-century value of stubborn pursuit of an unrealistic goal.

The next major set of values concerns individualism. Discussions of individualism suggested that it would be best to break this concept down into more delimitable components. Any such subdivision is necessarily arbitrary, and later in this report it will appear that somewhat different subgroupings might profitably have been made. Three pairs of antitheses were employed, as follows: self-reliance versus mutual aid; individuality versus "fitting in"; independence and freedom versus authority and tradition. The descriptions are as follows:

I. *Self-reliance.* The most worthwhile accomplishments are those we achieve by ourselves, depending entirely on our own resources. The strong person struggles through difficult tasks on his own, while the weak person calls on others for help. A man can take real pride in what he knows is entirely his own achievement in a way that he cannot when the achievement is that of several persons. The competent person gives more to the group then he receives.

Mutual aid. The principal value in accomplishment lies in working co-

[8] Cf., for example, Joseph A. Kahl, *The American Class Structure* (New York: Rinehart & Co., 1957), pp. 193–201, 205–210.

[9] Richard Hoggart, *The Uses of Literacy* (London: Chatto and Windus, 1957), pp. 27–61.

operatively with others. The finest persons are those who are equally ready both to give and to receive aid from others. An effective system of mutual aid, of pooling knowledge, skills, and resources is the best way of getting the most out of everyone.

II. *Individuality*. The discovery and development of one's personal uniqueness is a prime satisfaction, and having some individuality is a point of pride. To be just like the common run of men is to be nothing. The effect of the group on the superior member is a leveling one. But whether one is superior or not, he should have some uniqueness to which he can point.

Fitting in. Excessive uniqueness is an obstacle to an effectively working system of mutual aid. The person who stands out too much from others, even because of his superiority, often creates friction. A person gets a more worthwhile sense of satisfaction from feeling that he has a great deal in common with his fellows than he does from feeling superior to them.

III. *Independence and freedom.* An important goal in life is to free oneself from restraints upon behavior imposed by friends or associates or society. To feel completely free to make up one's own mind whether to do something or not to do it is the greatest satisfaction man can have. Working under the supervision of others is stultifying. Tradition is merely the tyranny of the past. Freedom is more important than accomplishment.

Authority and tradition. A man gains most by accepting the supervision of those who are more experienced or better qualified, and by following the wisdom of the ages as it is incorporated in tradition. One should have more sense than to set his opinions against those of authorities in a field. The ability to accept supervision constructively and make good use of authorities, and to understand and use the time-tested recipes for behavior is the mark of a mature person.

Citation of various aspects of individualism as "middle-class" characteristics is so extensive that only a few examples need be mentioned. Allison Davis is one of those who has described a system of mutual aid by which the "underprivileged workers" sustain one another during periodic lay-offs and unemployment and punish the individualistic pursuit of self-advancement.[10] Selig Perlman's classic statement concerning the character of working-class movements stresses the lack of self-confidence among laboring people, which precludes the adoption of individualistic ideologies.[11] Albert Cohen has made the distinction between norms of individualism and of reciprocity (mutual aid) the basis for his analysis of delinquency and the working-class boy.[12] An

[10] Allison Davis, "The Motivation of the Underprivileged Worker," in William F. Whyte, ed., *Industry and Society* (New York: McGraw-Hill, 1956).

[11] Selig Perlman, *A Theory of the Labor Movement* (New York: Augustus M. Kelley, 1949).

[12] Albert K. Cohen, *Delinquent Boys: The Culture of the Gang* (Glencoe: Free Press, 1955).

early empirical study by Useem, Tangent, and Useem, comparing the high stratum in a small South Dakota town with the lowest stratum, reports that the former are more individualistic and the latter higher in community mutual aid.[13] In Steiner's study of high-school students, already noted, the word "conceited" was among those rated distinctly more favorably by middle-class students.[14]

There are dissident notes regarding individualism, however. The individualism of the middle classes has often been tempered by a value placed upon charitable activities. A standard complaint of the would-be successful against those already in established positions has been the alleged practice of reserving positions for relatives and friends. August Hollingshead described the lowest class of boys in Elmtown as marked by a notable individualism, as not fitting well into any group activity.[15] And Marvin Sussman has stressed the existence of a mutual-aid system involving middle-class families.[16]

Four items were selected as representing a choice between self-reliance and mutual aid, one of which has already been included under the secular success rubric. The alternative is presented in its least complicated form in two items: (22) the pride in doing things on one's own without help from others, and (28) endorsement of the slogan, "neither a borrower nor a lender be." Question 36, which opposes success through breaks and pull to hard work, may be viewed partially as pitting self-reliance against secular success. Question 23 presents self-reliance as a more idealistic principle than the other items—respect for the other person's self-reliance rather than the assertion of one's own rights in this respect.

Six items were included to reflect individuality in various applications. The reputation of conceit is balanced against the advantage of being known for one's real abilities (18), and respect is balanced against being easy to get along with (26). Being superior to one's friends is opposed to being on a par with them (24). While these three items incorporate a passive aspect of individuality, two others express the manipulation of others, combining in different degrees the acceptance of difference and disagreement in a group. Moderate repudiation of the value of "fitting in" is expressed by (25) trying to get the group to do things one's own way rather than going along with the group, and the more extreme form is in (14) showing people how

[13] John Useem, Pierre Tangent, and Ruth Useem, "Stratification in Prairie Town," *American Sociological Review*, 7 (June, 1942), pp. 331–342.

[14] Steiner, *loc. cit.*

[15] August B. Hollingshead, *Elmtown's Youth: The Impact of Social Classes on Adolescents* (New York: Wiley, 1949), pp. 443–444.

[16] "The Help Pattern in the Middle Class Family," *American Sociological Review*, 18 (February, 1953), pp. 22–28.

to argue intelligently rather than smoothing over disagreements. A final item presents individuality in a special form, as (8) the choice between doing a few things perfectly or many things fairly well.

The third form of individualism produced more contradictory evidence and may, in retrospect, lack sufficient unity. Genevieve Knupfer observed that among low-status persons friendship contacts were confined to a narrow area, and suggested that this might possibly reflect a "deeply ingrained habit of doing what they are told." [17] Useem and associates had noted in 1942 that the top strata of women were more modern than the bottom strata.[18] However, a tendency for working-class people to vote more heavily for radical and liberal parties than the middle classes do appears to contradict the association of authority and tradition with the lower classes. Steiner's working-class students lent support to this counterevidence by rating the word "radical" more favorably than the middle-class students.[19] Attitude studies have generally supported the view that middle-class people are more receptive to the idea of change and experiment when political alignment and economic interest are not involved. H. J. Eysenck designed an attitude study to show that, when a variable of tough- and tender-mindedness was factored out, the conservatism of the working classes could be clearly demonstrated.[20]

Four items cover this somewhat heterogeneous area. The earlier question pitting (17) independence against success through taking orders is applicable here. A preference for (10) having things work out naturally is opposed to having groups quite organized. Defending one's opinion against that of the best authority (question 19) and trying new ways of doing things rather than sticking with time-tested ways (question 20) complete the authority and conservatism aspect of this value grouping.

Another item which is treated with the "youth-culture" grouping might properly be included here, though it has not been formally so classified. This is the (27) preference for making new friends, rather than sticking with a few tried and true friends.

Deferred gratification is the third major value-grouping included in the questionnaire. Since deferred gratification and impulse control have been so thoroughly linked in the sociological and psychological literature, it is appropriate to treat the latter as a corollary of the former.

17 Knupfer, *op. cit.*
18 Useem *et al., loc. cit.*
19 Steiner, *loc. cit.*
20 H. J. Eysenck, *The Psychology of Politics* (London: Routledge & Kegan Paul, 1954).

Deferred gratification. One should always act with the future in mind, treating the fleeting present in a calculating fashion for its contribution to the much longer future. The sacrifice of some immediate or momentary pleasure or gain when such sacrifice will help to secure a more worthwhile or pleasurable goal in the future is highly valued. The logic is that of thrift, in which one forgoes the pleasure he could have at the moment by spending his money as he gets it so that he can buy something more desirable later on, or invest the money and secure even greater returns.

Carpe diem. One should always live in the present, treating the future as undependable, unpredictable, and often a mere illusion. One should never pass up an opportunity to enjoy the present to its fullest, for no one can anticipate whether such opportunities will come later. Thrift is an illusion because of the unpredictability of the future. Those who save are no wealthier in the future than those who spend, but they will have had less enjoyment along the way

Impulse control. The expression or satisfaction of impulses as they occur must be restricted when they afford a threat to future benefit. A word unwisely spoken or a careless action may follow one for years. Since the long range consequences of any action or word are not usually immediately apparent at the moment they occur, it is generally better to control impulses rather than express them, or at least to delay their expression until a reasonable time has been allowed to explore their possible effects.

Impulsivity. The best time to satisfy an impulse is at the moment when it occurs. The satisfaction is fuller because it is spontaneous. Those who practice impulse control never fully enjoy anything because even when they do decide to act they are likely to feel ambivalent, to have lingering doubts as to the wisdom of expressing the impulse.

Association of middle class and deferred gratification is at least as old as recognition that the modern middle classes have been linked to the rise of capitalistic economics. The "spirit of capitalism" and the related "protestant ethic" include deferred gratification as a principal component.[21] In their classic study of child-raising, Allison Davis and Robert Havighurst concluded that middle-class methods served to make a more responsible, orderly, and tame individual.[22] Eli Ginsberg applied this idea in interpreting the socioeconomic differences in rates of premarital sex behavior reported by Kinsey and associates. Ginsberg suggested that middle-class boys were trained to defer gratifications of all kinds, including sexual consummation, for the sake of fuller gratifi-

21 Max Weber, *The Protestant Ethic and the Spirit of Capitalism* (London: Allen & Unwin, Ltd., 1930).
22 Allison Davis and Robert J. Havighurst, "Social Class and Color Differences in Child-Rearing," *American Sociological Review,* 11 (Dec., 1946), pp. 698–710.

cation in the future.[23] Leshan noted that when children from different backgrounds made up stories, the middle-class children placed theirs in a longer time span than did the working-class children.[24] In an effort to test the deferred-gratification hypothesis comprehensively by the use of a questionnaire, Schneider and Lysgaard found adequate support, though the differences between classes were not very great and some of the elements of the hypothesized value complex failed to correlate with socioeconomic status.[25]

Not all evidence is positive regarding deferred gratification. Steiner's middle-class high-school subjects rated "pleasure-loving" more favorably than did his working-class subjects.[26] Harry Beilen found no difference in willingness to postpone immediate satisfactions between high-I.Q. male students from low socioeconomic backgrounds who intended to go to college and a comparable group who did not. The finding was based on content analysis of responses to an open-ended questionnaire. He concluded that the investigator interprets as postponement what the subject regards as immediate gratification.[27]

The key item for this group was the choice between giving up all of one's pleasure now for the sake of the future and enjoying the present (question 35). The search for something better versus being satisfied with what one has (37), which was included under success, is also an indicator of deferment. The remaining items are special applications of this value. The preference for (11) dropping the subject until tempers cool rather than having it out right now stresses impulse control. The choices between (12) saving money for the future and spending money on friends and between (17) taking orders to get ahead and avoiding supervision deal with the deferment of peer relations and independence, respectively. The final choice between (33) a man of judgment and a man of action combines both deferment and impulse control in the "judgment" alternative, though it is clear that other broad values might be more relevant in the minds of our subjects.

The language of present-day intellectuals is full of references to "middle-class morality" and similar expressions. Such references are often vaguely all-encompassing. Frequently they refer to sex codes,

23 "Sex and Class Behavior," in D. P. Geddes and E. Curie, eds., *About the Kinsey Report* (New York: New American Library, 1948), pp. 131–145.

24 Lawrence L. Leshan, "Time Orientation and Social Class," *Journal of Abnormal and Social Psychology*, 47 (July, 1952), pp. 589–592.

25 Louis Schneider and Sverre Lysgaard, "The Deferred Gratification Pattern," *American Sociological Review*, 18 (April, 1953), pp. 142–149.

26 Steiner, *loc. cit.*

27 "The Pattern of Postponability and its Relation to Social Class Mobility," *Journal of Social Psychology*, 44 (August, 1956), pp. 33–48.

which we have not included in this investigation. But one of the aspects often implied is a code of strict personal integrity and responsibility. We have described this last general value as follows:

Strict integrity. Personal integrity is the greatest source of self-respect a person can have. A man's strength of character is indicated by his refusal to compromise a matter of principle, especially when there is much to lose and little to gain from strict adherence. A weakling shuns responsibility when he has made mistakes. Right and wrong are not to be judged by the consequences of action apparent to the actor; they can only be judged by reference to an established code of behavior.

Moral opportunism. Personal integrity is a good thing only when its effect on people is to facilitate their adjustment and happiness. Excessive concern with honesty and personal integrity makes people rigid and unkind. It is better to be an adjusted, effective person who can rationalize to himself when necessary than to assume unrealistic responsibility for following any strict code of conduct.

As early as the Hartshorne and May studies of character in children, empirical evidence was found that children from lower socioeconomic backgrounds were less rigidly honest in experimental situations than children from higher backgrounds.[28] Svend Ranulf argued from a variety of considerations that righteous indignation is a distinctively middle-class sentiment.[29] Irwin Smigel found that working-class subjects were more tolerant of "chiseling" on unemployment benefits than middle-class subjects.[30] B. M. Spinley concluded from personality tests administered to English slum and "public-school" children that the former lack the strict and efficient conscience that characterizes the latter.[31]

The most direct formulations of this broad alternative are found in items which contrast (15) sticking by the truth to telling a small lie to help a friend out of trouble, (30) taking full blame for mistakes and failures to laughing off mistakes and failures, and (38) being completely honest about feelings toward others to avoiding the truth when it would hurt others' feelings. In addition, two items already included under success contain an element of integrity. The choices between

[28] Hugh Hartshorne and Mark A. May, *Studies in Deceit* (New York: Macmillan, 1930).

[29] Svend Ranulf, *Moral Indignation and Middle Class Psychology* (New York: G. E. Stechert, 1938).

[30] Irwin Smigel, "Public Attitudes toward 'Chiseling' with Reference to Unemployment Compensation," *American Sociological Review,* 18 (February, 1953), pp. 59–67.

[31] B. M. Spinley, *The Deprived and the Privileged* (London: Routledge & Kegan Paul, 1953), pp. 129–133.

(21) being a smooth operator and being too kind to take unfair advantage, and (36) getting ahead by breaks and pull rather than strictly hard work may be examined in connection with the foregoing. Not included in this grouping, but related to concepts of right and wrong, is the choice between (31) defending one's honor or laughing off an insult.

VALUE CONTRADICTION AND VALUE DISCREPANCY

The classic configuration of the marginal man assumes *contradictions* rather than mere *discrepancies* between the value systems in which the individual is involved. Contradictions characterize the society in which distinct class subcultures coexist in a relationship of mutual accommodation. Discrepancies prevail where the classes have merely developed variations on a common society-wide system of values. Two kinds of evidence will be employed in order to discern whether contradiction or discrepancy is the rule. (1) The degree to which students from different backgrounds endorse different values. (2) The degree to which differences in goals correspond to differences in values not presented as personal goals.

Values Related to Background and Ambition

In Table 13, we report those value items which were found to be significantly associated with our measures of family background. Since we are interested in the most general conception of position in a system of stratification, we have used two measures: the family-breadwinner's occupation and the composite index of socioeconomic background. As described earlier, the latter is a simple summation of arbitrary weights assigned on the basis of breadwinner's occupation, education, and employer-employee status. Each measure of background (and of ambition) was trichotomized and each value item dichotomized as close as possible to the median in making these and subsequent cross tabulations in this chapter. Significance is accordingly measured by chi-square with two degrees of freedom.

Of the thirty-one items employed, eight for the men and nine for the women were significantly related to both of the measures at the two percent confidence level or better. For both men and women, another three items showed significant association with one of the two measures, revealing a similar but nonsignificant trend in relation to the other measure. The number of significant associations at the indicated levels of significance is not likely to be a product of chance, so we may safely conclude that there is some relationship between values and class background.

The relationships, however, are far from overwhelming on two counts. First, the number is not striking when we note that nearly all of the items were selected because there was some rationale for supposing that they should be correlated with class position. Thus, while some class differences exist, they do not cover the range of value choices which might have been anticipated from the contemporary literature on stratification.

Second, the magnitude of associations is small. The value most highly related to the background index is that placed on knowledge of serious subjects rather than popular subjects, and the biserial correlation with the background index is only .25 (males). Thus, there are many individuals within each class whose values are atypical. In light of this room for deviancy and the narrow range of values related to class position, the adjustments in the realm of values required in the course of upward mobility within the subject population would not seem excessive.

In order to impose a discipline upon the interpretation of correlations involving specific items, it is useful to consider them in the groups of related values. There is no support for the deferred-gratification hypothesis, nor for the hypothesis that strict integrity is a "middle-class value." Because of some negative correlations, it is even possible that moral opportunism may be the value associated with higher class position. Secular success and individualism, however, do supply several differences between high and low backgrounds.

In secular success it appears to be the acceptance of risk over security and the antithesis between secular, tough-minded success and tenderness which differentiate the classes. The choice between business success and family responsibilities, between the smooth operator and kindness, and between getting ahead by taking advantage of "breaks" and "pull" rather than by hard work document the latter difference.

Under individualism there is no support for viewing self-reliance as opposed to mutual aid, as a middle-class value, but some support for individuality and independence. Four of the six individuality items are clearly related to background for the women, but only two for the men. Neither for men nor for women does a concern to be free from authority and tradition relate to background. For women it is only individuality which differentiates according to background with any consistency, while for men none of the forms of individualism do so.

However, four of the individualism items which do correlate with

Table 13. Value Items Significantly Related to Background

Value item[a]	Male		Female	
	Bread-winner's occupation	Background index	Bread-winner's occupation	Background index
10. Likes things to work out naturally vs. likes groups quite organized	.02[b]	--	--	--
11. Believes in having it out right now vs. drops subject until tempers cool	--	--	.02	.02
13. Real success in business vs. real family man	.001	.01	--	--
14. Shows people how to argue intelligently vs. smooths over disagreements	.02	.02	.001	.01
15. Will tell small lie to help friend vs. sticks by the truth	--	--	.001	.001
17. Rather be own boss vs. will take orders to get ahead	.001	.01	--	--
18. Conceited, respected for abilities vs. has reputation for modesty	--	--	.05	.001
21. Smooth operator always comes out on top vs. too kind to take unfair advantage	.02	--	.001	.001

Value item[a]				
22. Prides self on doing things on his own vs. likes advice and help from others	--	--	--	.02
23. Good at making decisions for others vs. tries never to influence others	.02	.01	.05	--
24. Does many things better than friends vs. does most things as well as friends	--	.05	.001	.001
25. Tries to get group to do things his way vs. quick to go along with group	.01	.001	.01	.001
28. Neither a borrower nor a lender be vs. often borrows and lends with friends	--	--	--	.05
29. Talks about foreign policy and politics vs. talks about popular music and sports	.001	.001	.01	.01
34. Risks what he has to get ahead vs. prefers small but secure position	.01	.01	.001	.001
36. Uses breaks and pull to get ahead vs. works hard, refuses breaks and pull	.01	.02	--	--

a/ The headings in the table are abbreviated from the full statement of each value item as it appeared in the questionnaire. For convenience in tabular presentation (but not in the question-naire itself), the alternative more often chosen by respondents with higher backgrounds has been listed first in each instance.

b/ The probability that the observed associations could have occurred by chance in a random sample is less than the figure indicated in each instance. Associations were tested by chi-square, using two degrees of freedom.

background for men appear to reflect a common emphasis. Items number 14, 23, and 25 all incorporate the manipulation of others. In light of the failure of high-background boys to favor independence from authority and tradition, item number 17 should probably be interpreted as merely freedom to pursue one's own goals. The four items together may reflect the traditional entrepreneurial freedom from controls which is applied unilaterally in order to enable one to control others. This combination might be labeled "manipulative individualism."

In addition to tough-minded secular success and manipulative individualism, men from high and low backgrounds are differentiated only according to the value placed on being able to converse on serious rather than popular topics (number 29). For women, individuality is most prominent: there is some emphasis on secular success; there is also a value on conversing on serious topics, and some other scattered items show associations.

From these items we find little support for the 'classic concepts of value contradiction. However, it is quite possible that the lack of a positive valuation upon tough-minded manipulative attitudes toward others might be an obstacle to easy adoption of higher-class values by the mobile man.

Value Relevancy

Two people may "believe in" a value, or regard a given value as equally worthy, yet do so in a different fashion. The use of a value in any given situation depends not only upon the sensed worth of that value, but also upon the felt applicability or relevancy of the value to the situation. Our hypothesis may be stated as follows: *Social classes differ not so much in the values which they endorse in general as in the extent to which they regard these values as applicable to themselves as goals for their own striving.* The hypothesis rests on the assumption that there is a society-wide uniformity of values which crosscuts class lines, and that apparent value contradictions between classes are largely based on mistaking differences in value relevancy for differences in the acceptance of values. Whenever the life situation of any group of people who have some sense of mutual identity, such as the members of a social class, makes the attainment of any given value difficult and infrequent, the members of that group will tend through their self-conceptions to de-emphasize the value as a goal for their own striving, though they may continue to acknowledge it in other contexts.

Theoretical treatments of social class frequently assume that the values which are acknowledged on a society-wide basis are most readily attainable in the upper-middle class and least attainable in the lower segments of the manual-laboring classes.[32] Not only does this assumption apply to values such as the ambition-success complex, but it applies also to the traditional morality, to aesthetic and literary values, to individualism and self-reliance, and to many others. On the basis of this assumption we should expect to find a far-reaching difference in the personal relevancy of the values which middle-class and working-class people share. The upper-middle class would compartmentalize their values relatively little in this respect, tending to apply the values which they endorsed in general as goals for their own striving. Working-class members, on the other hand, should accept a great many values without applying them as goals for their own activity. If values were tested both in reference to the self and in reference to a more removed object, the representatives of different classes should differ less in relation to the latter than in relation to the former.

An attempt has been made to test this hypothesis by employing parallel forms of the questionnaire. The basic form on which the major analysis of values has been conducted presented each value item with the question, "Which kind of person would you rather be?" Four fifths of all questionnaires were worded in this fashion, so as to assure sufficient cases for the general examination of correlations of values with background, aspiration, mobility, and sociometric variables. This type of question was designed to identify values which the subjects applied to themselves. An alternate form was devised with the question in each instance stated as follows, "Which kind of person do you admire most?" [33] The question was framed in this fashion on the assumption that admiration is compatible with a maximum of social distance between the admirer and the admired. Thus, admiration was thought to indicate values held in a more general or abstract fashion, apart from their application to oneself. Every tenth questionnaire took this form. Our hypothesis was as follows: The answers to value items will differ by class background on Form A of the questionnaire (person you want to be), but not on Form B (person you admire most). Any finding that class differences were smaller in size or fewer in number on Form B than on Form A would suggest that observed differences were at least partially a matter of value discrepancy rather than value contradiction.

[32] Herbert H. Hyman, "The Value Systems of Different Social Classes," in Reinhard Bendix and Seymour M. Lipset, eds., *Class, Status, and Power* (Glencoe, Ill.: Free Press, 1953), pp. 426–442.

[33] The third alternate form which made up the remaining tenth of the questionnaires will be described in Chapter Six in connection with the discussion of youth subculture.

Unfortunately, the data of this investigation are not decisive with respect to the hypothesis because of the small number of cases employing Form B of the questionnaire. At the time the study was designed, somewhat larger correlations between values and the background and ambition measures were anticipated so that the size of the subsample required for significance was underestimated. Consequently, the comparison between forms of the questionnaire must be made in an impressionistic manner for whatever suggestive light it may shed on the hypothesis. None of the following speculations can be interpreted as conclusions fully warranted by the data.

When the value responses for males are cross-tabulated with the breadwinner's occupation (i.e., background) for Form B of the questionnaire, only one relationship is sufficient to reach minimum significance. We cannot conclude that there are no genuine relationships from the fact that only one out of thirty-one items reached the .025 level, however, since several of the relationships are of a magnitude equal to those which were accepted as significant on Form A with the larger number of cases.

We cannot proceed by a simple comparison of size of correlations based on Form A and Form B because the tabulation contains an intrinsic bias against the hypothesis, which is an artifact of the difference in sample sizes of the two questionnaire forms. By virtue of the much smaller sample on Form B, normal random variation would lead to a greater number of class differences of a given magnitude than in the larger sample of Form A. The difference in sample size can, however, be eliminated by employing a sample of the questionnaires from Form A. A sample approximately equal in size to the group of students who filled out Form B could be secured easily because of the system of numbering questionnaires. Questionnaires were distributed in serial number order, and all questionnaires ending with the digit "five" were Form B. As a sample of Form A respondents, all questionnaires ending in the digit "two" were used in the following analysis.

Because of the small size of the two samples, no attempt was made to identify relationships as significant or nonsignificant. Instead, attention was paid to the *degree* of relationship between background and each value item. If the relationship based on Form A of the questionnaire exceeded the relationship based on Form B, the hypothesis was confirmed. Since no confidence could be placed in the findings with respect to a single item, the number of positive and negative findings for the thirty-one items was regarded as the crucial indicator. As a measure of relationship the phi coefficient was employed, with the background index dichotomized near the median and the value items dichotomized as usual.

Table 14. Summary of Sample-Value-Relevancy Test

Sex	Form A minus Form B	All corre-lations	Correla-tions≥.10	Correla-tions≥.15
Male	Positive	19	13	9
	Negative	11	5	1
	No difference	1	--	--
	Total	31	18	10
Female	Positive	10	7	3
	Negative	19	10	7
	No difference	2	--	--
	Total	31	17	10

The differences which support and refute the hypothesis are summarized in Table 14. The latter table tells us that of thirty-one pairs of correlations, nineteen are in the predicted direction, eleven are in the opposite direction, and one pair shows no difference. There is clearly a modest preponderance in favor of the value-relevancy hypothesis. There is some tendency for men students to reflect their class backgrounds more strongly when translating values into their personal goals than when expressing admiration for someone.

The inadequacies of the data have still not been entirely circumvented in the latter findings. It is clear that several of the value items—perhaps even a majority—do not correlate with class background at all. Consequently, we have inadvertently included in the foregoing summary a number of differences between relationships which are too small to merit consideration. Differences of this sort will be random, dividing evenly between support of the hypothesis and disconfirmation. Inclusion of several such pairs will tend to obscure whatever relationship there is. Ideally, we should eliminate from consideration all items for which neither form of the questionnaire produces a "real" relationship. With large samples, we could do this by examining only relationships which are significant at one of the accepted levels. With the present samples, such a procedure would eliminate most of the items.

In order to achieve the purpose without eliminating too many items, we have adopted another expedient. If we disregard all items on which *both* coefficients fall below some arbitrary minimum, we can eliminate some of the "unreal" relationships without introducing any bias either favorable or unfavorable to the hypothesis. If the hypothesis is valid, any step which eliminates some of the random differences based on unreal relationships should produce more clear-cut support for the hypothesis. To this end we have adopted .10 as a minimum correlation, thus reducing the number of items from thirty-one to eighteen. Of the eighteen items, thirteen now support the hypothesis as compared with five which negate it. The result is clearly as predicted. By eliminating irrelevant items, we have secured a clearer confirmation of the hypothesis.

The minimum of .10 undoubtedly still includes some instances in which the relationships would disappear in a more adequate sample to which significance tests could be applied. If our logic is correct, each succeeding elimination of more unreal relationships should sharpen the findings further. If the hypothesis of value relevancy is both true and important, a second increase in the minimum acceptable correlation coefficient should provide even more decisive confirmation. Consequently, the differences between pairs of coefficients have been summarized a third time, setting .15 as the minimum. Of the remaining ten items, nine now confirm the hypothesis and one contradicts it.

Not only is there a preponderance of differences in support of the hypothesis, but also two steps taken to reduce the obfuscating effects of excessively small relationships successively improve the support for the hypothesis. Hence, we feel justified in saying that there is considerable presumption in favor of the relevancy hypothesis.

The data for women do not fit the relevancy hypothesis. If there is any tendency, it is in the opposite direction. It is for values to be more clearly differentiated with respect to admiration than personal goals. The elimination of random variations does not produce quite so clear a picture for women as for men. However, it is of interest to speculate that, in relation to women's role, value relevancy may have a special import. If a woman's station in life is determined more by the characteristics of the man she marries than by her own, then whom she admires (and is likely to marry) may have more relevance to her social status than what values she selects as her personal goals.

We have assumed that it is the men from lower backgrounds who shift their values when we ask about admiration rather than personal goals. While we can be even less confident of findings on this score than on the relevancy hypothesis itself, it is of interest simply to observe whether this is the case. Three of the items (24, 29, 34) which give strong support to the relevancy hypothesis show high-background students answering the two forms very similarly and low-background students answering quite differently. Admiration for the risk-taker, for the expert on serious topics, and for the person who excels his friends is uniformly shared by men from high and low backgrounds. The latter, however, are unwilling to make these values their own personal goals, probably because the working-class situation does not reward them as the middle-class situation does. On the other hand, two items (13, 21) show the opposite kind of shift. The high-background men admire the family man and the person who is too kind to take advantage of others, though their personal goals are more ruthless. Perhaps the middle-class boy is forced by his life situation to sacrifice the value he places on family and kindness because of the competitive and precarious nature of his station. Just as the lower-class boy may admire risk-taking but recognize that it does not pay in his situation, the middle-class boy may admire those who value being kind before being a "smooth operator," but realize that such a choice would be dangerous for him.

No effort will be made to determine how many items correspond to each of the types of shifts. It is sufficient to have illustrated the observation that both kinds of shifts are found, that each social class may make certain of the society-wide values less tenable as individual goals.

ANTICIPATORY SOCIALIZATION

The theory of anticipatory socialization can be briefly restated. Social classes (or other groups) tend to differ in the values their members espouse. But when a person who is objectively a member of one class thinks of himself as belonging to another *and* strives to attain membership in that other class, he will adopt the attitudes and values characteristic of his aspiration class before he actually becomes a member. Thus there will be members in most classes who do not exhibit the characteristic values because they are oriented toward future membership in some other classes.

Operationalizing Anticipatory Socialization

Anticipatory socialization can best be studied in a group that can be followed for several years, noting alterations in their values. But lacking such data, we can nevertheless determine whether the interrelationships of background and ambition with values are such as would be predicted from an assumed process of anticipatory socialization.

We cannot depend merely upon the correlation of values with ambition to justify the assumption of anticipatory socialization, because such correlations may well be products of the intercorrelation of ambition with values. Hence, the first requirement for evidence of anticipatory socialization is that correlations of some consequence between ambition and values remain when statistical correction to remove the influence of background has been made. The question of which set of correlations is causally prior cannot be adequately resolved by partialing and similar statistical methods, so it is desirable to treat each in turn as causally prior in order to compare the results. It is essential for the process of anticipatory socialization that any statistical correction which eliminates the influence of ambition should substantially reduce the apparent correlation between background and values. It must be shown that much of the seeming relationship between "class values" and background can result from the fact that ambitious persons, who acquire values appropriate to their destinations, are likely to have high backgrounds, rather than from direct connection between background and values.

The relationship is further complicated by linking the idea of anticipatory socialization with the concept of reference group. Unless anticipatory socialization is taken to imply some intuitive grasp of values which are not known firsthand, there must be a reference group of persons who already adhere to the appropriate values and from whom the ambitious person learns them. The reference group may be an adult group of some sort. But if ambitious students seek acceptance into a high stratum of society, it is likely that they pursue affiliation with those of their peers who already represent the high level they seek. Hence, they will adopt the students who come from high backgrounds as their reference group. Anticipatory socialization will then proceed by their learning from high-background students the values which the latter have already acquired in the home.

For a process of this sort to work, the students must begin with values appropriate to their social origins, gradually trading these for values appropriate to their destinations. It is not necessary that the shift be entirely complete, since even established adults show some trace of the values appropriate to their origin, compromising their acceptance of perspectives appropriate to the positions they have attained.[34] At any point during the process, then, we should look for some degree of independent correlation linking both background and ambition with values. The independent correlation with background indicates persis-

[34] Cf. Ralph H. Turner, "Life Situation and Subculture: A Comparison of Merited Prestige Judgments by Three Occupational Classes in Britain," *British Journal of Sociology*, 9 (Dec., 1958), pp. 312–314.

tence of the initial value commitments which allowed the anticipatory socialization process to be set in motion by supplying a value-differentiated reference group. The independent correlation with ambition shows that the relationship between ambition and values is not a mere artifact or the intercorrelation between background and ambition.

The case for anticipatory socialization will be more impressive if the data show that the "class-value" differentation of students is greater by ambition than by background. In this case it will be clear that a future-orientation has shaped the dominant organization, and the likelihood that the findings for anticipatory socialization are an artifact will be lessened. The best support for anticipatory socialization will consist of finding that the correlations between values and background are smaller than those between values and ambition. Support will also be found in the related finding that correlations between ambition and values account for more of the apparent correlation between background and values than the correlations between background and values do for the correlation between ambition and values.

Analysis by Individual Items

In Table 15 there is a list of the items that appear to be associated with ambition. Two measures were employed: occupational ambition and the ambition index. Both were trichotomized and related to the value items dichotomized. Comparison with Table 13 shows that more items are significantly related to ambition than to background.

For men, nine items are significant by both measures and a total of sixteen are significantly related to one of the two measures. When the results are compared index by index, eleven items are significantly related to occupational ambition as compared with ten significantly related to occupational background, and fourteen items are related to the ambition index as compared with nine significantly related to the background index. All of the items related to background are significantly related to ambition by at least one of the two measures, and the directions of significant associations are uniformly the same for ambition and background. Thus the correlations of values with ambition subsume the correlations with background and go beyond them, rather than bringing in a different set of associations. From such evidence we can draw preliminary support for the anticipatory-socialization theory.

For women, twelve items relate significantly to both indexes and another four or six to only one of the indexes. Fifteen items are related to occupational ambition as compared with ten to occupational back-

Table 15. Value Items Significantly Related to Ambition

Value item[a]	Male		Female	
	Occupational ambition	Ambition index	Occupational ambition	Ambition index
8. Can do a few things perfectly vs. can do many things fairly well	--	--	--	.05[b]
10. Likes things to work out naturally vs. likes groups quite organized	--	.05	.02	--
12. Spends extra money on friends vs. saves extra money for future	--	--	.02	.01
13. Real success in business vs. real family man	.05	.01	.001	.001
14. Shows people how to argue intelligently vs. smooths over disagreements	.001	.001	.01	.001
15. Will tell small lie to help friend vs. sticks by the truth	--	--	.001	.001
17. Rather be own boss vs. will take orders to get ahead	.01	.001	.001	.001
21. Smooth operator always comes out on top vs. too kind to take unfair advantage	.02	.001	.001	.001
22. Prides self on doing things on his own vs. likes advice and help from others	.05	--	.001	.02
23. Good at making decisions for others vs. tries never to influence others	.05	.05	--	--
24. Does many things better than friends vs. does most things as well as friends	--	.05	.001	.001

Item				
25. Tries to get group to do things his way vs. quick to go along with group	.001	.001	.001	.001
26. Respected but hard to get along with vs. easy to get along with	--	--	--	--
28. Neither a borrower nor a lender be vs. often borrows-lends with friends	.01	.01	.01	.01
29. Talks foreign policy and politics vs. talks popular music and sports	.001	.001	.001	.001
30. Laughs off his failure and mistakes vs. takes full blame for own failures	--	--	--	.05
31. Laughs off insult to his honor vs. never lets insult to honor go by	.02	--	--	--
34. Risks what he has to get ahead vs. prefers small but secure position	.05	.001	.001	.001
35. Gives up pleasure now for future vs. enjoys present	.001	.05	--	--
36. Uses breaks and pull to get ahead vs. works hard, refuses breaks and pull	--	.05	.001	--
37. Always looking for something better vs. satisfied with what he has	--	.001	.001	.001

a/ Each value item has been stated with the alternative favored by the respondents with higher ambition listed first.

b/ The probability that the observed associations could have occurred by chance in a random sample is less than the figure indicated in each instance. Associations were tested by chi-square, using two degrees of freedom.

ground. Fifteen items are related to the ambition index as compared with eleven to the background index. There are, however, three items that may only be related to background, though the directions of all relationships are the same for ambition and background.

No attempt has been made to use the relative size of correlations because all are initially so small. The more important step is to observe what happens to correlations when the two stratification variables are held constant in turn. Because of the only partial adequacy of each technique, two procedures have been employed to the same end.

In the first procedure we have treated each value item which was significantly correlated with the background index separately, employing a standardization procedure which avoids all assumptions of linearity. The objective of the procedure is to compute a set of adjusted expected frequencies which can be compared with the observed and unadjusted expected frequencies employed in the chi-square tables used to determine the relationships reported in Tables 13 and 15. The adjusted expected frequencies for given value endorsements are computed for high, middle, and low backgrounds, respectively, on the basis of the observed distribution of ambition in each category and the overall rates of endorsement by gradations of ambition. The result is a set of expected frequencies by background which are adjusted for the unequal distribution of ambition within each background category. The same procedure is then repeated, reversing the priority of ambition and background.

The result of the foregoing procedure is that, if ambition can account for none of the relationship between background and values, the adjusted expected frequencies by background will be identical with the unadjusted expected frequencies. If ambition accounts for exactly all of the relationship, the adjusted expected frequencies will be identical with observed frequencies.

Because of the uncertain effect of the standardization procedure on degrees of freedom, it is not possible to compute an adjusted chi-square and judge the significance of the remaining relationship in the manner in which a coefficient of partial correlation can be interpreted. However, we can employ the simple expedient of comparing the total size of the differences between observed and adjusted expected frequencies, so long as relationships are linear among the three categories of high, middle, and low. In Table 16 we have stated the difference based on unadjusted expected frequencies as a fraction of the difference based on unadjusted expected frequencies for each of the relevant value items. If we treat the magnitude of these differences as a measure of size of relationship, the table can be read in the following manner: on item

13 for males, 57 percent of the relationship between background and response to this value item remains after correction for the correlation between background and ambition. A slightly larger proportion, 67 percent of the relationship between ambition and response to the value item, remains after correction is made for the intercorrelation. Since magnitudes in this procedure are measured by the simple sum of differences, they cannot be equated in absolute terms with the magnitudes of correlation coefficients or other standard measures of relationship.

Examination of the table reveals that in most instances a substantial portion of each relationship is independent of the other, and that neither variable is overwhelmingly more important. In eight of the nine pairs for men and in nine of the twelve pairs for women, the residual is larger for ambition than for background though the individual differences are small. Thus, in general, we find support for the hypothesis that ambition has more power to account for relationships between background and values than background has to account for relationships between ambition and value.

Class-Value Index

In order to permit an alternative approach to such problems as this, we have devised a *class-value index* which can be treated by correlation methods. The nine value items that correlate significantly with both background and ambition for men are employed in this index. The response to each item is assigned the arbitrary weight of either "one" or "zero," indicating an endorsement associated with high ambition and background, or the opposite. The sum of these numbers for each individual, with a possible range from zero to nine, constitutes the basis for his class-value index.[35] The distribution of index values for the entire population of the study approximates a normal curve. Because the index has been constructed on the basis of the findings for males, it is a less adequate measure in the analysis of female data.

Correlations of the class-value index with background and ambition are summarized in Table 17, and reveal similar patterns for men and women. The zero-order correlation with ambition is larger than the correlation with background, but not greatly so. When partial coefficients are computed, the correlation between class values and ambition after background is held constant is still as large as the zero-order

---

[35] The nine items, with the alternative weighted "1" noted in parentheses, are as follows: 13 (a), 14 (b), 17 (b), 23 (a), 24 (a), 25 (b), 29 (b), 34 (a), and 36 (a). Responses to each item were dichotomized near the median before assigning the arbitrary weights.

Table 16. Adjustments for Background and Ambition[a]

Value item	Percent of difference remaining after adjustment			
	Male		Female	
	Attributable to background	Attributable to ambition	Attributable to background	Attributable to ambition
11. Believes in having it out right now vs. drops subject until tempers cool	--	--	74%	44%
13. Real success in business vs. real family man	57%	67%	--	--
14. Shows people how to argue intelligently vs. smooths over disagreements	63	83	52	79
15. Will tell small lie to help friend vs. sticks by the truth	--	--	68	44
17. Rather be own boss vs. will take orders to get ahead	58	64	--	--
18. Conceited, respected for abilities vs. has reputation for modesty	--	--	74	78
21. Smooth operator always comes out on top vs. too kind to take unfair advantage	--	--	63	52
22. Prides self on doing things on his own vs. likes advice and help from others	--	--	63	73
23. Good at making decisions for others vs. tries never to influence others	73	59	--	--

24. Does many things better than friends vs. does most things as well as friends	53%	73%	47%	70%
25. Tries to get group to do things his way vs. quick to go along with group	64	65	50	75
28. Neither a borrower nor a lender be vs. often borrows-lends with friends	--	--	56	82
29. Talks foreign policy and politics vs. talks popular music and sports	45	69	20	73
34. Risks what he has to get ahead vs. prefers small but secure position	06	92	52	77
36. Uses breaks and pull to get ahead vs. works hard, refuses breaks or pull	59	73	58	122

a/ Relationships between value items and stratification were initially measured as the difference between observed and expected frequencies in a six-fold table. Adjustments were then made by a simple standardization procedure. The expected frequencies of response to the value item were calculated on the basis of the distribution of ambition in each background category. The difference between observed and adjusted-expected frequencies is attributable to background independently of the correlated influence of ambition. The latter difference is stated as a proportion of the initial difference in the first column of the table. The entire operation was simply reversed in the second column. The larger the proportion, the greater is the fraction of the relationship between the specified variable and the value item which is independent of the relationship with the other stratification variable.

Table 17. Correlation of Class-Value Index
with Background and Ambition Indexes[a]

Variables correlated	Variable(s) constant	Male	Female
CVI with background index	None	.24	.25
CVI with ambition index	None	.32	.40
CVI with school	None	.28	.27
CVI with background index	Ambition index	.14	.10
CVI with ambition index	Background index	.25	.33
CVI with background index and school	None	.31	.30
CVI with background index and school	Ambition index	.21	.16
CVI with ambition index	Background index and school	.22	.31

a/ Coefficients include zero order, multiple, first-
and second-order-partial, and multiple-partial coefficients,
as indicated by the number of variables correlated and held
constant.

coefficient between class values and background. However, there remains a small but significant partial correlation between background and class values when ambition is held constant.

In order to insure against overestimating the evidence in support of anticipatory socialization, we should also consider the school neighborhood as an element of background. School neighborhood is probably partially an additional element of background and partially a "climate" constituted out of the future-orientations of students. If we attribute the entire "influence" of school neighborhood to background, we make the most conservative possible assumption in testing anticipatory socialization.

Returning to the table, we note that the coefficient of correlation between class values and school is less than the correlation with ambition but more than the correlation with the background index. The correlation of class values with background and school together (multiple correlation) is about the same as the simple correlation of class values with ambition. Similarly, the correlation of class values with background and school together while ambition is held constant (multiple partial correlation) is about the same as the correlation of class values with ambition while background and school are both held constant (second-order partial correlation). Thus, the introduction of the conservative assumption that neighborhood is wholly a part of background does not greatly alter the impression already gained that anticipatory socialization is an important reality. There remains, in addition, some independent correlation between background and values, indicating that class-of-origin values have not yet been fully exchanged for class-of-destination values.

We have spoken as if aspiration accounts for values, while it might be as reasonable to suppose that values account for aspiration. The anticipatory-socialization formula gives priority to aspiration and employs aspiration to account for the adoption of values which do not correspond with those of one's membership group. Except for calling into question the specific mechanism of anticipatory socialization, the issue in its simplest form does not seem to be the key issue in this investigation. If one assumes a tendency toward equilibrium between values and future-orientation with respect to group membership, causation in the individual instance might begin from either direction. For purposes of describing the social milieu within which the mobile person must work out his adjustments, the substantial correlation with membership group is the crucial finding.

The observation that direction of causation cannot be inferred from correlation may be modified in slight degree. We know by the nature of the variables that background must be causally prior to both ambition and class values. Hence the possibilities are three: either background determines both of the other variables, or class values constitute the intervening variable between background and ambition, or ambition is the intervening variable between background and class values. The last of these alternatives expresses the principle of anticipatory socialization best, since the adoption of values is contingent upon ambition. The partial-correlation analysis has shown that no one of these alternatives can account fully for the relationships observed. However, a tentative choice can be made by employing the same formula used in dealing with I.Q.

It is possible to compare the fit of the three correlations, between background and ambition (.24 for men, .38 for women), background and the class-value index (.25, .24), and ambition and the class-value index (.40, .32), with models based on the three alternatives. Of the three, the view that background leads to class values which cause ambition is least supportable. By contrast, the data fit best the anticipatory-socialization pattern, with ambition as the intervening variable between background and class values. While the conclusion is highly tentative because of the necessary assumptions that all variables have been measured equally well and that other variables are acting independently upon those under investigation, it is worthy of note that our data supply slightly firmer support for the standard interpretation of anticipatory socialization than for other lines of interpretation.

VALUE DIFFERENCES BETWEEN HIGH BACKGROUND AND HIGH AMBITION

Correlates of Ambition: Males

From the thirty-one value choices employed in the investigation, three seem to be clearly associated with ambition but not with background for male respondents (Tables 13 and 15). These items are preferences for (28) "neither a borrower nor a lender be," (35) "giving up all of his pleasure now so that he can be sure of the future," and (37) "always looking for something better than he has." In addition, the ambitious person may be distinctive in the degree to which he (22) "prides himself on doing things on his own, without asking anyone else for advice or help," and (31) "tries to overlook or laugh off any insult to his honor or his family's honor."

Two of the first three items represent the purest instances of the general value of deferred gratification. Postponing pleasure and looking for something better, rather than trying to enjoy what one has, express the core idea of deferring gratification. The items classified under deferred gratification which do not differentiate the ambitious from the high born either employ some antithesis other than immediate satisfaction or depict an element from an extended value complex rather than deferred gratification in the narrow sense.

An endorsement of self-reliance is suggested by the ambitious boys' acceptance of the adage, (28) "neither a borrower nor a lender be," and by their possible preference for (22) doing things on their own. Although the ambitious and the high born both tend to reject the self-reliant alternative in the other two items in this category, they differ in degree. The ambitious boys show a less marked preference for (23) making decisions for others rather than trying never to influence others, and for (36) using breaks and pull rather than getting ahead by hard work alone, than do the boys from high backgrounds. While the ambitious boys share the success values and some of the manipulative values of students who start from high backgrounds, they appear to weigh self-reliance a little more heavily, thereby lessening the impact of success and manipulation in these two choices. The four items together, then, supply a consistent picture of the ambitious boy as stressing self-reliance more than the merely high-born boy. With considerable confidence we conclude that self-reliance is an element in the value complex of destination stratification, but not of origin stratification.

It is noteworthy that under certain conditions of social structure there is a functional interrelationship between these two values of self-reliance and deferred gratification. Deferral of gratification often means the repudiation of mutual aid. In the "underprivileged-worker" complex described by Allison Davis [36] the two go hand in hand. In order to save for the future, the worker must defy the informal obligations of mutual aid to his less fortunate fellows. The assurance of mutual aid in turn eliminates the necessity for planning future security. If we keep in mind that both the high born and the ambitious are marked by a disproportionate success orientation, the interrelation of self-reliance and deferred gratification reinforces a picture of upwardly mobile men which has been documented from other sources.[37] The upwardly mobile men seem to be more controlled and socially reserved, having learned to extricate themselves from the mutual-aid patterns which would be of service to them only to the extent that they sought their principal satisfactions in their present social settings.

Correlates of Ambition: Females

Among the women a larger number of items appear to be associated with ambition but not background. Those which seem fairly clear are as follows: (12) "spends most of his extra money on his friends," (13) "real success in business, but isn't much of a family man (woman)," (17) "rather be his own boss than get ahead by taking orders," (26) "has everyone's respect but is very hard to get along with," (36) "watches for 'breaks' and . . . 'pull'," (37) "always looking for something better." The more questionable items are the following: (8) "can do a few things perfectly, but can't do many things fairly well," (10) "likes to see things work out naturally without much organization," (22) "prides himself on doing things on his own," (28) "neither a

---

[36] Allison Davis, "The Motivation of the Underpriviliged Worker," in William F. Whyte, ed., *Industry and Society* (New York: McGraw-Hill, 1946).

[37] For example, cf. W. Lloyd Warner and James C. Abegglen, *Big Business Leaders in America* (New York: Harper & Brothers, 1955); Melville Dalton, "The Industrial 'Rate-Buster'; a Characterization," *Applied Anthropology*, 7 (Winter, 1948), pp. 5–18.

borrower nor a lender be" (30) "can laugh off his failures and mistakes."

Two themes are repeated in this list of items. First, the emphasis on secular success which correlates with both ambition and background among the men differentiates the ambitious women, regardless of background. Three items among the clearest group (13, 36, 37) show this difference. Second, various types of individualism are reflected by two items in the first group (17, 26) and four among the less certain (8, 10, 22, 28). Two of the latter are the same self-reliance items which distinctively characterized the ambitious men. Two other items (one from each group) are independence items which correlated with both ambition and background for men. The remaining two items enlarge the area of individuality which already sets the high-background women apart from their peers, but even more markedly sets those of high ambition apart from others.

The two remaining items (12, 30) fit no pattern, except that both may be parts of the youth subculture.[38] Since other youth-culture items correlate in the opposite direction, however, it would be inappropriate to generalize on this basis.

As compared with the men, ambitious women appear to be more extensively differentiated in values from the merely high-born women. In one respect both ambitious men and ambitious women are differentiated on the same value: self-reliance is more highly valued by the ambitious than by the unambitious, regardless of sex.

Ambitious men are distinguished by their valuation of deferred gratification, while ambitious women are distinguished by a heightened emphasis upon individuality (8, 26). It is difficult not to find more than a chance correspondence between these differences and the distinctive sex roles within which ambition must be pursued. Traditionally, the male pursues his advancement by his own active efforts. In a sense he must actively grasp what he wants. Under these circumstances he must be ready to hoard his resources and to forgo immediate gratifications in order to make best use of the opportunities which are to come. The woman, on the other hand, succeeds by being chosen. While she may plan and scheme, it is ultimately a passive pose—that of being chosen— through which she succeeds or fails with respect to socioeconomic standing. Individuality, distinctiveness, standing out from the group— these are qualities which enhance the possibilities that the woman will not be overlooked when the choices are being made. In light of the changing character of modern business and professional activity, the

---

[38] The youth subculture is discussed in Chapter Six.

virtue of individuality gives way in the face of the importance of fitting in, so this quality ceases to differentiate the ambitious male. But individuality, which distinguishes the high-background female, distinguishes even more the woman with high ambition.

The remaining values which mark the woman of high ambition irrespective of background are values which distinguish the men of both high ambition and high background. These are the values of secular success and independence. When we found that men of high ambition held the same values as men of high background, we attributed the finding to a process of anticipatory socialization. We assumed that the ambitious boy from a lower background adopted boys from higher levels as his reference group and acquired a set of values which accorded with his destination. Since the girls from high backgrounds exhibit no more endorsement of secular success and independence than girls from lower levels, there can be no anticipatory socialization based upon adoption of high-level girls as a reference group. But another possibility suggests itself. There is extensive correspondence between the values which differentiate high from low strata, regardless of sex, and the values which distinguish males from females. The "male" values are for the most part the higher-strata values; the "female" values are those of the lower strata.[39] If the constellation of values which belong with high strata also constitutes the male values, it is conceivable that the ambitious girls should adopt the higher-stratum boys as their reference group, and thereby acquire such values as secular success and the strong valuation of independence.

These interpretations of the characteristics of ambitious men and women can only be regarded as an effort to suggest one set of explanations for some sparse findings. They do indicate that the upwardly mobile individual may adhere to values which set him somewhat apart from the peers of his origin or his destination, and that the ambitious girl may be set apart by a wider range of such values than the boy.

Manipulative Individualism

Inspection suggests that the four items which we called manipulative individualism correlate less strongly with ambition than with background. In addition, the items are notable for the fact that three of them show a similar degree of association with background on both Form A and Form B of the questionnaire.

In Table 18 we offer a comparison of correlations with the *manipula-*

[39] Twenty-one items are significantly related with sex (P < .01), and these subsume most of the items related to either background or ambition. In only two instances is the female alternative associated with higher ambition or background.

Table 18. Correlation of Class-Value Index
and Manipulative Individualism with Background
and Ambition Indexes[a]

Sex	Independent variable(s)	Variable(s) held constant	Dependent variable	
			Class-value index	Manipulative individualis...
Male	Background index	None	.24	.23
	School	None	.28	.20
	Ambition index	None	.32	.14
	Background index and school	None	.31	.25
	Background index and school	Ambition index	.21	.22
	Ambition index	Background index and school	.22	.03
Female	Background index	None	.25	.19
	School	None	.27	.18
	Ambition index	None	.40	.24
	Background index and school	None	.30	.21
	Background index and school	Ambition index	.16	.12
	Ambition index	Background index and school	.31	.17

a/ Zero order, multiple, second-order-partial, and multiple-partial coefficients are included, as indicated b... the numbers of variables correlated and held constant.

tive-individualism index and the *class-value index,* the latter includ- ing the four items in the former index along with five others. The table repeats correlations presented earlier which show that the class-value index is more highly correlated with ambition than with background. But the relationships with manipulative individualism follow a different pattern. For men, the correlation with background is greater than the correlation with ambition. Correlations with background are practically the same for class values and manipulative individualism, but the correlation between class values and ambition is more than twice as large as the correlation between manipulative individualism and ambition. A rather similar pattern applies to the women, but is less marked.

There are already indications that anticipatory socialization cannot be a simple process of absorbing the values possessed by members of a reference group. The ambitious boys exhibit values of deferred gratification and self-reliance which are not exhibited by their presumed reference group of boys from high backgrounds. These values must have been acquired elsewhere, or at the very most they must have come from mistaking a ceremonial image of the higher stratum for the private convictions of the members with whom the mobile boys have come in contact. The correlations involving manipulative individualism suggest a respect in which the upwardly mobile boys may have failed to acquire one type of value which is a part of the private convictions of the youthful members of their higher-stratum reference group.

The use of partial correlation can supply a more decisive indication of whether upwardly mobile youth characteristically fail to acquire the *manipulative-individualism* value while undergoing anticipatory socialization with respect to other values. The appropriate hypothesis is as follows: background will exhibit relatively similar correlations with class values and manipulative individualism when ambition is held constant; ambition will correlate with class values but not with manipulative individualism when background is held constant. In order to deal with background comprehensively, we have combined family background and school by multiple correlation in testing the hypotheses. The pattern of correlations for males corresponds exactly to these hypotheses. The first three partial correlations are practically identical in magnitude, and relationships of such magnitude would occur by chance less than once in a thousand times. The correlation between ambition and manipulative individualism when background and school are held constant is practically nil. There is no correlation between manipulative individualism and ambition apart from that which can be explained by the family backgrounds and schools from which the ambitious boys disproportionately come.

Table 19. Neighborhood Variation in Correlation of Class-Value Index and Manipulative Individualism with Background and Ambition Indexes

Neighborhood	Independent variable	Variable held constant	Dependent Variable			
			Male		Female	
			Class value	Manipulative individualism	Class value	Manipulative individualism
Nonethnic; high-level schools	Background index	None	.12	.14	.20	.18
	Ambition index	None	.18	.16	.33	.22
	Background index	Ambition index	.06	.09	.07	.10
	Ambition index	Background index	.15	.12	.28	.16

Nonethnic: middle-level schools	Background index	None	.17	.17	.18	.13
	Ambition index	None	.32	.22	.36	.20
	Background index	Ambition index	.08	.11	.07	.07
	Ambition index	Background index	.28	.18	.33	.17
Nonethnic: low-level schools	Background index	None	.07	.22	.02	.06
	Ambition index	None	.04	.01	.28	.10
	Background index	Ambition index	.06	.22	-.08	.03
	Ambition index	Background index	.03	-.02	.29	.08
All: low-level schools	Background index	None	.06	.07	.05	.03
	Ambition index	None	.10	-.02	.20	.11
	Background index	Ambition index	.06	-.08	-.01	--
	Ambition index	Background index	.10	-.03	.19	.10

Neighborhood and Class Values

The impact of neighborhood on class values can be noted in Table 18. For both males and females the coefficients of correlation between class values and neighborhood are about the same as those between class values and family background. If background is held constant, the partial correlations between school and the class-value index are .20 and .17 for men and women, respectively. These coefficients are small, but surpass the .001 requirements for significance. Herein lies further documentation for the effect of neighborhood in addition to the individual family background of the child. Schools that draw their students disproportionately from higher-family backgrounds tend to be more middle class in values than the individual backgrounds would warrant. Schools which draw their students disproportionately from lower family backgrounds are less middle class in values than the individual backgrounds of their students would warrant. The impact of neighborhood (as we interpret the difference between schools) is to accentuate the predominant tendencies, both with respect to ambition and with respect to values.

Whether the relationships among variables differ according to the type of neighborhood can be explored by the use of correlations computed separately for the high-, middle-, and low-area schools. The correlations with the class-value index reported in Table 19 suggest that there may be such differences, although the small size of all coefficients prevents the differences themselves from being significant. For men, the class-value index correlates most highly with both background and ambition in the middle-level schools, and is probably unrelated in the low-level schools. For women, the highest correlation with ambition is likewise in the middle level, but substantial correlations exist in all three kinds of areas. Background reveals no relationship in the lower-level neighborhoods, but exhibits approximately equal relationships in the middle and higher areas. To the extent to which it is safe to generalize from these correlations, it appears that the standard relationships with class values either fail to apply or apply less well in the lower-level neighborhoods than in the higher-level.

We have assumed that an important feature of the preparation for mobility is the learning of values appropriate to one's ambitions. The general pattern of anticipatory socialization insures that the ambitious individual will already have partially familiarized himself with the adjustments he must make and will have begun to accustom himself to thinking from the standpoint of a member of the stratum to which he aspires. When ambition is divorced from such learning, the precipitating conditions for a marginality crisis are maximized. The upwardly mobile individual lacks the perspective for consolidating the social position to which he is given access by his occupation, and he lacks the affinity of values which is important in gaining personal acceptance at the higher level. The general indication from the present data is that anticipatory socialization may not work in the low-level schools, especially for males from native, white, Anglo backgrounds.

The patterns for manipulative individualism and the class-value index are similar in the middle- and high-level schools and among girls in the low schools. But a strikingly different pattern appears among native white Anglo boys in the lower neighborhoods. Here, there is apparently a correlation between manipulative individualism and background when ambition is held constant (P < .01), but no correlation with class values and no correlation of either value index with ambition. Absence of the standard value subcultures by either origin or destination in these neighborhoods has been noted already. But manipulative individualism does suggest a value subculture by background which is not made a basis for anticipatory socialization. The only part of the value complex which remains characteristic of the higher-background boys in the low neighborhoods is manipulative individualism. The success values and other individualistic items are no more characteristic of them than of others.

This segmentation of the whole value complex relating to background level which characterized the boys from higher family backgrounds in the low neighborhoods might be explained in several ways. It might reflect the kinds of families that locate themselves nearer to lower sections to the city than they need to. Such families may live by servicing lower groups, or may live where they do because their value system is segmental to begin with. Or the segmentation may occur because of the lack of neighborhood support and implementation for a rounded pattern of higher-strata values. Still a third explanation for the segmentation may lie in the lack of prestige assigned boys from higher family backgrounds by their peers in lower-level schools, as discussed in the next chapter.

Whatever the reason for the pattern, the distinctive emphasis on manipulative individualism is not adopted by the ambitious boys. In all but the low neighborhoods, manipulative individualism is a part of the complex of values associated with socioeconomic level. It is probably learned by the ambitious through anticipatory socialization, though perhaps a little less readily than other value elements. In the low neighborhoods, however, the pattern is amorphous, only the higher-background nonethnic boys standing out because of their valuation of manipulative individualism. Within higher neighborhoods, the ambitious boys do not fail to learn the manipulative-individualism pattern when it is presented to them as part of the high-stratum subculture. But ambitious boys taken as a whole without respect to neighborhood are less likely to have absorbed manipulative individualism than other aspects of the class-value complex.

INTELLIGENCE QUOTIENT AND CLASS VALUES

Two hypotheses concerning class values and I.Q. should be acknowledged. (1) The endorsement of middle-class values may be a simple function of intelligence, the brighter children learning the middle-class or official "school culture" more adequately than others. Consequently, the relations with I.Q. would subsume the other relationships. (2) I.Q. may serve as an intervening variable in some of the relationships we have observed.

The first hypothesis applies separately to background and ambition as follows: (a) the relationship between background and I.Q. fully accounts for the apparent relationship between background and values; (b) the relationship between ambition and I.Q. fully accounts for the apparent relationship between ambition and class values. To test these hypotheses, we have employed partial correlation. No attempt has been made to examine relationships with specific value items. None of the value groupings showed a correlation with I.Q. The class-value index correlates modestly with I.Q. for both men and women (Table 20). Coefficients of partial correlation between the class-value index and background and the class-value index and ambition, in each instance holding I.Q. constant, are smaller than the original zero-order relationships, but remain significant beyond the .001 level for both men and women. While I.Q. may play a part in the relationships involving social-class values, our evidence does not justify the conclusion that it is sufficient to account for the relationships between values and either background or ambition.

Earlier we suggested that the plausibility of an intervening-variable hypothesis can be examined by comparing sizes of correlation coefficients, provided some rather exacting assumptions are made. By this criterion, the hypothesis of class values as the intervening variable is less plausible than the hypothesis of I.Q. as the intervening variable, though the coefficients are not sufficiently different in size to be decisive. When interrelations among ambition, class values, and I.Q. are considered, ambition is the more satisfactory intervening variable. If we add the present analysis to that in the preceding chapter, the causal

Table 20. Correlation of Class-Value Index with I.Q. and Stratification Indexes[a]

Variables correlated	Variable constant	Male	Female
CVI with I.Q.	None	.27	.25
CVI with background index	I.Q.	.18	.19
CVI with ambition index	I.Q.	.23	.34

a/ Coefficients include zero order and first-order partial correlations, as indicated by the variable held constant.

chain which finds best support in our data is as follows: background affects ambition and ambition affects both I.Q. and class values; in addition to the principal "Y-shaped" relationship there is a lesser influence directly from background to class values, directly from background to I.Q., and directly between I.Q. and class values.

SUMMARY

In this chapter the effort has been to estimate the degree to which the upwardly mobile student will encounter value contradictions, to ascertain whether his transition will be fostered by anticipatory socialization, and to explore some of the relationships between values and stratification in detail. The evidence in general suggests value discrepancy rather than contradiction, and is consistent with the hypothesis that considerable anticipatory socialization is taking place.

Relatively few of the items are related to background, and these are principally items measuring secular success and the preference for serious interests over popular ones. In addition, for men a sort of manipulative individualism and for women a stress on asserting individuality are associated with high background. The hypothesis that the classes differ more in the values they convert into personal goals than they do in the values they accept impersonally receives support in the case of men but not women, although the data are not decisive in this matter. If the hypothesis is correct, it further appears that in some instances the lower classes are forced to adopt goals not fully in keeping with their values and in other instances the higher-level men modify their goals because of the pressures of their class situation.

The anticipatory-socialization hypothesis requires evidence that students are relinquishing the values from their strata of origin in favor of values applicable to their strata of destination, but there should continue to be some anchorage to strata of origin so that persons from high backgrounds can serve as a reference group for the upwardly mobile. Evidence that a few more items are correlated with ambition than with background and that there is generally more association with ambition which is independent of background than there is with background independent of ambition is adjudged consistent with the hypothesis.

The reference group-anticipatory socialization theory cannot account fully for observed relationships, since there are values associated with high ambition which find no counterpart among students from high backgrounds, and there is one component of the high-background values which is not fully adopted by ambitious men. Self-reliance is clearly a part of the ambitious mens' value systems, and deferred gratification is probably a part, though neither is associated with high background. On the other hand, the manipulative-individualism component of high-background values appears to be less fully learned by the ambitious through anticipatory socialization than other elements. Ambitious women also value self-reliance, and place even more emphasis on individuality than women from high backgrounds. In addition, their endorsement of certain secular success and independence values suggests that they may have adopted high-background men as their reference group, because of the sex-linkage of high-stratum values.

Neighborhood operates as it does with ambition to augment the tendency toward high- or low-strata values based on prevalent background levels. The amorphous structure of ambition for males in low neighborhoods is further documented by an absence of relationship between class values and either background or ambition. Anticipatory socialization apparently does not apply to upwardly mobile men in the low neighborhoods, perhaps because the men from high backgrounds do not themselves hold higher-level values. The latter do endorse the manipulative-individualism component, however, but this is apparently not learned by the upwardly mobile.

Although the I.Q. is related to the endorsement of higher-class values, the data do not support the conclusion that class values are merely a reflection of I.Q.

CHAPTER FIVE

Social Desirability and Stratification

THE MARGINAL MAN is a person who seeks to change his identification from one stratum to another, but who is unable to resolve the related choices between value systems and between organized-group ties. The choices are necessary because the strata have incompatible value systems and because it is difficult to maintain ties across stratum boundaries. If marginality is a frequent consequence of upward mobility in American society, it is because the higher and lower social strata espouse different values and because members of each stratum refuse to accept fully and intimately persons who are known to have ties to other strata.

Our analysis thus far has shown some stratum differences which may be conducive to marginality, but which are sufficiently moderate that marginality is probably not inescapable. The aim of this chapter is to determine whether the patterns of interpersonal preference impede or facilitate the transitions in social ties which the upwardly mobile person must make. Are the students from one background valued more highly as friends by their peers than students from other backgrounds? Are there cleavages in friend preference along class lines which make it difficult to cross class lines? Is there evidence of an anticipatory-socialization principle organizing lines of cleavage in accordance with ambition as well as with background? To what extent does the future orientation of these students lead to the admiration of ability? The answers to such questions can be placed alongside the answers to questions concerning values to supply a balanced picture of the marginality potential of the high-school situation.

The principal issues were summarized in Chapter One under the distinction between class consciousness and prestige identification. Members of different strata may look upon each other with suspicion and hostility, viewing the person who tries to move up as a traitor. Or the dominant attitude may be respect for higher strata, with the result that friends and relatives of the upwardly mobile person themselves gain prestige through identification with him. If class consciousness is predominant, marginality is the almost inescapable fate of upwardly mobile persons. If prestige identification prevails, there are abundant opportunities to avoid marginality.

PRIOR EVIDENCE AND METHOD

Prior Research

The impression is quite generally encountered in sociological and educational literature that adolescent peer social organization incorporates the socioeconomic stratification of the larger community, and that this is especially true within the high school. The impression often coexists, however, with the view that adolescent social organization is a protest against adult values. As we have suggested earlier, the relationship between the youth subsociety with its special culture and social-class subsocieties with their special cultures has yet to be carefully delineated.

An impressive array of evidence can be cited to support the view that the peer group incorporates the class separatism of the community. Among the most influential studies have been August Hollingshead's investigation of social life in the high school of a small city in Illinois,[1] and a study of elementary-school children in the same city by Bernice Neugarten.[2] Similar observations at a higher age level come from a study of a small Eastern women's college by George Lundberg and Virginia Beazley.[3]

A British study with contrasting findings has been the basis for some speculation regarding national differences in school peer group stratification. A. N. Oppenheim failed to discover cliques along social-class lines in a number of London grammar schools.[4] It is plausible that the early separation of boys with high ability in special schools, regardless of background, helps to prevent the perpetuation of background differences.

However, other studies in the United States have not consistently produced findings comparable to those of Hollingshead, Neugarten,

[1] Hollingshead, *Elmtown's Youth*, pp. 204–242.

[2] Bernice Neugarten, "The Democracy of Childhood," in W. Lloyd Warner, *Democracy in Jonesville* (New York: Harper, 1949), pp. 77–88.

[3] George A. Lundberg and Virginia Beazley, " 'Consciousness of Kind' in a College Population," *Sociometry*, 11 (Feb., 1948), pp. 59–74. Cf. also, Merl E. Bonney, "A Sociometric Study of Relationships of Some Factor to Mutual Friendships on Elementary, Secondary, and College Levels," *Sociometry*, 9 (Feb., 1946), pp. 21–47; and Reva Potashin, "A Sociometric Study of Children's Friendships," *Sociometry*, 9 (Feb., 1946), pp. 48–70.

[4] A. N. Oppenheim, "Social Status and Clique Formation among Grammar School Boys," *British Journal of Sociology*, 6 (Sept., 1955), pp. 228–245.

and Lundberg. For example, H. Otto Dahlke failed to discover any association between economic class and high-low choice status in the elementary school, although there was "a small association between father's occupation of chooser and chosen in terms of positive choices." [5] A college study of 100 leaders and nonleaders among college fraternity men showed a disproportion of the leaders from lower socioeconomic backgrounds,[6] and a sociometric study of 163 girls in a women's residence hall in college showed no relationship between popularity and father's occupation or attendance at college.[7]

Christopher Sower offered the opinion that there is less social cleavage by occupation in suburban communities than in either cities or rural areas. To test this hypothesis he studied sociometric preferences in the seventh and eleventh grades in two schools in Flint, Michigan. He found no wide differences in fathers' occupation between the very popular and the very unpopular, and he found no significant cleavage among white-collar, craftsmen-foreman, and un-skilled-semiskilled workers.[8] A study of sixth-grade children in a small city, by Beverly Grossmann and Joyce Wrighter, showed a correlation between selection-rejection scores and the Barr Scale rating of father's occupation in the lower portions of the scale but not in the upper portions.[9]

A study of 88 marriages among Purdue University students suggests an approach which might profitably be applied to the more general phenomenon of clique formation.[10] The couples were divided into those who were acquainted before college and those who met on campus. Among the former there was some tendency toward homogamy by family background; among the latter there was no such tendency. Residential and organizational propinquity undoubtedly reinforce socioeconomic differentiation among young children. But a wider sphere of movement and less supervision of associations by parents

[5] H. Otto Dahlke, "Determinants of Sociometric Relations among Children in the Elementary School," *Sociometry*, 16 (Nov., 1953), pp. 327–338.

[6] Harold M. Hodges, Jr., "Campus Leaders and Non Leaders," *Sociology and Social Research*, 37 (March, 1953), pp. 251–255.

[7] Jean Waid Reilly and Francis P. Robinson, "Studies of Popularity in College: I. Can Popularity of Freshmen Be Predicted?" *Educational and Psychological Measurement*, 7 (Spring, 1947), pp. 67–72.

[8] Christopher Sower, "Social Stratification in Suburban Communities," *Sociometry*, 11 (August, 1948), pp. 235–243.

[9] Beverly Grossmann and Joyce Wrighter, "The Relationship between Selection-Rejection and Intelligence, Social Status, and Personality amongst Sixth Grade Children," *Sociometry*, 11 (Nov., 1948).

[10] Gerald R. Leslie and Arthur H. Richardson, "Family Versus Campus Influence in Relation to Mate Selection," *Social Problems*, 4 (Oct., 1956), pp. 117–121.

characterizes the older child. Hollingshead speaks of the attempts by parents to control their children's friendships, and the frequent resistance by the youths. In a small high school (circa 400 students), in a substandard school system, in a tightly knit small community like "Elmtown," there may be less opportunity for a genuine school peer organization to develop than in the large high schools in more amorphous metropolitan areas. In Flint, Michigan, the high school very likely affords greater opportunity for students to transcend the propinquity- and parent-imposed cliques of the elementary school. Oppenheim's British study applies to a metropolitan community and to a school system which keeps the parents "at arm's length" from the school. It is more appropriate to compare his findings with the study of Flint and the present investigation of Los Angeles than with Hollingshead's on Elmtown. We are led to the conclusion that while the stratification dimension in elementary-school cliques in the United States has been rather consistently substantiated, there is justification for supposing that the situation in senior high schools varies according to the type of community and its relationship to the school.

Sociometric Indexes

No attempt is made in this investigation to secure information on actual patterns of friendship, except insofar as the relatively factual question asking for "big wheels" gets at the operating peer-prestige structure. We are prepared to accept current characterizations of youth culture as a functioning system. Because of our emphasis on the ritual and transitory character of the system, however, we are more concerned with preferences for enduring association. So long as stratum lines cannot be wholly obliterated we should expect associations within levels to be a little easier than associations between levels. But it is the more private attitudes toward the highborn and the ambitious which are important in distinguishing between a system of class consciousness and a system of prestige identification.

The principal tool for this investigation is a simple and conventional sociometric index which we shall call the *friend rating*. The *friend rating* reflects the number of choices an individual receives from other students in his classroom. The index ranges from zero for the person who is not chosen at all to an arbitrary maximum indicating that the student is among the few most often selected by other students in the class. The exact nature of the computation will be described after the nature of the choices has been explained.

In order to insure that students made choices of the sort desired, we phrased the instructions to stress the closeness and duration of the friendship and referred to a hypothetical choice rather than an actual one. The exact wording of the item is as follows:

Suppose you wanted to pick some people to be your *close friends*—people you would enjoy doing things with and would like to have as close friends for a *long time*—. What *three* people who are *in this classroom right now* would you pick?

The question restricted the chooser to persons in the classroom at the time so that it would be possible to identify all the persons chosen, to match all choosers and chosen, and so that the choices each person received could be stated as a fraction of all the choices he could possibly have received. The number of choices was also specified so as to facilitate the computation of various indexes permitting individual comparisons.

When this method is employed, there is an important possibility that the individual may be forced to choose people he would not spontaneously select, with the result that choices are arbitrary if not erroneous in character.[11] In some instances students asked the investigator how they could make choices when none of their friends was in the classes where the questionnaire was administered. If, however, friendship is a relative matter, there is no reason why a subject should not be able to make choices as far down a continuum as desired. When we ask for hypothetical choices rather than existing friendships the problem is less severe. We need only assume that the students know others in the class well enough to be able to make some guesses as to who are most nearly the kind of persons they would like to have as friends. Questionnaires were deliberately administered in the second half of the school semester so as to insure that most students would have been together in the same classroom for ten weeks or more and would have formed some acquaintance with each other.

The actual index involved two stages of computation. First, the number of choices any given individual received was divided by one less than the total number of students in the classroom when the questionnaires were filled out. Since no person could choose himself, the index, when multiplied by 100, ranged from 0 for no choices received to 100 for choice by everyone in the class. However, in two of the ten schools it was not practicable to administer the questionnaires in individual classrooms, so students from several classrooms were assembled in a single large room for the study. It seemed likely that under the latter circumstance far more of the students would not know each

11 Helen H. Jennings, *Leadership and Isolation* (New York: Longmans Green, 1950).

other than when administration was by individual classes. Consequently, the range of index values would be quite different, rendering the indexes noncomparable between schools. To make the indexes comparable, we simple assigned arbitrary values from one to six according to the rank order of each individual's index within his own school, departing from the policy only to retain the arbitrary value of "one" for those students who received no choices at all. Since the percentage of isolates was amazingly constant, ranging only from thirteen to sixteen percent among the ten schools and in spite of the manner of administration, this departure from rank ordering is of minor consequence and enables us to identify the total isolate whenever desired. The final index, then, measures each student's relative "friendship desirability" as compared with other students in his school, and the distribution of index values is constant from school to school.

Two other sociometric questions were asked and similarly converted into indexes to clarify the elements in peer choices. The first was intended to identify the socially prominent and powerful individuals, as recognized by their peers. These individuals were identified in the vernacular of the adolescent peer group as "big wheels," and the rate at which any individual was named by his classmates in this connection will be referred to as his *wheel rating*.

The second question was intended to identify the students reputed by their peers to be the best students, those who achieved most effectively according to the distinctly academic codes. With such information it should be possible to determine whether conformity to the academic value scheme is a help or a hindrance to peer acceptability. The rate at which an individual was named by his classmates in this connection will be designated as his *brain rating*, again following an adolescent vernacular.

Since the latter two questions are phrased more as factual questions—who *are* the *wheels* and *brains*—there is much more agreement among the students in their answers than in their preference for friends. Slightly more than two thirds of the students are not named as *big wheels* by anyone and slightly less than two thirds are not named as *brains*. The indexes were initially computed in the same manner as the *friend rating*, but were classified into four categories for each school, namely, the top five percent, the next five percent, the next fifteen percent, and the remaining seventy-five percent.

Preference and Cleavage

Choices can be examined for evidence of the kinds of people who are preferred by their peers or for evidence of cleavage. Preference is measured by counting the number of times each person is chosen. The *friend rating* is the basic measure for this purpose. In computing such an index only the characteristics of the chosen are examined. Cleavage analysis is based on a comparison of the characteristics of chooser and chosen, measuring tendencies for students to select others who are similar or dissimilar to themselves. We have employed simple fourfold tabulations, dichotomizing the variable under consideration (e.g., high versus low background) and placing characteristics of the chooser on one axis and of the chosen on the other.[12] If the product of the number of choices falling in the two cells in which chooser and chosen are alike exceeds the product of the number of choices in the other two cells, a positive cleavage exists. If the reverse is true, there is a tendency for people to choose opposites. If the two products are equal, there is no cleavage.

It is possible to find clear preference patterns without cleavage, or to find cleavage without a preferred group. When socioeconomic background is the variable under examination, each combination of findings tells a special story. The absence of both preference and cleavage indicates a "classless society," one in which no attention is paid to the individual's background in selecting desirable friends. The presence of both preference and positive cleavage indicates an ingroup and an outgroup, the members of each preferring others from their own subgroup. Cleavage without preference indicates the same division into cliques, but with neither clique able to command numerical precedence over the other. Preference without cleavage indicates some agreement on the most desired individuals with no outgroup clique to challenge the preferred group.

These combinations correspond well to the patterns in which we are interested. The classless society suggests that youth culture has effectively eradicated class divisions derived from the larger society. Either the second or the third combination suggests that class consciousness is the governing relationship between strata. In schools in higher-level neighborhoods we expect the students with lower backgrounds to be the outgroup. In the lowest neighborhoods students with high backgrounds should form an outgroup. Preference in the first instance would be for students from high backgrounds and in the latter for students from low backgrounds. Cleavage without preference might exist in the middle schools where neither clique dominates. The fourth

---

[12] In order to keep the statistical properties of the fourfold tables as nearly equivalent as possible throughout the range of schools, the background index and ambition index were separately dichotomized for each school, as near to the median for the school as possible.

Table 21. Correlation of Sociometric Indexes with Background and Ambition

Variables correlated and type of correlation	Male	Female
Background index with:		
Friend rating (r)	.11	.01
Wheel rating (r_{bis})	.10	.12
Brain rating (r_{bis})	.22	.09
Ambition index with:		
Friend rating (r)	.14	.08
Wheel rating (r_{bis})	.13	.26
Brain rating (r_{bis})	.44	.24

combination, preference without cleavage, describes a social system in which the strata are related by prestige identification. It is conceivable that under special circumstances the identification might be inverted, higher-background students taking some pride in identifying with prestigious persons from lower levels. As a general pattern this seems so unlikely that it has not been treated as an alternative in the theory guiding the investigation.

SOCIOMETRY OF BACKGROUND AND AMBITION

Preference and Stratification

The impact of stratification variables upon preference can be summarized in a set of correlation coefficients between the sociometric indexes and the stratification measures. If we examine the correlations in Table 21 for men first, stratification does appear to enter into peer structure, though quite moderately. Each of the sociometric indexes correlates significantly with each of the stratification indexes. Correlations with *friend rating* and *wheel rating* are small. Correlations with *brain rating* are notably larger. Although the differences are not large enough taken singly to be worthy of note, in each case the correlation with ambition is larger than the correlation with background.

For women, likewise, the correlations with ambition exceed those with background, and the differences are greater than for men. *Friend rating* is unrelated to background for the girls, and the relationship with ambition is at the borderline. Desirability as a friend is apparently less related to background for girls than for boys, and may or may not be less related to ambition. In the case of *brain rating*, the differences between boys and girls are more striking. Both stratification measures are more strongly related with *brain rating* for boys than for girls. In contrast to these relationships, *wheel rating* is more closely related with stratification for girls than for boys, especially with ambition.

The student social system can be viewed as a product of two sets of tendencies. One set is the assignment of prestige according to the "official" value system of the school, awarding highest standing to students who perform best academically. The other set derives from the youth values which are independent of academic accomplishment. The *brain rating* was included in the investigation so as to make it possible to discover to what extent students allow the first set of tendencies to shape their social organization. The correlations of stratification with *wheel* and *brain ratings* can be interpreted in this light. In the case of men, stratification is quite clearly incorporated into the system reflecting official school values, though the "stratification of destination" is more important than the "stratification of origin." The lower correlations for *wheel rating* than *brain rating*, especially with ambition, indicate that stratification is a less important component of the extraofficial system. The correlations with *wheel rating* would undoubtedly not be significant if the effect of *brain rating* were partialed out. This observation affords support to the conception of a youth society which transcends class boundaries, insofar as the class-laden official school society allows.

The female social organization does not exhibit this contrast, however. While stratification is a less important dimension in the official school social system as it applies to girls than as it applies to boys, there is little difference between the girls' official and extraofficial systems. The stratification variable is clearly a part of the extraofficial system for girls, again more strongly on the basis of destination than of origin. But the presence of stratification in the extraofficial system cannot be attributed to the influence of the official system, as it could be for the boys. Hence, it appears that the extraofficial social system for girls contains a more important intrinsic stratification dimension than that for boys.

The cleavage analysis on the basis of friend choice is reported in Table 22. A preference summary made from the tabulations employed in cleavage analysis supports two general conclusions from the fore-going discussion.[13] Stratification enters into the preferences of students, favoring those of higher level. But stratification of destination appears to be somewhat more pervasive than stratification of origin.

Cleavage and Stratification

The cleavage summary tells a surprisingly clear story. There are exactly as many classes in which students from high backgrounds are preferred as there are in which low backgrounds are preferred. For the sample as a whole there is no cleavage according to background. There is, however, a marked cleavage according to ambition. In more than two thirds of the classrooms there is an apparent tendency for students to select as friends others with ambitions like their own.[14]

According to the models proposed at the beginning of the discussion, stratification of origin fits the prestige-identification pattern while stratification of destination fits a class-consciousness pattern in which the higher strata command stronger support than the lower. These observations place the distinction between types of relations among social strata in a somewhat different perspective by linking them more specifically with anticipatory socialization. Prestige identification in the stratification of origin is a necessary and facilitating condition for the emergence of anticipatory socialization on a widespread scale. The pervasive preference for persons who have the attributes of high stand-ing encourages ambition and the adoption of the outlook of a higher stratum. The failure of lower-level students to develop effective cliques which define their peers of high status as an outgroup permits the admiration to be translated into an active pursuit of mobility. Future-orientation permits youth with low ambition to form a minority ingroup in which the criterion of membership is destination rather than origin. This future-oriented cleavage may well contain the seeds of class consciousness which will emerge when the students leave school and establish their stable positions as adults.

Sex Differences

Up to this point the cleavage analysis has disregarded sex, and sex

[13] Preference is identified very simply from each fourfold cleavage tabulation. If the number of "highs" chosen exceeds the number of choices made by "highs," the highs are preferred. The labor of securing row and column totals can be avoided by subtracting the number in the high chooser-low chosen cell from the number in the low chooser-high chosen cell. If the difference is positive, the "highs" are preferred; if negative, the "lows" are preferred.

[14] Other investigations, such as that of Merl E. Bonney, *loc. cit.*, have shown a tendency for friendships to be structured according to occupational interests at the secondary and college levels.

Table 22. Preference and Cleavage by Background and Ambition

Type of pattern	Number of classrooms	
	Background index	Ambition index
Highs preferred	51	63
Lows preferred	29	17
Equal preference	9	9
Total	89	89
Positive cleavage	44	62
Negative cleavage	44	26
No cleavage	1	1
Total	89	89

differential has been introduced into the preference analysis only with respect to the recipients of choice. A full separation of sex patterns is made possible by repeating the cleavage tabulations in four separate groups, based on sex of both chooser and chosen. Thus, one full preference and cleavage analysis is performed for all choices in which a boy selects another boy. A second analysis is performed for all choices in which a boy selects a girl. The four possible analyses of this sort are reported in Table 23.

With respect to the background index, the preference patterns are surprisingly consistent for each of the four types of choice. The slightly larger number of classrooms revealing high-background preference when girls choose girls is far from conclusive. For each type of choice there is some indication of preference for friends from high backgrounds. None of the types of choices produces as clear indication of preference as the combination of all choices. Hence we are justified in believing that the admiration for the qualities of high status pervades all the relationships, whether same sex or opposite sex.

Likewise we find no evidence of cleavage by background in any of the four types of choice. Indeed there is even the suggestion that negative cleavage exists in like-sex choices. If there is any general tendency

Table 23. Sex Differentials in Preference
and Cleavage by Background and Ambition Indexes

Type of pattern	Number of classrooms (n=89)			
	Male chooser, male chosen	Male chooser, female chosen	Female chooser, male chosen	Female chooser, female chosen
Preference: background index				
Highs preferred	41	42	41	46
Lows preferred	34	32	35	33
Equal preference	14	15	13	10
Cleavage: background index				
Positive cleavage	33	31	39	38
Negative cleavage	50	34	34	48
No cleavage	6	24	16	3
Preference: ambition index				
Highs preferred	52	38	43	51
Lows preferred	25	38	34	24
Equal preference	12	13	12	14
Cleavage: ambition index				
Positive cleavage	45	39	43	53
Negative cleavage	40	32	27	34
No cleavage	4	18	19	2

to see disproportionately the favorable features of that which we do not
know intimately, there is good reason to suppose that members of a
very loosely structured class system might privately admire and desire

the friendship of members of other strata than their own. In case of cross-sex choices there is sufficient mystery in the opposite sex itself that stratum difference is a less conspicuous component of attraction. In addition, there are undoubtedly stronger sanctions from the adult community against cross-stratum attractions to the opposite sex than to the same sex.

In the analysis of preference by ambition we find again that none of the separate types of choice produces as clear results as all the choices combined. But here we find rather impressive evidence that preference patterns are not uniform. The clearest patterns of preference for persons with high ambition are found among same sex choices. There is no difference between the boys and the girls in this respect; the principle seems to be that the members of each sex tend to prefer the more ambitious members of their own sex. When boys choose girls, however, ambition appears not to be a factor. This contrast in the effect of a girl's ambition upon her acceptability to other girls and to boys is so fully in keeping with popular beliefs that it requires no discussion. The intermediate character of the evidence for preference when girls choose boys suggests compromise between the general preference for the ambitious and the romantic pattern which disparages consideration of such characteristics in the loved one.

When we move to the examination of cleavage by ambition, we first encounter evidence to support the popular stereotype that girls are more class conscious than boys. Here we find that cleavage by ambition pervades all the types of choice, but that the cleavage is only marked in choices made by girls. The evidence for cleavage in the choices made by boys, whether choosing other boys or girls, is so minimal that we should discount it except for its consistency with the general pattern. But among girls the cleavage is apparent, whether boys or girls are being chosen.

The separation of choices according to the sex of chooser and chosen has introduced no evidence which weakens or alters the general characterizations of stratification of origin and of destination. Prestige identification dominates the former, preference for those from high backgrounds characterizing all sex types of choices, and cleavage being absent from all types. The possibility that there may be a modest tendency toward cross-stratum preference in like-sex choices lends even greater emphasis to the picture. Class consciousness dominates the stratification of destination, though preference for the highly ambitious does not apply when boys name preferred girl friends, and cleavage is quite minimal when boys are making the choices.

There is one respect in which these data contradict the data in Table 21. The absence of relationship between *friend rating* and *background* for women is not confirmed in Table 23. Since students made choices only within classrooms, the deliberate or accidental grouping of students within classrooms can produce different results depending upon whether the classroom or the whole sample is the unit of analysis. Since this contradiction is tangential to the major issues of the investigation, it will suffice to observe that a slight relationship appears within classrooms which is not apparent for the entire sample when classroom units are disregarded.

NEIGHBORHOOD VARIATION

If the neighborhoods dominated by different social strata are causally different universes, the differences should be clear in the realm of interpersonal preference and cleavage.[15] The common view that lower-class peer groups punish the ambitious would be supported by a negative correlation between ambition and *friend rating* in lower areas and a negative relation between *brain rating* and *friend rating*. In broader terms, there would be a sharper separation between the official school social system and the working patterns of attractions and prestige among the students, and class consciousness rather than prestige identification would dominate the relationship between social strata in the lower neighborhoods.

Interrelation of Indexes

The correlations between pairs of indexes reported separately for the levels of school neighborhoods in Table 24 supply evidence bearing on the hypothesis of opposition between the two sets of tendencies. There are no extreme differences between neighborhoods. The associations are positive throughout the table. Evidently the consistency between the tendencies which was remarked for the entire sample also applies to each of the levels of neighborhood.

If there are differences of degree among the neighborhoods for boys, they are in the direction of a closer association between *brain rating* and the other indexes in the lower areas, and a more modest relationship between *friend* and *wheel ratings*. The closer association between *wheel* and *brain ratings* combined with the latter observation could lead to the inference that the official school social system had "captured" the system of student leadership, leaving the pattern of interpersonal preferences less well reflected in the student social structure. However, the substantial correlation between *brain* and *friend*

---

[15] Mortimer R. Feinberg has supplied evidence that the criteria of social acceptability are much the same for adolescent boys at different economic levels.

Table 24. Correlations among Sociometric Indexes by Neighborhood

Sex	Variables and types of correlation	Nonethnic students			All students, low-level schools
		High-level schools	Middle-level schools	Low-level schools	
Male	Friend-wheel rating (r_{bis})	.68	.56	.50	.52
	Friend-brain rating (r_{bis})	.33	.42	.44	.45
	Wheel-brain rating (phi)	.32	.22	.48	.40
	Number of cases	236	692	129	337
Female	Friend-wheel rating (r_{bis})	.60	.62	.32	.48
	Friend-brain rating (r_{bis})	.24	.44	.42	.43
	Wheel-brain rating (phi)	.40	.35	.25	.40
	Number of cases	255	727	136	373

ratings vitiates this interpretation. Perhaps the value of school achievement permeates the social system more completely in the lower neighborhoods, but student leadership per se is less highly valued. That the "big wheel" should be less sought as a personal friend is consistent with the finding that a manipulative kind of individualism is less highly valued in the lower levels than in the higher.

The lesser association between *wheel* and *friend ratings* in the low neighborhoods is even clearer for the women than it was for men. However, the correlation between *wheel* and *brain ratings* is less rather than greater in the low neighborhoods. Among the girls, the system indicated by *wheel rating* is more loosely tied to the whole peer organization in the low neighborhoods than elsewhere. *Brain rating* and *friend rating* bear about the same correlation for men and for women, and the possibility of a less developed connection between school success and the criteria of valued friendship in the high-level schools is even stronger for the girls. The findings for the girls may be interpreted as simply a fuller development of the tendency remarked among the boys. Perhaps the more serious consequences of school achievement for male success prevent as much separation between the student leadership system and the rest of the peer social organization as prevails among girls. For girls, the student leadership system in the lower neighborhoods shows a general tendency toward being independent of the organization which places academic performance as an important contributor to friendship desirability.

In sum, the interrelationships of indexes fail to support a view that academic excellence is punished in the lower-level neighborhoods because of a contradiction and separation between official school values and the informal system of interpersonal preference among peers. The preponderant evidence is that the same pattern of positive relationships among the systems prevails in all neighborhoods. If school success and interpersonal preference are less closely related anywhere, it is in the highest rather than the lowest neighborhoods. The one apparently distinctive characteristic of the lower neighborhoods is a greater separation between the student leadership system and patterns of interpersonal preference.

Stratification of Choice

The question of class consciousness and prestige identification in different neighborhoods can be answered by examination of preference and cleavage tabulations made separately for the three types of neighborhood (Table 25). The general preference for persons of high background applies to the high- and middle-level neighborhoods but not

Table 25. Preference and Cleavage for Neighborhoods

| Type of pattern | Number of classrooms | | | | | |
| | Background index | | | Ambition index | | |
	High-level schools	Middle-level schools	Low-level schools	High-level schools	Middle-level schools	Low-level schools
Highs preferred	11	30	10	15	32	16
Lows preferred	5	14	10	1	13	3
Equal preference	3	4	2	3	3	3
Total	19	48	22	19	48	22
Positive cleavage	8	25	11	12	34	16
Negative cleavage	10	23	11	7	13	6
No cleavage	1	--	--	--	1	--
Total	19	48	22	19	48	22

to the low areas. This observation initially lends support to the view that prestige identification in the middle and higher levels is replaced by class consciousness in the low areas. Examination of cleavage patterns is required to complete the assessment, however. For high and middle neighborhoods the pattern of prestige identification is confirmed by the absence of cleavage. For low neighborhoods a similar lack of cleavage negates the class-consciousness characterization. Rather, lacking either preference or cleavage by background, the lower areas are amorphous; they represent the "classless society."

There appears to be no stratification according to origin in the low neighborhoods. Such a pattern might impede or facilitate mobility aspirations depending upon the accompanying pattern of stratification according to destination. A similar absence of stratification by destination would create an environment lacking in peer recognition of the value of high socioeconomic position. But further examination of Table 25 shows that both preference for persons of high ambition and cleavage

Table 26. Sex and Neighborhood Differentials in Preference and Cleavage

Type of pattern		Number of classrooms by school level											
		Male chooser, male chosen			Male chooser, female chosen			Female chooser, male chosen			Female chooser, female chosen		
		High n=19	Middle n=48	Low n=22	High n=19	Middle n=48	Low n=22	High n=19	Middle n=48	Low n=22	High n=19	Middle n=48	Low n=22
Preference: background index	Highs preferred	11	23	7	10	22	10	10	23	8	7	30	9
	Lows preferred	5	18	11	6	20	6	5	20	10	9	15	9
	Equal preference	3	7	4	3	6	6	4	5	4	3	3	4
Cleavage: background index	Positive	6	20	7	7	20	4	9	22	8	7	22	9
	Negative	12	26	12	7	18	9	9	17	8	12	26	10
	No cleavage	1	2	3	5	10	9	1	9	6	--	--	3
Preference: ambition index	Highs preferred	16	21	15	6	24	8	12	20	11	10	29	12
	Lows preferred	3	19	3	9	19	10	6	19	9	7	14	3
	Equal preference	--	8	4	4	5	4	1	9	2	2	5	7
Cleavage: ambition index	Positive	9	22	14	8	24	7	9	23	11	11	30	12
	Negative	7	25	8	9	14	9	7	14	6	7	18	9
	No cleavage	3	1	--	2	10	6	3	11	5	1	--	1

according to ambition prevail at all levels. There may be less cleavage in the high-level schools, indicating failure to develop an unambitious outgroup. But otherwise the marked stratification of destination exists at all levels and takes a class-conscious manifestation in middle and lower neighborhoods. The cleavage could mean that a student in a middle or lower neighborhood finds it more difficult to adopt high ambitions once he has allowed himself to become affiliated and identified with a low-ambition group. But it would be his early ambitions rather than his background which led to this entrapment. At all levels, the ambitious student finds himself in harmony with the values of the preponderant student element.

Sex Differences

In order to complete the assessment of neighborhood variations, we have made separate tabulations of choices by sex of chooser and chosen for each of the three neighborhood levels (Table 26). The pattern of preference by background shifts by neighborhood in both instances in which the male is the person chosen, but not in the other instances. High-background males are preferred for friendship by both males and females in the high-level schools, and are also preferred, but less so, in middle schools. In the low schools, however, there is a small reversal in favor of low-level boys. A consistent slight preference for high background exists at all levels when boys choose girls, and a preference for high background is found in the middle schools when girls choose girls. No evidence of cleavage by background occurs with any type of choice at any level, however. The earlier conclusions about stratification of origin are not altered by the refined tabulation, except to note that it is a different evaluation of the male as an object of choice which accounts for the difference between the lower neighborhoods and others. It would not be correct to ascribe the difference to the attitudes of males, since the pattern exists whether males or females are the choosers. It appears simply that the higher the neighborhood, the more the high-background male is adjudged a desirable friend by his peers.

The absence of preference according to ambition when males choose females appears at all neighborhood levels. The rather limited preference when females choose males appears to be principally a reflection of patterns in the high-area schools. The relatively slight importance attached to ambition in the girls' statements regarding the occupations they would accept in their husbands finds its counterpart here in choices by girls outside of the high-area schools. The major preference in Table 23 was concentrated in the same-sex choices, both of which reveal some variation by neighborhood. We have no ready explanation for the finding that preference among boys for male friends with high ambition is overwhelming in high and low neighborhoods, but is apparently absent in the middle level. The preference for high ambition when girls choose girls appears at all levels, but there is a progression from a small preference in the high areas to considerable preference in the low areas. The cleavage by ambition appears to be consistent throughout the levels when girls are making the choices, but varies somewhat in boys' choices. The cleavage is quite moderate when boys choose boys, and it is possible that the only appreciable cleavage is in the low neighborhoods. When males choose females there appears to be no cleavage except possibly in the middle neighborhoods.

Again the detailed tabulation does not require important revisions in the conclusions drawn from the general tabulation. However, the suggestion that cleavage in male-male choices according to ambition exists only in the low-area schools combined with the absence of preference for high-background boys in these schools qualifies the generalization of destination-oriented class consciousness. These two characteristics may not be unrelated. Cleavage by ambition suggests an organized outgroup of the unambitious. Perhaps the most stable kind of respect for the ambitious person is a generalization from a pre-existing admiration for high socioeconomic standing. Where admiration of the ambitious is anchored in the respect for established standing, it may signalize a pervasive system of values, with the result that the unambitious are unlikely to organize their own informal system.

These peculiarities in the male-male choice pattern do suggest that the boy with ability is confronted with a more formidable choice regarding ambition in low neighborhoods than he is in higher areas. He must choose between alternative group identities within his peer group, and the prestige of high future-orientation cannot be stabilized and reinforced by reference to a prestigeful present high group among his peers. The earlier finding that ambition among boys is less closely correlated with background and with measured intelligence in the lower neighborhoods than in other neighborhoods is entirely reasonable in relation to these observations.

REFERENCE GROUPS OF THE UPWARDLY MOBILE

In application of the marginal-man theory and the concept of anticipatory socialization, we have assumed that reference-group theory supplies the mechanism by which the mobile person learns values which are foreign to his stratum of origin. Two problems involving reference groups have been created by the data. The first concerns the source of the relatively low ambition in low neighborhoods in light of the findings regarding preference patterns. The second concerns the failure of mobile boys in low neighborhoods to exhibit anticipatory socialization, in spite of other indications of future-orientation.

Goals and Standards

In Chapter Three it was observed that students from equivalent family backgrounds reflect the levels of their neighborhoods in setting their ambitions. A finding of either negative preference with respect to ambition or absence of stratification of destination in the low-area schools would have supplied a simple explanation for the finding regarding ambition. Although we cannot offer additional data at present, the issue is important enough for marginality theory to justify a speculative discussion of a plausible alternative.

Reference-group theory has suggested two important ways in which groups affect an individual's ambition.[16] One way is in the determination and selection of goals, according to the objects which are valued in the reference group. Identification with the group and its prestigeful members inclines the member toward adoption of the goals which are conspicuously held by them. Supplementing this process are the group sanctions which reward conformity and punish deviance.[17] This is the process which would have led to the hypothesis that a general disparagement of ambition in low-area schools accounted for the effect of neighborhood on ambition.

The other reference-group process has to do with the setting of standards rather than goals. Goals such as material, occupational, and educational success are continua. Two persons may value material success, but their conceptions of how much wealth constitutes success may be quite different. "Goal" refers to the direction of ambition; "standard" refers to the level of attainment which is regarded as success. Standards are set partly by the same processes we have described for goals. But they are also set by a process of comparing oneself with others. The question, "How far is up?" is answered in relation to how far others are known to have ascended. One may set his standards by reference to public figures and groups, but we suspect that standards are more often based upon individuals and groups who are close at hand. In a community of manual workers such comparison readily

[16] Harold H. Kelley, "Two Functions of Reference Groups," in Guy E. Swanson, Theodore M. Newcomb, and Eugene L. Hartley, eds., *Readings in Social Psychology* (New York: Henry Holt, 1952), pp. 410–414.

[17] These processes have been investigated by Theodore M. Newcomb, and reported in *Personality and Social Change* (New York: Dryden, 1943).

leads to the judgment that the well-established craftsman and the independent small tradesman have achieved a high degree of success. In a community of professionals and corporation officials, the same level is unimpressive. This standard-setting by comparison with a reference group is supplemented by the group's effects upon courage and opportunity to learn the means for ascent. Ambition always contains an element of risk. The evidence that others like oneself have achieved similar objectives, or even that many others like oneself hold the same ambitions, is a source of courage to take the necessary risk. Ambition also implies some assessment of the means. Persons who have immediate contact with other people who have achieved a given level are more likely to feel that they understand how to get there, and consequently are more willing to set their standards accordingly.

A reasonable speculation from the data at hand would be that the reference groups of students in low neighborhoods foster the *goal* of ambition in the same manner as those in higher neighborhoods; but, by comparison with those around them, these students are led to set lower *standards* of success than their high-neighborhood peers. They are less likely to have a confident sense of understanding the steps to a given high level; they are less likely to have the support of shared high ambition to build up their courage; and they are likely to receive the praises of their peers and adult associates for a lower standard of success. Such an interpretation reconciles the positive attitude toward ambition with the depressed level of ambition in low areas.

Unsupported Choice Pattern

The failure of ambitious boys in the low neighborhoods to exhibit the values appropriate to their destination suggests either that they do not have a reference group from whom to learn the values, or that some complication must be introduced into reference-group theory to account for the finding. Initially it seemed simple and adequate to accept the absence of correlation between class values and background as the explanation. Boys of high background could serve as a reference group from whom the mobile learned appropriate values, except when the former did not themselves show such values. However, discovery of a correlation between manipulative individualism and background which is not carried into anticipatory socialization complicates the situation.

Earlier it was taken for granted that mobile boys adopt boys of higher backgrounds than themselves as a reference group, though no evidence was actually adduced. Even if this assumption should hold in general, there remain at least two important ways in which the reference-group behavior of boys in the low neighborhoods might differ from that in higher areas. On the one hand, mobile boys in all neighborhoods may name high-background students as desired friends, but for some reason they fail to learn the values of manipulative individualism. Such failure in turn might stem from the unpleasant character of such values when they are divorced from the full complex of class values. Or failure might stem from the fact already noted that the lower neighborhood as a whole does not accord the prestige to high-background students that higher neighborhoods do. Perhaps a person may prefer a group of people, but not learn the group's values unless the community supports the preference by the assignment of prestige.

On the other hand, mobile boys in the low neighborhoods may simply fail to adopt boys from high backgrounds as their reference group, largely because their peers fail to accord prestige on the basis of background. This explanation would be consistent with the findings regarding friend preference and background, and would suggest a special dimension not usually incorporated into reference-group theory.

Some exploration of these alternatives is possible by examining the relationship between "upward choice" and mobility. We can test the basic assumption that upwardly mobile boys tend to choose peers from higher backgrounds than their own as desirable friends. We can further note whether the same tendency applies in all neighborhoods, as our first broad alternative implies, or whether it fails to apply in the low neighborhoods only. Finally, we can compare the tendency for upward choice in mobile and nonmobile boys, in order to clarify further the sources of the special prestige given high-background students in all but the low neighborhoods.

A cross-tabulation has been prepared between direction of choice and the mobility index [18] (Table 27). Chooser and chosen have been compared for each choice, employing the background index. The direction of difference has then been cross-tabulated with the mobility index, which compares the standard score on ambition with the standard score on background for the chooser. Since the possibilities of upward mobility and of upward choice are both related to the backgrounds of the students, a correction must be introduced for spurious correlation. This has been done by computing an expected frequency of upward, same, and downward choice for persons in each mobility category, based on the actual number of persons above, equal to, and

---

[18] The mobility index is the difference between the standard-score equivalents of the background index and the ambition index with the addition of a constant to make all values constant.

Table 27. Direction of Friend Choice
by Background, for Males

School level	Relative mobility	Observed/expected choices		
		Upward choice	Hori-zontal choice	Downward choice
High	Very low	7/9	10/8	31/31
	Low	49/42	24/23	70/78
	Average	86/83	51/46	97/10!
	High	98/90	20/24	33/37
	Very high	47/41	0/3	0/3
Middle	Very low	31/18	10/16	104/11.
	Low	122/132	80/77	255/24!
	Average	278/283	128/105	216/23.
	High	227/209	87/82	105/12.
	Very high	131/122	31/33	19/26
Low	Very low	1/3	3/3	33/31
	Low	20/22	19/22	85/80
	Average	95/91	46/49	80/81
	High	83/72	32/35	38/46
	Very high	66/63	23/25	14/15

below them. The estimate is not exact, since it was done for neighborhoods rather than for each classroom within which students made their choices.

The table shows first that there is some general tendency for the more mobile boys to make upward choices more frequently than a random selection would indicate. The underlying assumption of reference-group process is thus supported, and there is justification for supposing that anticipatory socialization does take place in the manner suggested. The table further shows that the tendency to make upward choices characterizes the mobile boys in all three neighborhoods. There is no striking difference in the extent to which mobile boys make upward choices from one type of neighborhood to the next. We must therefore rule out the hypothesis that anticipatory socialization fails to take place because mobile boys in low neighborhoods do not prefer students from higher backgrounds than their own.

There are differences in the rates of upward and downward choice according to mobility-orientation and neighborhood. In the low neighborhoods there is very little upward choice apart from the tendency among mobile boys. As we anticipated, there is no peer support for the mobile boys' choice of high-background students as a reference group. In the high neighborhoods, on the other hand, the tendency to make upward choices extends to boys who are less mobile than the average. There is, then, general peer support for the mobile boys' tendency to make upward choices and for their selection of a reference group.

The middle neighborhood shows a peculiar configuration. There is some upward choice among the upwardly mobile and the downwardly mobile, but there is a pattern of downward choice among the average and just-below-average groups. The upwardly mobile boys are not alone here in their preference for friends from high backgrounds, but the middle group poses a peculiar problem. We shall delay further consideration of this problem until certain other peculiarities of the middle neighborhoods are noted in the next chapter.

In response to the initial question, we must note that the choice aspect of reference-group process takes place in all neighborhoods, but that the relationship of these choices to those by nonmobile peers is obscure because of the peculiarities of the middle-level schools. If only the contrast between high and low schools were taken into account, we might claim support for the interpretation that mobile boys learn the values of the group which they prefer only when that preference is reinforced in the larger community of peers. The apparent presence of another variable in the middle neighborhoods makes it impossible either to support or reject the interpretation. On the other hand, the hypothesis that manipulative individualism is unattractive when divorced from the rest of the class-value complex, or when viewed in a dominantly working-class setting, remains plausible but unexplored.

SUMMARY

The findings and inferences from this chapter can best be reviewed in connection with some of the principal observations from the two preceding chapters. The impact of social stratification upon ambition, values, and interpersonal preference will be considered as a whole.

That stratification according to socioeconomic criteria pervades the lives of these youths is indicated by its relationship to ambition, values, and peer-preference patterns. Educational, occupational, and material ambition all reflect the advantages of high socioeconomic background. In a number of respects the values of students from different levels of backgrounds differ. And there is a fairly general pattern of preference for students of high backgrounds when desirable long-time friends are named.

However, by absolute standards, the impact of stratification in all areas is modest. Correlations of ambition with background, though comfortably significant, are low, and there are instances of high ambition among students from the lowest backgrounds. Three hypothetical systems constitute a continuum from the closed to the most open class system. Under a closed class system, each child aspires only to the position of his parents. When the system of stratification is a ladder, then the best that each can do is aspire to climb a few rungs from where he starts, and extensive mobility is a matter of generations. When success is sought after the model of a race or sporting event, each person starts on a par with all others in setting his level of ambition. The evidence of student ambitions reveals a compromise between the latter two systems, background remaining a factor but not to the extent that a ladder pattern would indicate.

Neither the number of value items which correlate with stratification nor the size of the relationships is impressive. The majority of items tested does not correlate, and more value items correlate with sex than with stratification. The values which correlate are chiefly those having to do with a fairly ruthless pursuit of secular success and certain kinds of individualism, but not deferred gratification or strict integrity. They are also, chiefly, values which distinguish males from females. There is a further possibility that certain of these values, notably those dealing with secular success, may vary by social strata only when applied to personal goals, and not when applied in judgment of others.

The impact of stratification upon interpersonal choices is likewise not great. Although the desired friend, the *wheel,* and the *brain* are all more likely to be students from high backgrounds than chance would dictate, the relationships are small. Furthermore, while there is preference for the person of high background, there is no cleavage by background. The absence of antagonistic groups of high- and low-background students indicates an interstrata relationship of prestige identification rather than class consciousness in the school.

A stratification so moderate in its effect might be entirely imposed upon the youth society by official school pattern. A comparison of relationships with friendship choice, *wheel rating,* and *brain rating* suggests that the sexes differ in this respect. It is possible that the school values import stratification into the naturally unstratified relations among boys. But socioeconomic stratification appears to be indigenous to the social relations of girls.

Evidence regarding both values and interpersonal preference indicates that the stratification of destination is more important than the stratification of origin among these students. A few more value items correlate with ambition than with background, and the correlations with ambition subsume more of those with background than those with background subsume of the correlations with ambition. Patterns of interpersonal preference are more consistently in favor of students with high ambition than of students from high backgrounds. The friend, *wheel,* and *brain* indexes all correlate more strongly with ambition than with background. Ambition forms a basis for social cleavage as well as preference, while background does not. It is even possible that with background there is a slight preference for opposites when same-sex choices are being made, in contrast to the cleavage by ambition. There is more suggestion of a genuine class consciousness in the stratification of destination than in the stratification of origin.

In spite of minor differences, stratification reveals much the same over-all pattern for boys and girls. Individuality may be a class-related value among girls, but not among boys. Less evidence was found among the girls to suggest that values differ among classes as personal goals rather than as abstract values. The clearest patterns of preference for friends with high ambition apply to same-sex choices, and boys' choices of girls are unrelated to the girls' ambitions. There is a more organized outgroup of unambitious girls than of boys, though the cleavage is more consistent when girls choose girls than when they choose boys.

Neighborhood, as identified by the school that the students attend, appears to affect the ambitions and values of the students in addition to whatever effect is attributable to their individual family backgrounds. Within school neighborhoods of different levels, predominantly the same relationships prevail. There is no evidence of relationships which are entirely reversed in different neighborhoods. However, there are some differences in degree which seem to fit into comprehensible patterns. There are a few notable peculiarities in the middle-level schools. But the principal unique patterns are found in the lower neighborhoods.

Although the level of ambition and the endorsement of high-strata values in low neighborhoods are lower than family backgrounds alone would lead us to expect, there is still an appreciable amount of high

ambition. Girls especially, in naming the most desirable occupation
for a husband, exhibit full awareness of the occupational ladder. While
no boys aspire to large-business ownership or officialdom, several in
each school have their sights on the professions.

Within the lower neighborhoods, the standard ambition constellations are less clearly operative. Level of ambition, background, and
measured intelligence are less interrelated. In relation to the standard
determinants, then, amount of ambition is a more fortuitous matter
than elsewhere.

When boys and girls from the lower neighborhoods name those they
would like as friends, they favor peers with good reputations for academic performance as much as students in other neighborhoods, but
it is the *wheel*—the leader in student affairs—who receives no preference. Only in these lower neighborhoods is there apparently no relationship between being a *wheel* and being desired as a friend. Like the
wheel, the boy from higher background receives no special preference
from his peers, in contrast to his favored position in other neighborhoods. In this double sense the lower neighborhoods are the nearest
to a classless society, discounting both family background and school
social prominence in the selection of desirable friends.

Ambition, like scholastic reputation, is as important in the low
schools as elsewhere. When girls name desired girl friends, ambition
is even more important than in other schools. But the relations with
ambition take a distinctive turn among the boys. Only in these schools
is the level of ambition clearly a source of cleavage among boys. The
unambitious tend to make their selections from among other unambitious boys.

The peculiarity of social organization among boys in the lower
neighborhoods may be stated comprehensively as a pattern of future-
orientation without anticipatory socialization. Ambition and academic
success are valued, but the distinctive values appropriate to the destination of the highly ambitious are not learned along the way. The failure
of anticipatory socialization to accompany future-orientation is probably a consequence of the absence of a high-prestige model from whom
to learn the values appropriate to higher strata. In other neighborhoods the students from high family backgrounds are a preferred
group, who already exhibit the values to which the mobile individuals
must be socialized. They can then serve as a prestigeful reference group
for the ambitious. In the lower neighborhoods there are similar groups
of students from higher backgrounds who are preferred as friends by
the upwardly mobile men. It may be that the students from high backgrounds do not exemplify the class values well enough to constitute

a model for the mobile boys. Of it may be that because they are not accorded recognition by their peers, the ambitious do not take them as a reference group and consequently do not learn their values.

Although the effect of the neighborhood is to depress the ambitions of students relative to their family backgrounds, the evidence does not suggest that this effect is brought about by social pressures directed against the ambitious person. In this connection it is important to distinguish between the absence of personal preference for the big wheel and the modest but unmistakable preference for the person with high ambition. It appears to be social climbing as a route to ambition which is less favored here than elsewhere, rather than ambition itself. Perhaps it is the standard-setting function of the reference groups, defining how much achievement constitutes success, which depresses these students' ambitions.

The lower ambitions of the boys may also be partially attributed to a danger of commitment to low ambition which is greater here than elsewhere. The presence of an outgroup made up of the unambitious boys, with its own preferred individuals, probably means that it is socially difficult for a boy who once becomes a member to adopt and pursue higher ambitions. In the higher neighborhoods where such outgroups are weak or absent, the "late bloomer" does not have to become a traitor to a group of his peers as he apparently does in the low neighborhoods. In the higher neighborhoods the boy has presented to him only one clearly sanctioned identity which he may achieve or not. In the low neighborhoods the boy must choose between two socially sanctioned identities, and the choice is accompanied by both the internal commitments of self-conception and the external commitments of group loyalty.

CHAPTER SIX

Youth Subculture

THE IDEA that there may be a special youth subculture in American society affects the applicability of the marginal-man hypothesis in two important ways. First, an age society with its own value system would obscure the class-value differences and facilitate the formation of ties irrespective of background. Hence it would ease the transitions of mobility, at least delaying the impact of marginality-producing experiences. Second, the devaluation of ambition and serious adult values in the youth subculture would constitute a generalized impediment to mobility. The peer social system would ostracise the ambitious, and its values would shift the students' goals away from serious adult ends.

Margaret Mead took the first major step toward the idea of a youth culture with her documentation of the view that cultural factors rather than physiological maturation account for some of the distinctive behavior of youth.[1] Willard Waller pointed out the existence of a youth society and culture, rather than a mere aggregate, with his description of the "rating and dating complex." [2] Talcott Parsons further proposed that youth subculture performs an essential function in freeing the individual from the excessive dependency ties induced by the nuclear family system, enabling him to assume the personal independence demanded by the role of the mature adult in American society.[3] Thus the conception of youth behavior has evolved from a set of behavior aberrations to a socially transmitted subculture reflecting the peculiar position of youth in American society and functionally supporting the adult role.

The present investigation has been guided by a slightly variant conception of the dynamics of youth subculture. We shall summarize this viewpoint before examining the relevant data.

[1] Margaret Mead, *Coming of Age in Samoa* (New York: Morrow, 1928).

[2] Willard Waller, "The Rating and Dating Complex," *American Sociological Review*, 2 (Oct., 1937), pp. 727–734.

[3] Talcott Parsons, "The Kinship System of the Contemporary United States," in *Essays in Sociological Theory* (Glencoe, Ill.: Free Press, 1954), pp. 177–196.

A CONCEPTION OF YOUTH SUBCULTURE

In his widely cited discussion, Talcott Parsons characterizes youth culture as emphasizing irresponsibility in contradistinction to the demands of an adult role, placing athletic prowess abnormally high on the prestige scale, and valuing persons according to some special non-utilitarian qualities—glamor in girls and a sort of all-around character in boys.[4] Along with these characteristics goes romantic love. Employing Parsons' characterization, Riley and Flowerman stress mediocrity as the central feature of youth culture, the restriction of goals to a level attainable by all.[5] Arriving at a very similar characterization from a different point of departure, David Riesman stresses the consumption-orientation rather than production-orientation of the "other-directed" peer group, and suggests that the crucial determinant of success in the peer group is the ability to express the proper tastes in all matters of concern to youth.[6] James Coleman shows the pervasiveness of athletic prowess and personal attractiveness in determining popularity in the high school.[7]

The Empirical Referent

There is relatively little serious disagreement among writers concerning the actual content of youth culture, but there has been a continuing series of efforts to identify more precisely the empirical referent for the youth subculture and subsociety. Charles W. Hobart in a recent study of college students found partial but not complete support for some deductions from the functional view of romantic love as a special facet of youth culture.[8] A number of investigators have asked how general and how typical such phenomena as Waller's rating and dating complex were. Samuel H. Lowrie concluded on the basis of a questionnaire administered to Bowling Green College students that the rating pattern did not assume the importance attributed to it by Waller.[9] Burgess and Wallin in their study of one thousand engaged

4 Talcott Parsons, "Age and Sex in the Social Structure of the United States," *American Sociological Review*, 7 (Oct., 1942), pp. 604–616.

5 Matilda White Riley and Samuel H. Flowerman, "Group Relations as a Variable in Communications Research," *American Sociological Review*, 16 (April, 1951), pp. 174–180.

6 David Riesman, *The Lonely Crowd* (New Haven: Yale University Press, 1950).

7 James S. Coleman, *The Adolescent Society: The Social Life of the Teenager and Its Impact on Education* (New York: Free Press of Glencoe, 1961).

8 Charles W. Hobart, "Emancipation from Parents and Courtship in Adolescents," *Pacific Sociological Review*, 1 (Spring, 1958), pp. 25–29.

9 Samuel H. Lowrie, "Dating Theories and Student Responses," *American Sociological Review*, 16 (June, 1951), pp. 335–340.

couples concluded that the dalliance pattern of dating had not been widely practiced by their subjects.[10] H. H. Remmers reported a surprising degree of conformity to adult, and especially parental, opinions among high-school students in response to a questionnaire.[11] Many researchers have wondered to what extent that which passes as youth culture is the "line" used by mass-media hucksters to address youthful audiences rather than the spontaneous pattern of behavior evolved within youth society itself. The most extreme challenge comes from Frederick Elkin and William Westley, who conclude from a study of forty middle-class youth in a Montreal suburb that the usual sociological characterization of youth culture is largely myth.[12]

Extended Primary Group

In the present view the most fundamental aspect of youth society-culture is its simulation of an *extended primary-group* society. The immediate experience of each participant in the youth society incorporates the exacting demands of loyalty, the penetration of conventional reserve and dignity, and the camaraderie which are universals in primary groups. At the same time, the composition of the immediate "primary" group is constantly changing, so that the loyalty, informality, and camaraderie may be directed toward those people who were strangers a few minutes ago and will never be seen again. Thus each face-to-face group is experienced as a portion of an extended group of the same sort, comprising all those age mates who accept the youth pattern. But because the primary group is extended in this fashion, the primary relations themselves must be largely simulated. It seems hardly conceivable that the subjective experience that Cooley discussed—the sympathetic interpenetration—could occur with the shifting composition and casual acquaintance of the face-to-face groupings.[13]

The youth subculture and youth subsociety emerge as formidable realities at about the time the child leaves the special and protective settings of his original primary groups. To the child, the family and the neighborhood have been primary groups, even though the neighborhood seldom has this character for adults. But as the child leaves

[10] Ernest W. Burgess and Paul Wallin, *Engagement and Marriage* (Chicago: Lippincott, 1953), pp. 126–149.

[11] H. H. Remmers and D. H. Radler, *The American Teenager* (Indianapolis: Bobbs-Merrill, 1957), pp. 248–249.

[12] Frederick Elkin and William A. Westley, "The Myth of Adolescent Culture," *American Sociological Review*, 20 (Dec., 1955), pp. 680–684.

[13] Charles H. Cooley, *Human Nature and the Social Order* (New York: Scribners, 1922).

the small neighborhood-based elementary school where he spent the entire day with a small number of peers and a single teacher and enters the large impersonal and heterogeneous high school, he is forced to cope for the first time with a genuine *Gesellschaft*.[14] Here, for the first time, he is without a well-defined and continuous identity, known to himself and his associates and passing with him from situation to situation. Any special reputation must now be made over again in each of the many new settings in which he constantly finds himself. Furthermore, he is now thrown more continuously and inescapably upon the good offices of his peers. There is no single adult following his fortunes from situation to situation, and peer activities in general are much freer from continuous effective adult supervision. Children can no longer depend upon an adult coming in to enforce the rules of fair play in any game. At this point, we suggest, *youth culture emerges out of the children's efforts to reinstate a primary-group system of identities and relations and controls in the context of constantly shifting peer associations.*

Solidarity of the we-group—the loyalty of members to one another and the adherence to group norms—is a central characteristic of any primary group. But the hiatus between an earlier close adult supervision with enforcement of rules and a later mature individual acceptance of responsibility for fair play makes the acceptance and enforcement of some kind of ground rules especially urgent. It is a reasonable hypothesis that intolerance of the unusual and of the superior are greatest when the observer and the observed are potential competitors and when there is no assurance that they will be restrained by any mutually accepted body of rules. Peer solidarity accordingly takes the place of institutionally imposed order. It is imposed without the sensitiveness and restraint of maturity, and an indiscriminate intolerance of the different takes the place of a finely graded system of rules.

Peer Identities

In the normal primary group, each individual has an established identity compounded of his shared identity as a group member and the distinctive identity derived from his role in the group.[15] Again it may

14 Ferdinand Tönnies, *Community and Association,* trans. by Charles P. Loomis (London: Routledge & Kegan Paul, Ltd., 1955).

15 The concept of identity is used in the sense suggested by Nelson Foote and Leonard Cottrell, Jr. in *Identity and Interpersonal Competence* (Chicago: University of Chicago Press, 1955); and by Anselm Strauss in *Mirrors and Masks* (Glencoe, Ill.: Free Press, 1959).

be assumed that the acceptance of divergent identities in any group is a function of confidence in the pre-eminence of shared group-membership identities. The long experience and intimate knowledge that members of a true primary group have of one another establish the grounds for such confidence and allow unique identities to flourish. However, the casual contacts with a great many peers, combined with prior experiences of unpredictable and threatening behavior by some of those peers, forestalls the development of similar confidence regarding each individual's peer-group identity. Hence, there is an urgent demand to demonstrate the shared peer identity conspicuously and repeatedly.

At the same time, the difficulties in the way of establishing any special identity of a stable sort, even apart from the intolerance of uniqueness, force the individual to rely more strongly upon his shared peer identity. The individual himself is led thus to rely upon shared identity to the degree to which he encounters difficulty in the establishment of an acceptable and continuous unique identity. As the youth finds difficulty in getting all of his relevant others to support a common identity for him, he tends to assert the youth identity more strongly.

Against the background of a uniform peer-membership identity, individual identities still tend to emerge and to acquire some continuity among situations. As they do, some of these identities constitute more of a threat to the peers than others. As in any group, uniqueness and even superiority may be displayed either in such a fashion as to demonstrate that the group identity is still pre-eminent or so as to suggest that the unique identity enables the individual to relinquish some of his shared identity. When the individual fails to make conspicuous demonstration of group identity, his peers readily assume that he views his uniqueness in the latter fashion and he is labeled "conceited" or "queer." But by demonstrating that he thinks of himself chiefly as one of the gang, the individual may cultivate considerable tolerated uniqueness and superiority.

The implications of uniqueness in various areas of accomplishment likewise vary. Some types of excellence make the individual highly acceptable to an important outgroup, and thus suggest that he may be disloyal to the peer group. Other forms of excellence are in areas less highly evaluated by such important outgroups and are less likely to imply rejection of the peer identity. The student who excels scholastically is required to make a more impressive demonstration that he is just an ordinary loyal member of the peer group at heart than the youth whose achievements are in athletics or popular music.

While solidarity is enforced by appropriate informal penalties, the positive base for solidarity and the symbolic means for demonstrating peer identity are found in the cultivation of special youth interests. Sports, popular music, special recreational and language fads acquire distinctive value to youth as interests that distinguish the ingroup from the outgroup and as the substantive focus for the maintenance of simulated primary relations.

Distinctive Features

In the foregoing statement there are two important points of difference from many of the usual discussions of youth subculture. First, we have not emphasized the strains arising out of crucial choices such as occupation and mate selection, nor have we stressed sex problems. While these problems demonstrably color the preoccupations of youth subculture, children of twelve and thirteen who may be as yet unconcerned about such decisions find themselves strongly drawn into the youth subsociety. The problems of identity and of insuring a controlled interpersonal environment appear to be prior to the decisions regarding mate and occupation and to continue throughout the years during which youth culture is an important feature of the individual's daily life. Once the youth subsociety is established, the shared preoccupations of its members at any given stage are taken up in the youth subculture. But these adolescent problems may exist, and do in many European countries, without the kind of youth culture that we recognize in the United States. It is not our intention to deny the pervasive impact of these problems on the character of youth culture, but merely to suggest that they are not primary in determining the existence of a youth subsociety and youth subculture.

The second point of difference from many discussions of youth subculture is the emphasis on strains in the relations among peers rather than upon the youths' relation to adults. Frequently youths are depicted as uniting largely for defense against the demands of their parents and teachers, youth subsociety constituting a coalition in a "cold war" against adult authority and projected adult ambition. But we suggest that the extent of peer rivalry and antagonism is often underestimated and that the youth-adult tension is more a consequence of youth subculture than its cause. Institutional arrangements place youths in competition with one another in both serious pursuits and recreational activities. Interpersonal suspiciousness and jealousy are openly expressed in the disguised form of banter. Indeed, trading insults, "chopping out" the other fellow and joining in riotous laughter at his loss of dignity are among the major preoccupations of peer communication. Meanwhile, the presence of a united front among youths is perceived by parents and teachers as a threat to their control, and adds to their apprehensions regarding the character of the unsupervised behavior of youths. In those instances in which youth preferences and adult preferences clash, the pressures upon youths from their peers do make them more intractable in the dealings with adults. Adults are likely not to understand the nature of the peer pressures and to interpret intractability as evidence that the youth respects and wishes the good will of his peers more than that of his parents and teachers. In fact, he often values the good will of his parents more, but is constrained because his position in the peer group is much more precarious than is his position in the family. As a consequence of the foregoing, the youth culture does take on a tint of anti-adultism, more deeply hued for some members than for others, and is likely to be viewed more strongly in this fashion by adults than by youths themselves.

Insofar as there is some opposition between youth society and adult authority, it is also important to note whether it is centered about important values or merely about day-to-day implementation. Well before the age of any real youth society, children form coalitions to resist close supervision of their activities and detailed direction by adults. But such resistance does not imply an opposition of long-range values. Indeed, such resistance is often made possible by the tacit confidence of the children that their parents will stop them before they get too far "out of line." The coalition of youth may mask a consensus with parents and teachers on many fundamental values behind the friction over matters of immediate supervision.

Segmentation and Ritualism

In addition to these points of emphasis regarding the etiology and dynamics of youth culture, the point of view which has guided our investigation also includes a special conception of the empirical referent of youth culture. In spite of the fact that there is ample documentation of the existence of the distinctive youth patterns and that the patterns are transmitted and enforced among the members, there are still two important respects in which the conditions of a true subculture are not met. First, the youth subculture is a *segmental* pattern rather than a comprehensive way of life, and is attached to a youth society which is likewise segmental. In the true subculture, such as characterizes regions, classes, and ethnic groups, the individual's whole social life is carried out with others who share the subculture. Furthermore, the subculture contains patterns pertaining to all phases of life. But youth culture pertains to only a segment of life, and relations with family and other groups continue to be at least as important as those with peers. Consequently, there must necessarily be a continuing accommodation between the ways of the youth subculture and those of other important groups.

Some of the prevalent ideas about the youth subculture derive from the vivid depiction of life among the "corner boys" of streetcorner society. However, as W. F. Whyte has taken pains to point out, the corner boys were actually young adults who had been prevented from assuming adult roles by the Depression of the 1930's.[16] Consequently, the youth patterns had become a considerably more comprehensive way of life for them than is normally the case.

Second, youth subculture is a *ritualistic* pattern. It is the nature of ritual that it can be perfectly executed without inner conviction. Whenever there is ritual there will be some who perform it from conviction, many who occasionally experience the feelings that are supposed to motivate the performance while often executing the ritual in the absence of feeling, and some for whom the ritual is merely a required demonstration of group acceptability. Because youth society is segmental and pertains more to the recreational than to the serious aspects of life, it is relatively easy for an individual to conform ritually while resisting or limiting internalization. The view here is that the average American youth comes into contact with youth subculture first as a system of norms intolerantly imposed upon him by other youth and only subsequently begins to incorporate elements into his own value system. The view, further, is that most youth do not acquire an inner conviction corresponding in degree to their external conformity.

The very solidarity of youth society is ritualistic in an important respect. A full-fledged solidarity would stress altruism and self-sacrifice for one's fellows and denial of forms of self-interest which array members competitively. Such is the solidarity ordinarily demanded by the family group, the gang, vital religious ideologies, and utopian social movements. In contrast to full-fledged solidarity is ritual solidarity with its studied avoidance of apparent individualism and constant conspicuous assertion of unity and fellow-feeling. The latter can prevail in the absence of altruism and with competitive self-interest only disguised.[17] We suspect that the real rivalries in courtship, school, occupational preparation, and student activities are only disguised rather than eliminated by the youth who feel that they have a chance

16 William F. Whyte, *Streetcorner Society* (Chicago: University of Chicago Press, 1943).

17 Ralph H. Turner, "Preoccupation with Competitiveness and Social Acceptance among American and English College Students," *Sociometry*, 23 (Sept., 1960), p. 313.

for success. The peer culture does not penetrate deeply enough to require that solidarity take precedence over pursuits related to long-range success goals.

If youth solidarity is of this ritual character, it is distinguished from the mutual-aid pattern so frequently ascribed to the lower classes in American society. The latter should be an impediment to ambition, punishing the ambitious with ostracism and other group penalties.[18] The former, however, can be handled by appropriate disguise and ritual compensation. Even more important, enough members of the youth group may privately admire the successful person and share his ambitions so that peer disapproval will only be inconsistently and unconvincingly registered. Sufficient admiration may be expressed in various ways so that the successful individual can offset a limitation of peer participation with the gain in prestige that he acquires. Thus, while the ambitious individual finds his relations within the youth society more complicated and ambivalent than others do, he is not confronted with an entirely negative reaction.

Upward Mobility and Youth Subculture

In sum, the youth subculture has been described as a segmental and ritual pattern which many youth enact in the spirit of a game while still retaining private standards and goals at variance with it. On the one hand, the pattern provides a ready identity for the individual in an otherwise amorphous situation and protects the individual by imposing controls on his peer environment. On the other hand, the special youth interests provide a basis for sociable enjoyment and a considerable degree of fellow-feeling. The ritual forms of interaction and subjects of communication provide a means for ready communication in casual and fleeting interpersonal relations. The declarations against success in fields of serious accomplishment are hardly to be taken other than as public disavowals to protect the individual's pride in the face of possible failure in highly valued pursuits.

The foregoing conception of youth subculture has implications for the position of upwardly mobile youth. A youth culture which is practiced largely as an enjoyable ritual has relatively less effect in eradicating differences in class background than a strongly internalized pattern. While accepting at face value a youth's peer identity for peer-group purposes, the individual is not prevented from also recognizing his social-class identity and making use of it from time to time. Because

18 Allison Davis, "The Motivation of the Underprivileged Worker," in William F. Whyte, ed., *Industry and Society* (New York: McGraw-Hill, 1946).

of the segmental character of youth society, the importance of family background wavers from situation to situation even in relation to the same group of associates. Suppression, rather than eradication of rivalry and competitiveness among peers, leaves many potential antagonisms ready to erupt when the smooth surface of youth subculture is broken. The mobile individual may then find himself accepted on the surface but unable to shed his class identity underneath. In some respects exactly the situation required for marginality might prevail. The ritual solidarity and classless equalitarianism of youth society might deceive the upwardly mobile person into supposing that he was fully freed from the identity derived from his family background. A subsequent discovery that he was not accepted as an equal by students from higher levels could then have the traumatic and disillusioning quality depicted in the classical marginal-man experience.

While the equalizing effects of a youth culture so conceived would be limited, the mediocrity values of such a youth culture would also be a less serious obstacle to ambition than otherwise. Much of the social disapproval of ambition would be tempered by private admiration. The ambitious youth might trade a certain amount of intimacy for genuine prestige in the eyes of his peers. But the social acceptability of the ambitious individual to his peers would be less a function of his ambition than of the manner in which he handled the ambition. The ambitious youth who joined in the requisite exhibition of peer solidarity could have both prestige and peer acceptance.

The preceeding chapter has already shown that the ambitious are more likely to be favored by their peers than are the unambitious. But two additional kinds of data supply evidence relative to the nature of youth subculture and its impact on the would-be mobile individual: (1) the interrelations among *friend, wheel,* and *brain ratings;* (2) the responses to twelve of the value items which correspond to components of youth subculture. In the remainder of the chapter these two sets of data will be examined, followed by a consideration of neighborhood variation.

SOCIOMETRIC HOMOGENEITY AND HETEROGENEITY

The three basic sociometric indexes supply clues to variations among private interpersonal preferences, student leadership, and scholastic reputation. Negative correlations among some of these would point to an opposition between peer subculture and school values. Cleavages among the students according to their ratings would reflect fragmentation into "ins" and "outs" which would lessen the homogeneity of youth society.

Interrelations among Indexes

Each index has been cross-tabulated with each other index (Tables 28–30), though summary measures have not been used because of the skewed distributions of *wheel* and *friend ratings.* Inspection reveals at once that there is considerable positive correlation within each pair of indexes. After allowance is made for the smaller proportion of women than of men with high *wheel ratings,* relationships are very similar for the sexes. In general, the students select for close enduring friendship individuals who have some reputation as *wheels* or as good students. Being good in schoolwork enhances rather than damages the student's chances of being selected as a potential friend as it enhances his chances of being regarded as a *big wheel.*

The character of the relationships among the indexes deserves some special note. When *friend rating* and *wheel rating* are cross-tabulated, it appears that no one has at the same time both a high *wheel rating* and a low *friend rating,* though a great many students combine a high *friend rating* with a low *wheel rating.* Either the qualities desired in a friend are essential but not sufficient for a peer leader, or by virtue of his prominence, the peer leader is sure to be desired as a friend, even when he lacks other favorable qualities.

A similarly unbalanced relationship exists between *friend rating* and *brain rating,* although the degree of the relationship appears to be less. Almost no one who is an isolate is also high in *brain rating.* However, many students are high in *friend rating* without also being regarded as excellent in academic endeavor. The parallel with *wheel rating* is clear. No one can be reputed as a *brain* or as a *wheel* without having qualities which lead at least a few people to name him as a desirable friend. But one can be quite desirable as a friend without being recognized as a *brain* or as a *wheel.* In connection with *brain rating* it is easier to select between the two interpretations than it was in connection with *wheel rating.* Parsimony favors the view that excellence in schoolwork is positively valued so that an appreciable number of persons take it into account in determining their friendship preferences.

It is also worthy of note that there is a slightly smaller relationship between *brain rating* and *friend rating* among men than among women. This difference is consistent with the widely held view that excellence in schoolwork is more fully accepted as a positive value for women than for men. While the extreme view that men are punished by their peers for "unmasculine" success in academic efforts finds no support in our

Table 28. Association of Wheel Rating with Friend Rating

Sex	Wheel rating	Distribution, by friend rating					
		1 low FR	2	3	4	5	6 high FR
Male	1 (low)	90%	84%	76%	57%	39%	14%
	2	8	14	17	27	24	28
	3	2	1	5	9	16	15
	4 (high)	--	1	2	8	20	43
	Total	100%	100%	100%	101%	99%	100%
	Total number	244	287	369	245	135	72
Female	1 (low)	95%	96%	88%	76%	53%	28%
	2	5	4	9	15	28	23
	3	1	--	2	5	9	22
	4 (high)	--	--	1	5	11	28
	Total	101%	100%	100%	101%	101%	101%
	Total number	163	282	505	299	123	69

Table 29. Association of Brain Rating with Friend Rating

Sex	Brain rating	Distribution, by friend rating					
		1 low FR	2	3	4	5	6 high FR
Male	1 (low)	91%	87%	77%	67%	62%	40%
	2	7	7	16	19	19	25
	3	2	3	3	6	13	18
	4 (high)	1	3	4	8	7	17
	Total	101%	100%	100%	100%	101%	100%
	Total number	244	287	369	245	135	72
Female	1 (low)	88%	86%	79%	66%	57%	28%
	2	9	10	14	22	23	33
	3	3	2	3	8	7	20
	4 (high)	1	3	4	5	14	19
	Total	101%	101%	100%	101%	101%	100%
	Total number	163	282	505	299	123	69

Table 30. Association of Wheel Rating with Brain Rating

Sex	Wheel rating	Distribution, by brain rating			
		1 low BR	2	3	4 high BR
Male	1 (low)	77%	53%	44%	32%
	2	15	25	23	26
	3	5	9	7	5
	4 (high)	2	13	26	37
	Total	99%	100%	100%	100%
	Total number	1031	187	69	65
Female	1 (low)	90%	68%	41%	42%
	2	7	21	26	18
	3	2	6	13	13
	4 (high)	1	5	20	27
	Total	100%	100%	100%	100%
	Total number	1071	229	70	71

data, the more modest notion that the "masculine" values partially offset the otherwise positive valuation of academic achievement among men is congenial with the data at hand.

Again there is an unbalanced relationship between *brain rating* and *wheel rating*, following roughly similar form for males and females. Many students combine high *brain ratings* with low *wheel ratings*, indicating clearly that the subjects have been able to distinguish the "bookworm" from the influential peer leader. However, very few students with minimum *brain ratings* are able to achieve high *wheel ratings*. Perhaps there is a halo effect, students overestimating the quality of school performance among their peer leaders. There could, however, be no halo effect unless students placed the same positive valuation upon both types of personal qualities. School policies undoubtedly play a part, discouraging student leadership among those who do not perform fairly well academically.

In light of a possibility that the correlation between *friend rating* and *brain rating* derives from a halo effect—a tendency for students to attribute academic excellence or recognize such excellence in their friends more often than in others—we have employed I.Q. as an external verification of academic ability. Since the distributions of both I.Q. and *friend rating* approximate normal curves and since the plotted relationships appear to be linear, product-moment coefficients of correlation are employed. The coefficients are +.14 and +.12 for men and women respectively. Though small in absolute terms, both coefficients are considerably larger than required for significance at the one percent level of confidence. With this corroborating evidence, then, there is more reason to take the positive relationship between *friend rating* and *brain rating* seriously as a genuine reflection of the consistency between the working values of the peer group and a considerable degree of academic accomplishment.

Lines of Separateness

Three *elite indexes* have been employed to measure the kind of quality of choices which any given individual received and to explore the interrelation of choice systems further. The *friend elite* index reflects the average *friend rating* of the persons who chose the individual in question as one they would like to have as a friend. Similarly the *wheel* and *brain elite* indexes reflect the average *wheel* and *brain ratings* of those naming the given individual as a would-be friend. As before, it was necessary to compute the indexes and then assign arbitrary values which would render the indexes comparable among the ten schools. The initial index in each instance was simply the average unadjusted *friend rating, wheel rating,* or *brain rating* of the individual's choosers. The final index was assigned on the basis of rank-order categories within each of the ten schools.[19]

The cross-tabulations of *friend rating* with each of the three *elite* indexes are summarized in Table 31. The most highly desired as friends are more often chosen by others who are highly desired as friends, by those who are generally identified as *wheels,* and by those who are thought to perform especially well in their schoolwork. Not only do the relationships hold for both men and women students; the relationships are quite similar in degree and character. After allowance has

19 For the *friend-elite* index arbitrary values were assigned as follows: 5 for the top 15 percent; 4 for the next 20 percent; 3 for the middle 30 percent; 2 for the next 20 percent; and 1 for the lowest 15 percent. For the *wheel elite* and *brain elite* indexes, values assigned were as follows: 4 for the top 10 percent; 3 for the next 15 percent; 2 for the next 15 percent; and 1 for the lowest 60 percent.

Table 31. Association of Elite Indexes with Friend Rating

Sex	Elite index[b]	Percentages of students[a]		
		Low friend rating (1, 2)	Medium friend rating (3)	High friend rating (4, 5, 6)
Male	High friend	45%	62%	78%
	High wheel	25	43	66
	High brain	22	37	55
Female	High friend	45	61	79
	High wheel	17	25	48
	High brain	20	33	53

[a]/ The figures in the table refer to the percentage of students with a given friend rating who have the indicated high elite-index score. Since the elite indexes were simply dichotomized (high and low) in this table, the complementary percentage in each instance would have been redundant and has been omitted.

[b]/ The elite indexes were dichotomized as follows: the high friend-elite index includes code numbers 3, 4, and 5; the high wheel-elite and high brain-elite indexes include code numbers 2, 3, and 4.

been made for the male-female difference in *wheel rating,* there may be a slightly greater relationship between *friend rating* and *wheel elite* for the men than for the women. Also *friend rating* may be slightly more strongly related to the *wheel-elite* index than to the other *elite* indexes among the men.

The foregoing relationships lend further support to the view that the friendship values among the students, the peer prestige system, and the academic prestige system are characterized more strongly by mutual support than by cleavage and opposition. Not only is the desired friend likely to be a *wheel* or a *brain:* he is likely to be especially favored for friendship by the *wheels* and the *brains* in his class at school.

Table 32. Cleavage and Friend Preference
by Wheel and Brain Ratings

Pattern of cleavage or preference[a]	Classroom units[b] (n=89)		
	Friend rating	Wheel rating	Brain rating
Positive cleavage	53	73	68
Negative cleavage	36	15	19
No cleavage	--	1	2
Positive preference	(89)	87	79
Negative preference	--	1	8
No preference	--	1	2

a/ Cleavage means a tendency for students to select others like themselves as desirable friends. Preference refers to a general tendency to select some kinds of persons in preference to others, regardless of the characteristics of the chooser.

b/ The units are the classroom groups in which the questionnaires were administered and within which sociometric choices were made.

Not only is the *brain* somewhat more likely than other students to have several persons pick him as a desirable friend and name him as a *big wheel,* but he is also more likely to conform to the prevalent peer patterns in his choice of desirable friends. Rather than representing a set of values at variance from those of his peers, the student with an academic reputation is especially likely to embody peer standards in his own choices.

In Table 32 there is a summary of unit-by-unit cleavage and preference tabulations for *friend rating, wheel rating,* and *brain rating.* There is some suggestion of cleavage according to friendship desirability, but the preponderance of positive over negative findings is not impressive. With respect to both *wheel rating* and *brain rating,* however, there are clear tendencies for cleavage between the "highs" and the "lows."

The unit findings regarding preference offer emphatic substantiation for the over-all correlation of *friend rating* with both *wheel rating* and *brain rating*. In eighty-seven of eighty-nine units the *wheels* are more often preferred as friends than the *nonwheels,* and in seventy-nine units the *brains* are preferred to the *nonbrains.*

The cleavages between the *wheels* and *nonwheels* and the *brains* and *nonbrains* indicate a partially organized outgroup in each instance. The fact that the scholastic achievers are the ingroup, as indicated by the relationship to *friend* and *wheel* systems, strongly suggests that the antischolastic values in youth subculture are of a ritual character and are at variance with private preference and the determinants of peer-group social prominence.

YOUTH-SUBCULTURE VALUES

Included in the questionnaire are twelve items which correspond to various aspects of youth subculture. Two kinds of hypotheses can be examined on the basis of assuming that a key feature of youth subculture is simulation of primary-group relations, and that youth subculture is normally practiced only segmentally and can be learned primarily as ritual. First, the kinds of items which should receive heaviest endorsement can be predicted. Second, differences in endorsement rates under three different forms of the questionnaire can be anticipated.

Item Endorsements

The following predictions are made on the basis of the conception of youth subculture which has been outlined. (1) An expression of peer solidarity should be especially strongly endorsed when it is specifically opposed to solidarity in the larger impersonal community. (2) Peer solidarity will not be strongly endorsed when it is opposed to long-range personal objectives such as those concerned with career. (3) Peer solidarity will not be strongly endorsed when it is opposed to values which are viewed as sacred in the parental world. Youth values which consist chiefly of mere interests will be more easily internalized than those at the sacred pole, if we assume that youth-parent opposition is a by-product of the youth culture rather than its essence. If, as some sociologists suppose, the latter were the case, then opposition to a value held particularly sacred by parents would have extra merit in the youth society and we should not expect the hypothesized relationship to exist.

Percentages of endorsement for the twelve youth-culture items are presented in Table 33. The table includes the three forms of the ques-

Table 33. Endorsement Rate for Value Items Related to Youth Culture, by Questionnaire Forms

Value item[a]	Endorsement rate					
	Male			Female		
	Form A	Form B	Form C	Form A	Form B	Form C
8. Can do many things fairly well vs. can do a few things perfectly	58%	70%	74%	66%	75%	79%
12. Spends extra money on friends vs. saves extra money for future	19	22	25	14	12	16
15. Will tell small lie to help friend vs. sticks by the truth	51	52	60	44	44	48
16. Puts friends ahead of community welfare vs. community welfare ahead of friends	73	71	72	70	76	73
18. Has reputation for modesty vs. respected for real abilities	67	62	76	66	66	67
24. Does most things as well as friends vs. does many things better than friends	60	68	84	74	68	82

Statement						
25. Quick to get along with group vs. tries to get group to do things his way	56	62	68	66	70	75
26. Easy to get along with vs. respected but hard to get along with	31	39	49	25	32	38
27. Always making new friends vs. sticks with few tried-true friends	62	63	55	60	69	59
29. Talks about popular music and sports vs. talks foreign policy and politics	75	70	81	78	77	83
30. Laughs off his failures and mistakes vs. takes full blame for own failures	47	40	43	49	42	46
38. Avoids hurting others' feelings vs. honest about feelings toward others	62	55	61	63	59	56

a/ Each heading in the table is abbreviated from the full statement as it appeared in the questionnaire. For convenience in tabular presentation (but not in the questionnaire itself), the alternative corresponding to youth culture has been listed first in each instance.

tionnaire, but for the present we shall be concerned only with the responses to Form A. The degree of endorsement is not recorded in the table, but merely the alternative chosen. For convenience, the youth-culture alternative is stated first and the percentage refers to those choosing the youth-culture alternative.

The two choices which draw overwhelming endorsement for the youth pattern are the choice between friends and community welfare (item number 16) and the choice between competence in popular and serious topics of conversation (item 29). The former was designed as a choice between primary-group ties and what is usually regarded as the ethically more sophisticated *Gesellschaft* obligation toward the community. The result is by no means a demonstration of the special view of youth subculture presented above, but it does accord with the first hypothesis.

In light of hypothesis (3), that private preferences will accord most with youth culture when the values are relatively devoid of sacred or moral significance, the finding regarding item 29 is also what should have been expected. Further support for this hypothesis is found in observing the four items least favorable to the youth-culture alternative. Three of these appear to involve some moral value. The preference for being respected though hard to get along with (item 26) is striking, while the respondents divided fairly evenly on the choices between lying for a friend and honesty (item 15) and between taking blame and laughing off failures (item 30). The preference for strict honesty would have been marked except that during pretests the question was modified in order to bring about an even split. Although these students participate in the youth society, share its interests in things popular rather than serious, and very likely give public endorsement to many of its behavioral rules, they apparently continue to accept privately the moral values that may from time to time be opposed by strictures of the youth culture.

The item which yields the smallest support for the youth culture opposes the spending of money on friends to saving money for the future (item 12). Here seems to be support for the general notion of ritual solidarity in contrast to altruism and mutual aid. Though the student would rather have his strong points unrecognized than be thought conceited and prefer to do most things as well as his close friends rather than better than they, his concessions to peer solidarity do not invade this more serious realm of self-interest.

Thus the general pattern of extreme items has consistently supported the image of the youth culture suggested above. In addition, there is a striking consistency between the sexes with respect to these items. The only sex difference with respect to the more extreme items is the overwhelming endorsement by women students of doing most things just about as well as one's friends rather than better (item 24). Probably girls have been pushed less toward individualistic performance than boys so that the youth value of equality among peers can be more readily internalized by them. The similar discrepancy between male and female responses dealing with conforming to the group as opposed to directing the group (item 25) supports such a view.

The items which supply a clear but modest majority for the youth-culture alternative all, with one exception, deal with obligations in interpersonal relations. The fact that these items do not draw heavier support is surprising when the prevalent conceptions of youth culture are held in mind. The fact that only a modest majority supports each of these youth alternatives suggests that there remains a strong private dedication to individualistic values which is not eradicated by several years of participation in the ritual solidarity of the youth subculture.

The remaining item (number 8) was intended to measure the choice between a balanced mediocrity and exceptional proficiency in a few areas. Here there is a strong majority for the former among women and a small majority among men. Again the classical values receive surprising endorsement.

Alternate Questionnaire Forms

Further light on the involvement of individuals with youth-culture values can be gained by examining answers supplied on alternate forms of the questionnaire. One fifth of the questionnaires were divided equally between Form B and Form C. In Form B of the questionnaire, subjects were asked which kind of person they admired most. And in Form C they were asked which kind of person they would like to have as a friend.

The answers supplied on Form C should be the most nearly indicative of the working pressures of the youth culture upon individuals, if isolation is the ultimate penalty and popularity the ultimate reward attaching to youth culture. The question will not correspond exactly to youth pressures, since there are undoubtedly differences between those who are chosen for association in youth activities and those who would be preferred as friends with a longer and less frenetic association in mind.

Form B, on the other hand, places values in a context most abstracted from the immediate concerns of the individual. By asking the subject whom he admires we allow him to acknowledge values in a way which is relatively divorced from any implication that he must adopt these values as his own goals or that he would like to have such persons about him as friends.

There are several possible patterns with respect to the similarities and differences among the responses to the three forms of each value choice. The pattern which most closely reflects the conception of youth subculture outlined here has endorsement rates which are highest on Form C, responses on Form C which are differentiated from those on the other forms, and responses on Forms A and B which are little differentiated. Such a pattern suggests that the individual is not greatly influenced in his private conception of his ideal goals by the youth culture. When he conforms overtly, as he may do often and extensively, his conformity is of a genuinely ritual character not reflected in his serious ideals for himself. The pattern also suggests that the person who is isolated for nonconformity to the youth pattern may nevertheless be privately admired and respected by the youths who isolate him.

A total absence of differentiation could have varied meanings. With a high rate of endorsement of youth value items, the absence of difference might plausibly indicate full internalization of youth culture rather than ritual acceptance. A low rate of endorsement without difference between forms might suggest that a minority of youth account for the apparent youth values—the not uncommon situation in which the actions of a conspicuous minority are mistaken by outsiders and insiders alike for the preponderant attitude within the group. Other patterns need not be explored unless they are encountered empirically.

The table shows that while differences are small, the most common relationship separates the higher rate of endorsement under Form C from the relatively less differentiated rates under Forms A and B. Disregarding statistical significance, we note that for men students eleven out of twelve items show a higher endorsement rate under Form C than under Form B and eight out of twelve show higher endorsement under Form C than under Form A. For women students nine of twelve items show higher endorsement rates under Form C than under Form A or under Form B. Differences between Forms A and B are more evenly divided.

Among five of the items (18, 24, 25, 26, 29), for men there is significantly higher endorsement of the youth alternative on Form C than on one of the others, though the nature of the difference between Forms A and B is less clear. These five items all seem to reflect the demands of peer solidarity, rather than the special values which are supposedly a part of youth culture. In each of these instances some potential conflict between peer solidarity and individual superiority or moral integrity is involved. In each instance, the demands of peer solidarity are not as strongly accepted on Forms A and B as on Form C. Some items express the pattern of setting one's goals as a compromise between peer values and values more abstractly acknowledged, while others exemplify the pattern which places admiration between youth-culture conformity and self-goals. A sixth item, the preference for balanced mediocrity (item 8), clearly falls in the latter pattern, suggesting a rather thorough belief in the youth culture, but a reluctance to convert belief into a goal for oneself. This distribution could occur if self-interest were at stake, or if pressures in the situation made the following of personal inclinations difficult.

Significant differences between the forms are fewer for women respondents than for men respondents. The pattern for balanced mediocrity resembles the pattern found among the men. Three of the five items mentioned as reflecting peer solidarity show modest tendencies similar to those uncovered for the men. But, in general, the picture is less clear. As a consequence, it seems likely that acceptance of the aspects of youth culture reflected in our twelve items is less characterized by ritual conformity-ambivalence among the girls than among the high-school boys.

A final comparison among the three forms of the questionnaire has been made, using the index which summarizes the twelve youth-culture items. Although the pattern of difference is in accord with expectation (higher mean index on Form C than on Forms A and B; larger differences for men than for women), the required level of statistical significance is not reached. Since the differences among forms were significant for several of the items, it appears that students do not tend sufficiently to adopt or reject the youth-culture items as a whole to make the composite index significant.

Correlations with Background and Ambition

If youth culture is an equalizing medium, there should be no correlation between youth-culture items and background. Out of the twelve items, nine or ten confirm this hypothesis for the men (Table 34). The two or possibly three exceptions, are all in the direction of linking the youth pattern with the lower levels. For women there are five exceptions, four linking youth culture to the lower level and one linking it to the higher. Higher-level youths of both sexes are less ready to accept the interest in popular music and sports and more resistant to losing identity in the group. Hence, the youth culture fails to equalize fully the patterns of students from different classes. Since

Table 34. Youth-Culture Values Correlated by Background and Ambition

Value item	Male vs. female	Male				Female			
		Background		Ambition		Background		Ambition	
		Occupation	Index	Occupation	Index	Occupation	Index	Occupation	Index
8. Many things fairly well vs. few things perfectly	-.001	--	--	--	--	--	--	-.05	--
12. Spends extra money on friends vs. saves for future	+.01	--	--	--	--	--	--	+.02	+.01
15. Lie to get friend out of trouble vs. strict truth	+.001	--	--	--	--	+.001	+.001	+.001	+.001
16. Puts friends ahead of community vs. community welfare first	--	--	--	--	--	--	--	--	--
18. Reputation for modesty vs. reputation as conceited	--	--	--	--	--	-.05	-.001	--	-.01
24. Does as well as friends vs. does better than friends	-.001	--	-.05	--	-.05	-.001	-.001	-.001	-.001

25. Goes along with group vs. gets group to go his way	+.001	-.01	-.001	--	-.01	-.01	-.001	-.001	-.001
26. Easy to get along with vs. respected	--	--	--	--	--	--	--	-.01	--
27. Always meeting new people vs. sticks to old friends	--	--	--	--	--	--	--	--	--
29. Talks about popular music and sports vs. foreign policy, political trends	--	-.001	-.001	-.001	-.001	-.01	-.01	-.001	-.001
30. Laughs off failures and mistakes vs. takes full blame	--	--	--	--	--	--	--	--	+.05
38. Won't hurt feelings vs. honest about attitudes	-.01	--	--	--	--	--	--	--	--

the number of items which correlate with class is not impressive for any of the value categories, we must regard the findings as providing no special support for the view that youth subculture is unrelated to social class.

From the assumption that youth culture is an obstacle to ambition there comes a second hypothesis, that there should be a negative correlation between youth culture and ambition. Since it appears that most of the relationships which are to be found are negative, some support is gained for the second hypothesis. For both hypotheses, however, the relationships are not comprehensive enough to warrant generalizations applying to the youth subculture as a whole. Since much the same correlations apply to background and ambition, the evidence which supports the second hypothesis is also the evidence which negates the first. Whether the correlations are easier to interpret as evidence of anticipatory socialization or as reflections of youth subculture can hardly be determined from the foregoing evidence.

When the twelve items are cross-tabulated with *friend rating*, separately for males and females, there are no significant relationships. When the youth-subculture index based on the twelve items is cross-tabulated with *friend rating*, separately for males and females, no relationships appear. A unit-by-unit cleavage tabulation with the youth-subculture index dichotomized, likewise shows no relationship (Table 36). Forty-one units are positive, forty-seven negative, and one "zero" with respect to cleavage. Concerning preference, there are forty-four positive, thirty-seven negative, and eight "zero." Not only are the youth-subculture adherents no more often named as desirable friends than the nonbelievers; there is no tendency for a cleavage by values as measured here.

NEIGHBORHOOD AND YOUTH SUBCULTURE

The relationship between youth subculture and class subcultures has never been carefully explored, although the typical descriptions of the former seem usually to have been drawn from middle- and lower-class neighborhoods. Because of the extent of overlap between the content of lower-class subculture, as it has been described in sociological literature, and youth subculture, it is doubtful that the latter could exist as an effective phenomenon in lower-class neighborhoods.

The youth-subculture index, based on the twelve value items covered in the preceding discussion, was found not to correlate with either background or ambition. But when the schools are separated into groups, the hypothesis that youth subculture should correlate negatively with ambition but should not correlate at all with background

Table 35. Correlation of Youth-Culture Index with Stratification, by Type of Neighborhood

Sex	Variables correlated	Level of nonethnic neighborhood			Ethnic and nonethnic low neighborhoods
		High	Middle	Low	
Male	Youth culture with background index	-.04	-.07	-.07	-.08
	Youth culture with ambition index	-.02	-.15[b]	.06	-.06
	Number of cases	168	521	96	223
Female	Youth culture with background index	-.04	-.09	-.04	-.07
	Youth culture with ambition index	-.14[a]	-.16[b]	-.06	-.11
	Number of cases	206	576	112	298

a/ P $\leq$ .05.

b/ P $\leq$ .01.

is supported in the middle-level schools for both boys and girls (Table 35). The coefficients are not large by absolute standards, but they are significant. There is also the predicted negative correlation for girls in high-level schools, but of borderline significance.

Higher correlations in middle-level schools might have been discounted on the grounds that these schools contain a higher range of variability in background than either the high- or low-level schools. But since there is an absence of correlation when all neighborhoods are combined, the finding cannot be so easily dismissed. It is even more important to note that whether the absence of relationships in the lower-level schools is a consequence of the truncated distribution of background or of some other circumstance, the value amorphousness which it indicates is no less real. For whatever reason, ambitions and values are less well integrated among the boys in lower-level schools, and the classic youth culture appears not to function as it may in middle-level schools.

The cleavage analysis employing the youth-subculture index can be examined separately by neighborhoods. In order to supply a context for its interpretation, it is presented with a similar analysis using the class-values index in Table 36. It should be noted that only one or two of the 31 value items correlated with *friend rating* at a level of borderline significance and that none of the value indexes was correlated with *friend rating*. When all the neighborhoods are taken together there is no clear preference or cleavage pattern for either index, although there is a slight negative preference relative to class values.

If there is any preference pattern, it is a preference for persons low on the class-values index in the middle schools. Similarly, the only suggestion of cleavage by class values is in the middle schools. There are no preference patterns by youth culture, except possibly in the high areas, and again the only possible cleavage by youth culture is in the middle-level schools. The apparent negative cleavage by youth culture in high and low neighborhoods may be simply chance, or it may indicate a tendency borne of ambivalence for students to admire those different from themselves.

If it were not for the consistency of these observations with the equally small neighborhood variations in correlation of youth culture with ambition, the patterns of cleavage would not warrant further discussion. But both tables indicate that if the classic conception of youth culture works at all, it works only in the middle-level schools. Youth culture is supposed to be an equalizing mechanism, erasing the distinctions of socioeconomic background among its devotees, but also discouraging high ambition by virtue of its values of irresponsibility

Table 36. Neighborhood Differentials in Preference
and Cleavage by Class-Value and Youth-Culture Indexes

| Type of pattern | Number of classrooms | | | | | |
| | Class-value index | | | Youth-culture index | | |
	High-level schools	Middle-level schools	Low-level schools	High-level schools	Middle-level schools	Low-level schools
Highs preferred	9	16	11	12	22	10
Lows preferred	10	29	9	5	21	11
Equal preference	--	3	2	2	5	1
Total	19	48	22	19	48	22
Positive cleavage	8	29	7	6	30	5
Negative cleavage	11	19	15	12	18	17
No cleavage	--	--	--	1	--	--
Total	19	48	22	19	48	22

and mediocrity. The predicted combination of no correlation with background and a negative correlation with ambition is found only in the middle neighborhoods. It is likewise in the middle neighborhoods that the only suggestion of friendship cleavage on the basis of adherence to youth culture appears. There may be a slight preference for values associated with lower background and ambition and some cleavage according to whether the students adhere to values of higher or lower strata. Likewise, the middle schools are the only group in which there is a possible cleavage by ambition when boys choose girls (Chapter Five).

Perhaps the less clearly defined and more mixed character of the schools in middle-level neighborhoods and the respectability concern of lower-middle-class parents makes the values of the students a criterion of social differentiation. These are the schools that draw most heavily from a population whose hold on "middle classness" is quite precarious. The cleavage finding is fully in keeping with the prevalent view of the lower middle class as a group of people who are upwardly oriented, and who make up for their lack of economic differentiation from upper-working-class groups by emphasizing a differentiation of values.[20]

If we draw upon our initial suggestion that the youth culture is more of a device to protect youth from one another than an organized opposition to the adult world, the combination of a sufficiently high general level of ambition and a sufficient level of insecurity regarding attainment may be the most fertile condition for a strong youth culture. As a ritual form, the denial of ambition is only possible when the level of private ambition is high enough that individuals can confidently separate their working ambitions from their public protestations. On the other hand, the social necessity to reduce the external appearance of great ambition is maximized when the attainment of personal goals is felt to be precarious. For the first reason, the youth subculture might be less relevant in lower-level schools, and for the second reason, it might be less potent in the higher-neighborhood schools.

A peculiarity in Table 27 in the previous chapter may also fit the pattern suggested here. It was noted that in the middle-level schools the men with average or moderately low mobility failed to choose friends from persons of higher backgrounds than their own to the degree that we had anticipated. Youth subculture, we suppose, is most distinctively a phenomenon of the undistinguished student, who is neither highly ambitious nor downwardly mobile. The modest negative correlation between youth subculture and ambition suggests that adherents are concentrated in the average and slightly below-average brackets with respect to mobility. If youth subculture is an obstacle to ambition, we should expect to see it reflected in deviation from any general pattern of upward choice of friends. The deviation is where we would expect it to be on the assumption that youth subculture is of especial significance in the middle schools.

SUMMARY

A youth subculture which obliterated distinctions of social class would facilitate mobility; but by disparaging ambition, responsibility, and academic values it would also impede mobility. The term *subcul-*

---

[20] Joseph A. Kahl, *The American Class Structure* (New York: Rinehart, 1957), pp. 202–205.

ture has been applied to youth behavior on the grounds that a widespread and distinctive pattern of behavior is transmitted and imposed within a youth society, and that it serves a function in preparing the child for the requirements of adult society. On the other hand, youth subculture is necessarily a more segmental part of the individual's life than the more common types of subculture. In addition, a suspicion is justified that youth subculture is frequently adopted ritualistically, so that it does not penetrate to the private convictions of its adherents. Although the usual theory of youth subculture stresses resistance to adult demands and responsibilities, an alternative conception is proposed. Release from the primary groups of childhood creates problems of control and identity in the youth's relations with his peers. Youth subculture is a device to resolve these problems, and arises more from the youth's problems of relations with peers than out of opposition to adults. If youth subculture is ritualistic and is not primarily anti-adult in character, it would neither obliterate class distinctions nor effectively oppose high levels of ambition among most students.

The finding of positive intercorrelations among *friend, wheel,* and *brain ratings* belies an effective youth conspiracy against academic excellence. The unbalanced character of the correlations suggests that both high *wheel ratings* and high *brain ratings* are assets but not requisites to being named as desirable friends. Since the more popular students receive a disproportion of their choices from *wheels* and *brains,* it appears that the latters' criteria are not at odds with those dominant in youth society. Cleavages exist between *wheels* and *nonwheels* and between *brains* and *nonbrains,* but the *brains* and *wheels* constitute the ingroups, as judged by friendship preference.

Endorsement rates on twelve value items which correspond to aspects of youth subculture are highest when the issues are primary-group values and youth interests and least when self-interest or moral values are involved. There is also a slight tendency for youth items to be endorsed more frequently when students are asked about the choice of a friend than when asked for personal goals or admirable qualities. The latter observation suggests that students impose upon one another by their friendship preferences a youth subculture which they do not accept equally for themselves. The hypothesis that youth-culture endorsement is related negatively to ambition, but unrelated to background, does not receive support.

When relationships are examined within neighborhoods, the standard hypotheses regarding youth subculture find possible support in the middle-level schools, whose core populations are from lower-middle-class backgrounds. The negative correlation between youth values and ambition, coupled with an absence of relationship between youth culture and background, appears here. Here also is found a possible cleavage according to youth-culture adherence and a possible preference for students low on the class-values index. These highly tentative findings are in accord with theoretical reasons for believing that the classic conception of youth subculture is only applicable to somewhat heterogeneous neighborhoods which are predominantly of this intermediate socioeconomic level.

The total impression from the chapter is that youth subculture probably has less effect in modifying the mobility experience than many social scientists suggest, but that the full impact of youth subculture may be experienced in some middle-level neighborhoods.

CHAPTER SEVEN

Emphases in Ambition

ONE MAJOR PROBLEM suggested in the opening chapter remains for consideration. The concept of mobility refers to a comprehensive change in position, including income level, educational level, place of residence, way of life (subculture), social ties and identity, and many other circumstances. General theories of mobility assume that the change is experienced comprehensively, that the mobile person values all aspects of the change. If he does not value all aspects initially, the social context makes them so interdependent that he eventually learns to value them in the course of being mobile. But, in the early stages of mobility, ambition is sometimes quite segmental, even the awareness being incomplete. Since the impact of experience upon an individual is relative to the things that he values, certain kinds of ambition probably facilitate marginality and others lessen it.

In the present chapter we shall repeat certain analyses specifically in relation to alternative emphases in ambition. The most important alternative is between a segmental emphasis on the material aspects of position and a segmental emphasis on a "cultural" style of life. For men, the special emphasis on ownership or self-employment deserves a little more exploration. Finally, the special case of intrastratum ambition will be examined for the light which it sheds on mobility.

TYPES OF EMPHASES

Two special measures are introduced into the investigation in order to make it possible to deal with emphases in ambition. One is the *material-educational polarization* index, and the other a special question dealing with *eminence*.

Material-Educational Polarization

People whose ambitions emphasize different segments of mobility will judge their achievements by different criteria. One person may be interested primarily in being able to buy whatever he wishes—to have a life of expensive comforts and amusements. Another is anxious for prestige, for high standing in the eyes of the community about him. Still another seeks a social environment which will be congenial to the pursuit of "cultural" interests—intellectual and aesthetic appreciations. Other sorts of rewards may be sought, but these three will interest us for the present.

In a general way our three principal measures of ambition highlight the three sorts of success goals just outlined. There is an important common core, but when any one goal is disproportionately high it is reasonable to suppose that the reward in question looms especially large in the individual's conception of success. If one respondent's level of material aspiration is higher than that of other respondents with comparable educational and occupational aspirations, it can be plausibly assumed that material comforts and luxuries constitute his major goal in mobility. Or a respondent whose occupational ambition is lower than that of others with comparable material and educational goals can be regarded as relatively indifferent to the prestige aspects of success.

Educational and material aspirations in particular are amenable to interpretations of this sort. While occupation may reflect prestige considerations somewhat more than the other two measures, it also serves as the most general measure of ambition. But educational and material ambition are segmental measures. Hence, it seemed useful to devise a special index of polarization between educational and material ambition. An index was sought that would differentiate those who were disproportionately high in one or the other kind of ambition from those whose ambitions in the two areas were roughly equivalent. In order to accomplish this purpose, measures of the two kinds of ambition were converted to standard scores; the difference between the two standard scores was employed as the index, with the addition of a constant to make all values positive. In the resulting distribution, values above four indicate a disproportionate material aspiration, and values below four indicate disproportionate educational aspiration.

In the theoretical context of this investigation, the character of adjustments which the upwardly mobile person is required to make should vary according to his principal emphasis in mobility. If his primary concern is with achievement of a culturally rich and satisfying way of life, he will be especially sensitized to similarities and discrepancies in the realm of values, while being relatively easily satisfied with his material rewards. If his primary concern is with the material reward, he may be relatively insensitive to value considerations and unaware that adjustments in interests and manners are requisite to the consolidation of the higher status toward which he strives.

Eminence Ambition

A special question was devised to identify a somewhat different kind of ambition, which we call *eminence*. One man seeks to use his skill in a specialized craft as a means of moving into the supervisory hierarchy where he will no longer be a craftsman but a manager. Another man is driven to excel as a craftsman, but has no desire to leave the crafts for a higher occupation. Each of these men is ambitious, but in a different way. Each must be distinguished from the man who wants nothing more than to "get along" in the occupation he is in.

The theoretical basis for such a difference has been formalized by Kingsley Davis in a distinction between *prestige* and *esteem* as forms of personal evaluation based upon occupational (or any other) status.[1] Each individual acquires a certain rank among his fellows by the sole criterion of the status with which he is identified. Merely by virtue of being a doctor rather than a clerk, a craftsman rather than a street sweeper, a business official rather than a retail salesman, a man is assigned higher prestige. Upward mobility, as we have defined it, is concerned with a change of status which brings an increment of prestige.

However, some doctors command more respect than others and some carpenters are ranked above others, especially in the eyes of their close associates. The distinctions which reflect how well an individual seems to be performing the tasks assigned to one in his position are called esteem. A manual laborer may have high esteem; a business executive may have low esteem. The general estimates people form of one another often merge or compromise prestige and esteem, but frequently note them separately. The individual's own self-estimate often plays off the more favorable against the less favorable.

Parenthetically, the possibilities of intraclass eminence striving and the existence of divergent emphases in ambition have relevance for the debate regarding comparative rates of mobility in different countries. S. M. Lipset and Reinhard Bendix have argued that differences in rates of vertical mobility among modern industrial countries are less than we have commonly supposed.[2] The empirical evidence consists of generational rates of movement between broad occupational categories. But cross-national comparisons of mobility rates require an assumption that the opportunities to improve oneself—to achieve a valued kind of success—within occupational classes do not differ from nation

---

1 Kingsley Davis, *Human Society* (New York: Macmillan and Co., 1949), pp. 93–94.
2 Seymour M. Lipset and Reinhard Bendix, *Social Mobility in Industrial Society* (Berkeley: University of California Press, 1959), *passim*.

to nation. Since correlations of occupational ambition with material ambition are imperfect, it is clear that some of our students seek a given standard of living without an equivalent change in occupational class. If high eminence striving is found among students with low occupational aspirations, it is clear that they believe in a considerable range of success within occupational classes.

The data in this report will not contribute toward answering the principal question of whether the intraclass range of opportunity varies from country to country. But if differentiations of emphasis in ambition and the differentiation between eminence and class ambition prove useful in this investigation, the importance of taking intraclass opportunity into account in cross-national comparisons is suggested.

As a measure of eminence striving, the student was asked to select an answer to the following question:

After you are in the occupation which will be your life work, when will you consider yourself successful enough that you can relax and stop trying so hard to get ahead?

The answers ranged from, "When I am doing well enough to stay in the occupation," to, "When doing better than everyone else in my occupation," and "Never." Originally the last two alternatives were not included. But in the pretest the majority of students chose the maximum alternative, "When recognized as one of the top persons in my occupation," and quite a number of students insisted in writing in the word, "never." Accordingly, the last two alternatives were added before the final questionnaire was printed. Women were asked, "After your husband is in the occupation which will be his life work, when will you consider him successful enough that he should relax and stop trying so hard to get ahead?" The same seven answers were supplied.

The actual responses (Table 37) reveal a high degree of eminence striving. Close to three quarters of the men students stated that they would not be prepared to relax their efforts until they were among the top persons in their occupation, if ever. And fully a third chose the extreme response of "never." While the demands of women on their husbands are lower, they are still high in absolute terms. The results are surprising in light of a widespread conviction that the nineteenth-century ideology of ceaseless striving is now a thing of the past, and that mediocrity, "getting by," is the major standard of the day. Whatever may be the dominant pattern among adults, these students appear to give overwhelming lip service to the traditional ideal of eminence striving.

For two reasons, we anticipate that responses to the eminence ques-

Table 37. Eminence Ambition

Eminence level	Distribution	
	Male	Female
...hen I am doing well enough to stay in the occupation	3.6%	4.1%
...hen I am doing as well as the average person in my occupation	2.4	5.4
...hen doing a little better than the average in my occupation	7.8	14.8
...hen doing much better than the average in my occupation	15.0	22.2
...hen recognized as one of the top persons in my occupation	31.8	33.8
...hen doing better than everyone else in my occupation	6.8	4.5
...ever	32.6	15.2
...otal	100.0%	100.0%
...otal number	1341	1435
...o answer	11	6

tion will not be as valuable as was initially hoped. First, the clustering of responses at the upper end of the continuum means that important gradations of eminence striving are not sufficiently revealed, the answers serving only to differentiate the small minority who are not striving for eminence from the great majority who are. Second, the bimodal character of the distribution of responses suggests that the question measures two dimensions rather than one. The response of "never" is not necessarily a greater degree of the same variable as is indicated by the other answers. The value of striving for its own sake might be held by a person who had no idea of ever becoming the greatest in his field. With the benefit of hindsight, we should have reworded the question in such a fashion as to rule out "never" as a response and force a more adequate spread of answers among the alternatives which reflected eminence less equivocally.

Keeping the foregoing qualifications in mind, we shall cautiously

examine the interrelations of eminence striving with the other measures. Since the eminence measure for women did not appear to be related to any of the other forms of ambition, the following analysis
applies only to men. A simple fourfold analysis reveals a positive correlation between occupational ambition and eminence, which is significant but very small (phi is .08), and a correlation which is only
slightly larger between eminence and the ambition index (phi is .15).
The fact that a youth aims at a high or a low occupational level tells
us rather little about the degree of eminence he seeks within his
chosen goal. The absence of strong correlation between prestige and
esteem means that students who are not ambitious in the conventional
interclass sense may be quite ambitious with respect to their intraclass
achievement.

By examining relationships between eminence striving and the other
forms of ambition while holding the basic occupational aspiration
relatively constant, we can determine whether a strong eminence
orientation is related to the *relative* amount of educational, material,
and ownership aspiration. Because of the minimal correlation with
occupational aspiration and the problematic character of the distribution of eminence responses, the cumbersome process of examining detailed cross-tabulations within categories of occupational aspirations
was employed, rather than the more comprehensive expected cases or
partial correlation methods. Within the three large ambition categories
of skilled labor, semiprofessions, and professions, the results are rather
consistent.

There appears to be no relation between eminence ambition and
material ambition. It is doubtful that there is any relationship between eminence ambition and ownership ambition except for a possible
small relationship among the skilled-labor aspirants. But a small
though appreciable relationship between educational ambition and
eminence ambition appears in each of these occupational ambition
categories.

The finding regarding ownership lends further support to the accumulating impression that the traditional view of ownership as the
crowning attainment and goal of ambition has largely disappeared
within the student society under examination. Not only is ownership
not the goal of high interclass ambition: it is also not the goal or
measure of high ambition within most classes. The impression that the
skilled crafts are the repository of the traditional values and conceptions of success is also reinforced by the relationship between eminence
ambition and ownership ambition among aspirants to that level.

The findings of no relation between eminence aspiration and material aspiration and of a consistent relation between eminence aspiration and educational aspiration further underline the view that these are alternative kinds of ambition and further clarify the nature of the difference. The goal of high educational attainment is associated with the goal of high achievement within one's occupational level. Those who seek only sufficient education to enter the occupation of their choice are also likely to regard themselves as having arrived when they achieve moderate success within their occupation. High monetary ambition, on the other hand, does not necessarily carry with it any concern for the cultural aspects of high position, nor does it necessarily imply any unusual pride in attaining excellence.

EMPHASES AND BACKGROUND

The student's background should be reflected, not only in his level of ambition, but also in the aspects of success which he emphasizes. Students from different value subcultures may adopt a society-wide value such as success or upward mobility while investing it with different value content. For example, interviews in our files suggest that students from working-class backgrounds are often urged to get an education because "an educated man can always get a job." It is unlikely that mere security from unemployment would loom large in the values which a professional man would give his son for seeking an education. Furthermore, the steps necessary to a given level of attainment probably appear quite different from the perspectives of higher and lower classes. The person closer to the level in question can see the requisites to success at that level more accurately. Or the person from a lower background may hope to achieve a given occupational level with a minimum of qualifications because of the disadvantage under which he operates in attaining those qualifications.

Common conceptions of the class system view the higher strata as more prestige and culture oriented, while the working classes are thought to be concerned with the more immediate, tangible, and "practical." [3] If such a difference prevails, the relative emphasis on material and educational aspirations will vary according to background. Viewed both as a means to success and as a type of emphasis in success, high educational ambition should be more strongly associated with high background than is high material ambition. If such a difference in ambition emphasis between students from high and low backgrounds were found, it would point to a likely source of

[3] Genevieve Knupfer, "Portrait of the Underdog," *Public Opinion Quarterly,* 11 (Spring, 1947), pp. 103–111.

Table 38. Correlations between Background Index
and Various Measures of Ambition

Type of ambition	Male	Female
Ambition index	.38	.42
Occupation[a]	.20	.37
Education	.37	.35
Husband education	--	.38
Material	.15	.17
Ownership[b]	-.12	--
Eminence	.14	.05
Material-educational polarization	-.17	-.17

a/ For women, this item is minimum husband occupatio
b/ For ownership, the biserial correlation was used.
In all other cases, the product-moment coefficient was
employed.

marginality-producing differences between the upwardly mobile students and their future peers.

Another difference in emphasis between students from high and
low background may revolve about the pursuit of esteem as distinguished from prestige. If students from lower backgrounds hesitate
to set as high goals as the students from higher backgrounds do, as
we have already shown, it is also likely that they should expect less
after they achieve a given occupational position. Since the occupational goal itself is more precarious, it would seem even more auda-
cious to set a goal of unusual success within the chosen occupation.
This observation should be reflected most directly in the level of
eminence ambition, but might also extend to material ambition.

We shall explore the two foregoing hypotheses with a combination
of linear correlation and expected cases methods. First, we shall examine the simple correlations between background and a measure
of each type of ambition. Then we shall attempt, chiefly by means of
the expected cases method, to determine whether certain of the special forms of ambition are correlated with background after all association attributable to occupational ambition has been removed.

In Table 38, we report correlations between the composite index of background and various kinds of ambition. Although none of the correlations is large, nearly all appear to be statistically significant. The largest correlations are with educational ambition for both men and women and with acceptable husband's occupation for women. It is notable that the composite ambition indexes do not correlate appreciably higher with background than does educational ambition or the girls' educational requirements for a husband. It is also worthy of note that the girls' own educational goals and the minimum acceptable education for a husband show just about the same degree of correlation with their backgrounds.

Educational ambition is often the easiest type of ambition to secure, classify, and manipulate statistically, and consequently is made to bear the principal burden in many researches. The observation that educational ambition correlates more strongly with background than other forms of ambition do suggests that excessive reliance on this single measure may create an exaggerated impression of the magnitude of relationship between ambition and background. Among the types of ambition with which we are dealing, education is probably most directly subject to the test of prior success and failure by the stage in life which these students have reached. If the student from lower backgrounds suffers some of the disadvantages that Allison Davis and others have enumerated in achieving success in school, he may well revise his educational ambition downward without necessarily lowering his ambition in other respects. Recognizing that there are alternative routes to success in American society, he may place his dependence more strongly on other routes than education, or on a combination of routes. The result is that the ambitious student from a lower background plans to go further with less education than the student from a higher background.

Perhaps also, recognition of the intrinsic advantages of high monetary and occupational attainment is less affected by class position than a similar recognition for education. The idea of securing more education than is necessary for one's other goals may be more comprehensible to the student who has learned to value the literate and cultured style of life through direct participation than to the student from a background where these things are known more by secondhand report than by direct experience.

While educational measures of ambition exaggerate the correlation between ambition and background in general, they may give a better prognostication of actual mobility than some of the other measures of ambition. They are subject to "reality testing" earlier in the individual's career, and insufficient educational attainment can turn out to be a more serious obstacle to other forms of success than the lower-background student realizes.

The correlation coefficients for occupational ambition should not be overinterpreted since the distribution departs considerably from normal. In spite of the generally low level of acceptable husband occupations specified by the women, the correlation with background is roughly the same as that for educational ambition. While we have no evidence to test such an interpretation, it is possible that the general romantic depression of acceptable occupational level makes the basic distinction between white- and blue-collar occupations, or between skilled and lesser occupations, a more crucial minimum for girls from higher backgrounds than the distinctions among groups of higher occupations are to boys from high backgrounds.

Correlations with material and eminence ambition are quite minimal, but are probably statistically significant. Like material ambition, the self-respect that comes from doing excellently at whatever level one finds himself seems also to cross-cut the lines of family background. Since high eminence striving is the rule, it seems reasonable to conclude that self-esteem is no monopoly of the higher levels in society, and is less diminished by lower-status background than is educational ambition.

If there is any relationship between background and ownership ambition, it appears to be a negative one. This observation adds further to our accumulating impression that ownership has ceased to be a differentiating criterion of high standing. Even the hypothesis that lower-background students avoid the more readily transmissible forms of success, such as ownership, in favor of those in which they are at less of a disadvantage in proving themselves is not borne out in this instance. The supposed advantage of boys from high backgrounds in securing capital is apparently not buttressed by a sufficiently strong evaluation of ownership in its own right. As before, we must conclude that the appeal of ownership is probably not in the high standing and other rewards which it offers, but more in the independence and security of a modest station which is felt to offer other advantages than success in the usual sense.

Finally, it is of interest to note the general similarity in the absolute and relative magnitude of relationships for men and women. Only in eminence does a small relationship for men become no relationship for women.

The relationship between background and ambition-emphasis is summarized in a slightly different way by using the material-educational polarization index. A small negative correlation between the index and background underlines a slight tendency for the ambition constellations of equally ambitious students from high and low origins to differ. As before, the evidence points to the disproportionate emphasis on material ambition on the part of the students from lower backgrounds.

For the men students, one further step has been taken to observe the relationships between various ambition measures and background while holding a central measure of ambition constant. Since the ambition index incorporates the measures of material and educational ambition, it is a less acceptable standard than occupational ambition. In order further to avoid linearity and normality assumptions we have used an expected cases method. Expected percentages of high educational, material, ownership, and eminence ambition were computed for men students from low occupational background, small-business background, and high background, on the basis of the observed distributions of occupational ambition within each background category. Comparison of these adjusted expected distributions with actual distributions will tell us whether students with comparable occupational ambitions but different occupational backgrounds differ in the extent of their other ambitions (Table 39).

An appreciable relationship with ownership ambition is wholly accounted for by the high ownership ambition of students from small-business families. There is otherwise no difference in the ownership ambitions of students from high and low backgrounds who have comparable occupational ambitions, unless it be a small negative relationship. Students from high backgrounds may be slightly more inclined toward high eminence ambition than students from low backgrounds with similar occupational ambitions. However, the relationship is so small as to be unimportant in comparison with the tendency for eminence to transcend class boundaries.

Appreciable relationships between occupational background and both material ambition and educational ambition emerge, though the relationship with education is notably larger. The earlier conclusion that the relative emphasis on education is greater among students from higher backgrounds continues to receive support.

As a final step in testing the variation in material versus educational ambition by background, we have followed the same expected cases procedure, employing the material-educational polarization index. The index is significantly related to occupational background (P < .001) in the expected direction when no correction is made for occupational ambition. But a comparison between observed and ad-

Table 39. Ambition Emphases in Relation to Background, for Men

	Percent of men with high ambition					
Type of ambition	Observed percent			Adjusted expected percent		
	High occupational background	Small-business background	Low occupational background	High occupational background	Small-business background	Low occupational background
Educational	72%	48%	29%	60%	45%	35%
Material	38	25	22	31	27	25
Ownership	50	39	64	55	50	58
Eminence	83	70	68	78	71	70
Material-educational polarization	45	51	63	48	54	60

justed expected percentages reveals only a trivial relationship in the hypothesized direction. The finding does not necessarily demonstrate that there is no difference in emphasis between students from high and low backgrounds who aspire to a given level. The finding may reflect a tendency for lower-background men students to implement their general emphasis on material over educational ambition by choosing occupations (such as the semiprofessions) which seem to promise relatively high material standards in proportion to their educational requirements. The unequivocal association between the MEPI (with its built-in standardization principle) and occupational background makes it reasonable to interpret the results as indicating that emphasis and choice of occupation are inextricably combined in the students' ambitions.

Intelligence and Emphasis

Table 40 allows us to review the place of I.Q. in the ambition emphases of the students. Educational ambitions bear the highest relationships with intelligence. However, they also continue to show the largest relationships with background after I.Q. has been partialed out. Material and eminence ambition appear to be a little more highly related to I.Q. than to background among the men students. Among the women students, eminence ambition is entirely unrelated to I.Q. The intelligence measure is negatively correlated with material-educational polarization, but there remain small negative correlations with family background after I.Q. has been partialed out. In general, the table suggests that the correlations between ambition emphases and I.Q. are somewhat like those between ambition emphases and background, but do not subsume them.

Neighborhood and Emphasis

It remains to be determined whether neighborhood adds its influence to family background in contributing to different emphases in ambition. Since eminence ambition does not vary importantly along the continuum from high to low schools, no attempt at further analysis is demanded. Apparently, it is desire for a high position rather than ambition to attain self-respect by performing well in whatever station one achieves that is affected by the prevailing class level of the school.

A nonlinear analysis of the relation of ambition to neighborhood, treating occupational, educational, and material ambition separately (for men only) was reported in Chapter Three. Material ambition

Table 40. I.Q. in Relation to Ambition and Background

Variable correlated	Correlation with I.Q.		Partial correlation with background index, I.Q. constant	
	Male	Female	Male	Female
Background index	.31	.30	--	--
Ambition index	.46	.39	.29	.35
Occupational ambition[a]	.38	.23	.09	.32
Educational ambition	.47	.32	.27	.28
Husband education	--	.30	--	.32
Material ambition	.23	.15	.09	.13
Material-educational polarization	-.22	-.17	-.11	-.13
Ownership ambition[b]	.03	--	--	--
Eminence ambition	.24	.05	.07	.03

a/ For women, this item is minimum husband occupation.
b/ For ownership, the biserial correlation was used. In all other cases, the product-moment coefficient was employed.

varies less than occupational and educational ambition from high to low neighborhoods, but a larger proportion of the variation is attributable to the neighborhood. In absolute terms the residual impact of neighborhood is small, however. Linear correlation analysis shows material-educational polarization to be quite modestly related to school (−.14, men; −.16, women), but partialing out family background reduces the coefficients to nonsignificance. Our data, then, suggest the conclusion that, unlike level of ambition, relative emphasis on material or educational components of ambition is chiefly a product of family background rather than neighborhood. Neighborhood is more important in promoting a comprehensive ambition level than in its effects on particular kinds of ambition.

Neighborhood as Causal Universe

If the relationship of total ambition to background and intelligence can vary between neighborhoods, it is likely that the emphases in ambition will be differently determined. Correlations between the material-educational polarization index and background in the three types of neighborhood (Table 41) show a clear progression for the men but not for the women. If we disregard the women, allowing for the more complex meaning of educational ambition in their case, a plausible explanation for the finding is readily available. In these lower neighborhoods with their more amorphous stratification, it is chiefly the boys from higher backgrounds who can afford to have relatively high educational ambitions, or who are likely to have the broader cultural conception of ambition rather than the simple material view. In the middle and higher areas there is sufficient awareness of the value of education and of the broader cultural conception of ambition so that individual background is less related to the dominant emphasis the individual's ambition takes.

Further simple fourfold tabulations for the men students indicate that eminence ambition is significantly related to occupational background in the lower-area schools, but not elsewhere. Material ambition appears to be related to occupational ambition in both high and middle neighborhoods and to occupational background in high-area schools, but not elsewhere, unless a small negative relationship with background in the low-area schools be credited. The relationship already suggested between eminence and educational polarization in ambition probably explains the first observation. The amorphousness of ambition patterns in the lower areas is further accented by the absence of relationship between occupational and material ambition.

Cautiously we may interpret the difference in background relationships with material ambition in conjunction with the findings on material-educational polarization and eminence ambition. As we move from the low to the high areas, we move from a possible negative relationship between occupational background and material ambition through a positive relationship just below the five percent level of confidence in the middle schools, to an unmistakably positive relationship in the high-area schools. At the same time, eminence ambition is related to background in the low-area schools, but probably not in the other schools. Background reveals a clear relationship to ambition emphasis in the low school areas only, whereas higher back-

Table 41. Correlations of Background and Ambition Emphases by Neighborhood

Sex	Variables correlated	Type of coefficient	High schools	Middle schools	Low schools
Male	MEPI with background index	r	-.06	-.14[b]	-.26[b]
	Material ambition with occupational background	phi	.22[b]	.07	-.19[a]
	Material ambition with occupational ambition	phi	.15[a]	.15[b]	.07
	Eminence ambition with occupational background	phi	.02	.05	.26[b]
	Eminence ambition with occupational ambition	phi	.08	.01	.15
Female	MEPI with background index	r	-.05	-.18[b]	-.03

a/ P ≤ .05   b/ P ≤ .01

ground conveys the somewhat more complete and "idealistic" kind of ambition. The students are less preoccupied with simple material gain, and more concerned with attaining self-respect through achieving excellence in whatever niche they find for themselves. But in the higher neighborhoods, and especially in the highest, the students from high family backgrounds are not distinguished in this fashion. They are distinguished only by wanting more of everything, but not by any special concern for eminence.

Here we find further justification for believing that the causal complex within which ambition occurs is different in neighborhoods of different level for the men students, though the same differences are not found for women students. It is the lower-area neighborhoods which are most sharply set apart from the rest.

VALUES AND FRIENDSHIP DESIRABILITY

The importance of distinguishing types of emphasis in ambition for our investigation lies in the expectation that the social ties and value transitions at the heart of the marginality experience will differ. Hence, we must look to see whether the student with one type of ambition has fewer of the values of his destination peers than the student with another type of ambition, and whether he differs in social desirability among his peers.

Material-Educational Polarization

The thirty-one value items have been individually cross-tabulated with material ambition and with educational ambition. The resulting tests of relationships have been presented so as to permit a comparison among items which are associated with both types of ambition, items associated only with material ambition, and items associated with only educational ambition. An examination of Tables 42a, 42b, and 42c shows that for men, ten items are associated with both types of ambition, eight with material ambition alone, and four with educational ambition alone. Eighteen items are associated with material ambition, including ten that meet the .001 criterion for significance —more than correlate with any other ambition or background measure. Only sex is significantly associated with more items.

Seven of the ten items that are correlated with both types of ambition are also among the ten items that probably have a linear relationship with background.[4] Two of the remaining three items which

4 This and subsequent statements are based upon comparison with Table 14 (Chapter Four), reporting association of value-items with occupational background and the background index.

Table 42a. Values Associated with Material and Educational Ambition, for Men

Value item[a]	$P \leq$ [b]	
	Material ambition	Educational ambition
13. Real success in business vs. real family man	.001	.01
14. Shows how to argue intelligently vs. smooths over disagreements	.01	.001
21. Smooth operator, comes out on top vs. too kind to take unfair advantage	.001	.05
22. Pride in doing things on his own vs. likes advice and help	.02	.01
23. Good at making decisions for others vs. tries never to influence others	.001	.01
24. Does many things better than friends vs. does most things as well as friends	.001	.02
28. Neither a borrower nor a lender be vs. often borrows-lends	.02	.01
29. Talks foreign policy and politics vs. talks popular music and sports	.01	.001
34. Risks what he has to get ahead vs. prefers secure position	.001	.01
37. Always looking for something better vs. satisfied with what he has	.001	.001

a/ The alternative associated with high ambition has been listed first in each instance.

b/ Significance is based on chi-square, with two degrees of freedom.

Table 42b. Values Associated with Material
Ambition Only, for Men

Value item[a]	$P \leq$[b]	
	Material ambition	Educational ambition
9. Makes very good living vs. enjoys art, music, books	.001	(-.02)
0. Likes things to work out naturally vs. likes groups quite organized	.01	--
1. Believes in having it out vs. drops until tempers cool	.001	--
5. Will tell small lie to help friend vs. sticks by truth	.001	--
6. Puts friends ahead of community vs. puts community ahead of friends	.05	--
0. Sticks with time-tested ways of doing things vs. tries new ways of doing things	.05	--
0. Laughs off failures and mistakes vs. takes full blame for failures	.02	--
6. Uses breaks and pull to get ahead vs. works hard, refuses breaks, pull	.001	--

a/ The alternative associated with high ambition has
been listed first in each instance.

b/ Significance is based on chi-square with two
degrees of freedom.

were earlier found to be associated with background are correlated
with educational ambition alone, and the other is associated with
material ambition alone. If it is appropriate to use the boys from
high backgrounds as a standard, there is no basis for concluding that
one type of ambition is associated with a more complete anticipatory

Table 42c. Values Associated with Educational
Ambition Only, for Men

Value item[a]	$P \leq$ [b]	
	Material ambition	Educational ambition
9. Enjoys art, music, books vs. makes very good living	(-.001)	.02
17. Rather be his own boss vs. will take orders to get ahead	--	.001
25. Tries to get things his way vs. quick to go along with group	--	.001
35. Gives up pleasure now for future vs. enjoys present	--	.001

a/ The alternative associated with high ambition has been listed first in each instance.

b/ Significance is based on chi-square, with two degrees of freedom.

socialization than the other. Insofar as merely the range of values is concerned, emphasis on one or the other forms of ambition does not point to a greater predisposition to marginality.

The different items which correlate respectively with material ambition alone and educational ambition alone seem to exhibit a pattern. The most striking point of contrast is the reversal in direction of relationship for item 9, which is as follows:

(a) Someone who enjoys art and music and likes to read books, but just barely makes enough money to live on; *or*
(b) Someone who makes a very good living but doesn't enjoy art or music or reading books at all.

Alternative (a) is preferred by boys with high educational ambition, and alternative (b) by boys with high material ambition. This contrast helps us to interpret the differences between the two types of ambition and to interpret correlations noted earlier between the material-educational polarization index and several other variables. Initially, we suggested that the polarization could indicate either different concepts of the most effective route to success or the pursuit of different types of success. The above finding suggests that at least some distinction in objective is included in the differences between the two indexes of ambition. Boys who stress either material or educational ambition are not merely choosing different routes to the same goal; the kind of success or mobility which they envisage is different. To one group the broad "cultural" component is a crucial element in what they value as success; to the other group it is less important.

To conclude that high material ambition signalizes an absence of interest in serious culture would not be correct. Both types of ambition are associated with (29) a preference for being able to talk about serious rather than popular topics. It is not the contrast between serious cultural interests and popular interests which differentiates the emphases in ambition; it is the contrast between serious cultural interests and business success. If the finding on item 9 is noted in conjunction with item 36, boys with disproportionate material ambition are distinguished by an augmented emphasis on secular success. Four of the seven secular success items (13, 21, 34, 37) are associated with both forms of ambition. Two of the remaining three (9, 36) are related to material ambition but not to educational ambition. No success items are related exclusively with educational ambition, except negatively. Boys with disproportionately high material ambition apparently differ from other ambitious boys in carrying the value of secular success to the extreme.

It is difficult to characterize satisfactorily the remaining six items which mark the boys with disproportionately high material ambition, though they appear to have some common features. Three of the items belong to the youth culture, while none of the items related to educational ambition do. The high material aspirant prefers to (15) tell a lie to help a friend, to (16) put friends ahead of community welfare, and to (30) laugh off his failures and mistakes. On the other hand, he seems to (20) favor tradition over novelty, a choice which runs counter to the youth culture, and shares with high education aspirations the rejection of youth culture in preferring to (24) do things better than friends and to (29) talk about foreign policy and political trends. However, five of the six items related exclusively to material ambition suggest the rejection of formal controls. The three items just mentioned (15, 16, 30) oppose particularistic to universalistic obligations,[5] thus disparaging a sense of respon-

[5] Talcott Parsons and Edward Shils, *Toward a General Theory of Action* (Cambridge: Harvard Univ. Press, 1952), pp. 81 ff.

sibility toward the larger community and its norms. Besides item 15, the item about whose relationship to material ambition we can feel most confident is the preference for (11) having it out right now rather than waiting for tempers to cool. Here, too, there is a clear rejection of an external standard of reasonableness and control. The remaining preference for (10) having things work out naturally rather than having groups organized again fits the pattern.

With this surprisingly clear picture before us, two items are on the surface disturbing. First is the possible preference for (20) time-tested ways of doing things. Since the relationship is of only border-line significance, it may be merely a product of chance. But the very absence of correlation in the opposite direction helps to clarify the nature of the independence from community restraint which goes along with high material ambition. It is apparently not a rejection in the interest of innovation, and therefore not the kind of anti-normative attitude characteristic of the liberal or radical.

The other datum of interest here is the unquestionable association between high educational ambition and preference for (17) being one's own boss rather than taking orders to get ahead. Apparently, the high material aspirant's dislike of normative regulation does not extend to the unwillingness to take orders as a means of getting ahead, while the high educational aspirant's independence in this respect does not encompass the anti-normative attitude. An explanation may lie simply in the relative valuation of the antithesis to independence, which in this case is secular success. The high material aspirant values secular success enough so that no over-all preference emerges between this value and independence, while the high educational aspirant does not value secular success so highly. On the other hand, a different kind of independence must be indicated or the boys with high educational ambition would share some of the five items which distinguish the high material aspirants. Acceptance of personal supervision must be a different matter from acceptance of organizational and impersonal norms. The independence of the high education aspirant is of the latter sort.

The manipulative kind of individualism which is related to both kinds of ambition (14, 23) is further evidenced by the high education aspirants (13, 25), and deferred gratification (35) is likewise present. The boys who emphasize education in their ambitions thus appear to take the themes of serious culture, independence from personal supervision combined with the manipulation of others, and deferred gratification, all of which they share with other high aspirants, and carry them to a greater extreme. The boys who emphasize material ambition similarly take the theme of secular success, which they share with other high aspirants, and make more of it. In addition, they exhibit a kind of rejection of group organization and formal norms which involves an acceptance of primary-group obligations.

A first glance reveals little correspondence between the findings for women and the findings for men (Tables 43a, 43b, and 43c). Six of the nine items which correlate with both types of ambition for women also correlate with both in the case of men. Beyond this, however, there is little resemblance. Insofar as these forms of ambition reflect the goals which ambitious persons seek, similar patterns should prevail for men and women. Insofar as they represent the means to success, however, the patterns might be rather different.

Although the specific items involved are not the same, the same pattern of extended emphasis upon secular success among those who disproportionately value material ambition is evident. High material ambition is exclusively related to preference for (21) being a smooth operator, (36) succeeding by breaks and pull rather than hard work, and (37) always looking for something better. Because of the generally greater success-orientation of men, the first and last of these items were related to both ambition indexes for men. Although the preference for (9) good living rather than enjoying art, music, and books does not occur, the reverse relationship does apply to high educational ambition just as it did in the case of men. With appropriate allowance for a somewhat less pervasive emphasis on secular success throughout, we can safely conclude that the two kinds of ambition are differentiated in this respect according to a similar pattern for men and for women.

Three items measuring individuality are preferred by the high material aspirants in addition to the three (14, 24, 25) they prefer in common with high education aspirants. The preferences for (8) doing a few things perfectly rather than many things fairly well, for (18) being respected rather than having a reputation for modesty, and for (26) being respected rather than easy to get along with represent an extension of a theme which differentiates both kinds of high ambition from low ambition. All six items classified under individuality are preferred by the girls with high material ambition, while only three are preferred by girls with high educational ambition.

In juxtaposition with the earlier discussion of the connection between individuality and women's ambition, these findings lend themselves to ready interpretation. Earlier, in Chapter Four, we noted that the importance of individuality in the value constellation of ambitious girls may arise from the fact that girls attain success largely

Table 43a. Values Associated with Material
and Educational Ambition, for Women

Value item[a]	$P \leqslant$ [b]	
	Material ambition	Educational ambition
13. Real success in business vs. real family man (woman)	.001	.001
14. Shows how to argue intelligently vs. smooths over disagreements	.01	.01
15. Will tell small lie to help friend vs. sticks to truth	.05	.05
17. Rather be his own boss vs. vs. will take orders to get ahead	.001	.05
24. Does better than friends vs. does as well as friends	.01	.01
25. Tries to get things his way vs. quick to go along with group	.001	.001
28. Neither a borrower nor a lender be vs. often borrows-lends with friends	.01	.01
29. Talks about foreign policy and politics vs. talks popular music and sports	.05	.001
34. Risks what he has to get ahead vs. prefers secure position	.001	.001

a/ The alternative associated with high ambition has
been listed first in each instance.

b/ Significance is based on chi-square, with two degrees of freedom.

Table 43b. Values Associated with Material
Ambition Only, for Women

Value item[a]	P $\leqslant$ b	
	Material ambition	Educational ambition
8. Can do a few things perfectly vs. can do many things fairly well	.02	--
8. Conceited, respected for abilities vs. has reputation for modesty	.02	--
1. Smooth operator, comes out on top vs. too kind to take unfair advantage	.02	--
2. Pride in doing things on his own vs. likes advice and help from others	.02	--
6. Respected but hard to get along with vs. easy to get along with	.02	--
). Laughs off failures and mistakes vs. takes full blame for failures	.05	--
5. Gives up pleasure now for future vs. enjoys present	.05	--
5. Uses breaks and pull to get ahead vs. works hard, refuses breaks, pull	.001	--
7. Always looking for something better vs. satisfied with what he has	.001	--

a/ The alternative associated with high ambition has
en listed first in each instance.

b/ Significance is based on chi-square, with two de-
ees of freedom.

Table 43c. Values Associated with Educational
Ambition Only, for Women

Value item[a]	P ≤ [b]	
	Material ambition	Educationa ambition
9. Enjoys art, music, books vs. makes very good living	--	.001
12. Spends extra money on friends vs. saves extra money for future	--	.001
31. Laughs off any insult to his honor vs. never lets an insult go by	--	.01
33. Man of judgment vs. man of action, goes right at job	--	.02

a/ The alternative associated with high ambition has been listed first in each instance.

b/ Significance is based on chi-square, with two degrees of freedom.

by being chosen, rather than by direct pursuit of success. It is very likely that the girls who stress material ambition disproportionately are the ones who are depending most heavily upon being "chosen" for the attainment of an appropriate station in life. Girls who stress educational ambition, on the other hand, are more likely attempting to win success in a manner similar to that of men. The fact that individuality is more fully related to high material ambition than to high educational ambition is exactly what would be predicted from the assumption that disproportionate material ambition indicates especial reliance upon favorable marriage for the attainment of high standing. Such a relationship should apply only to women and not to men.

We hesitate to make further interpretation of the differences, since the remaining items do not fall readily into groups. Rejection of deferred gratification (35) by high material aspirants differentiates them from high educational aspirants in the same direction as for men, but further toward the *carpe diem* end of the continuum. The preference for (33) a man of judgment rather than a man of action was originally classified as belonging to a deferred-gratification group. In the absence of endorsement of (35) giving up pleasure now for the future, however, it would probably be more reasonable to interpret the item in this context as a further indication of a sort of serious intellectual or aesthetic culture. Interpreted in this fashion, the item simply reinforces the preference for (9) art, music, and books rather than a good living. It characterizes those girls whose ambition emphasizes education disproportionately.

While we are left with some uninterpreted items, we conclude that the pattern differences between the findings for men and women are not so great as appeared at first glance, and should have been anticipated from an earlier stage in our analysis. The two types of ambition carry with them selective emphasis on either secular success or genteel culture, just as they did for men. Similarly, the emphases may differ on the deferred gratification-*carpe diem* dimension. In both of these instances, the general difference between males and females affects the relationships with specific items. One item for the women (30) touches on the strong antinormative value among boys with disproportionate material ambition, but, in general, this pattern is lacking in both groups of girls. Whereas boys whose success orientation is segmental in favor of material level show a strong antinormative and antiorganizational control value, the comparable group of girls shows a heightened emphasis on individuality.

The discussion of material and educational emphases in ambition will be concluded by an examination of their respective relationships with social acceptability. To this end, the *friend rating* has been correlated with the two measures of ambition, and a cleavage analysis has been performed employing the material-educational polarization index. When associations are tested in nine-fold tables, both types of ambition show low but significant correlations with *friend rating* for the boys (Tschuprow's $T = .09, .10$, respectively). For the girls, there is an association of borderline significance with educational ambition ($T = .07$) but not with material ambition. The polarization index is negatively correlated with *friend rating* at the borderline level for boys ($T = -.07$), but not for girls. Among boys, the student who places a relative emphasis on educational rather than material ambition is slightly more likely to be named as a desirable friend. While we might have expected a curvilinear relationship making students who balanced the two types of ambition most acceptable, such is not the case.

Table 44. Preference and Cleavage
by Material-Educational Polarization

Type of pattern	Number of classrooms			
	High schools	Middle schools	Low schools	All schools
Material preferred	7	21	10	38
Educational preferred	12	25	11	48
No preference	--	2	1	3
Total	19	48	22	89
Positive cleavage	8	27	17	52
Negative cleavage	11	21	5	37
No cleavage	--	--	--	--
Total	19	48	22	89

No separation between men and women has been attempted in the cleavage tabulations (Table 44). Students whose ambitions are polarized toward education are preferred in a few more classes than students polarized toward material ambition. If such a preference is more than an artifact of chance, it seems clearer in the higher-level schools.

The evidence is a little better for some tendency toward cleavage between those whose ambitions are differently polarized. In addition, a rather clear pattern of neighborhood difference emerges. The cleavage is marked in the low neighborhoods, more moderate in the middle neighborhoods, and entirely lacking in the high neighborhoods. Socially, the choice between emphasizing material or educational ambition is of least consequence in the high neighborhoods. In the low neighborhoods, we find again that group boundaries may make change in ambition difficult for the student. Just as the initial choice between the high and low ambition places the student in a social group, so the choice between cultural and material paths of ambition assigns him to one group and erects barriers to identification with other groups.

Ownership Ambition

Only three value items are significantly correlated with ownership ambition. The entrepreneurial values of risk-taking (34) and of being a smooth operator (21) appear, but both are less strongly associated with ownership than with material ambition. The largest correlation is with preference for being one's own boss (17), but again, it is no larger than the item correlation with educational ambition. Just as the determination to be independent rather than employed is unrelated to the complex of ambition with which this investigation is concerned, it is not distinctively related to any of the complexes of values.

Eminence Ambition

If there is an important form of ambition which does not involve mobility between social strata, it should have its own distinctive value constellation. Identification of this value constellation is not only interesting in its own right; it supplies a base of comparison from which values distinctively linked with mobility ambition can be identified. If eminence ambition were associated with some but not all of the values which are correlated with mobility ambitions, we should conclude that a combination of high eminence and low mobility ambition leads to or reflects an incomplete absorption of the values associated with ambition. If eminence ambition were associated with a different pattern of items, the conclusion would be that distinctive values relate to the two types of ambition.

Table 45 shows that eminence ambition has an appreciable value constellation that is rather more extensive for the women than for the men. Initially, we expected individuality to loom large in the complex, since eminence is defined in terms which strongly imply such a value. The high eminence ambition score is a way of saying that a man is unwilling to be merely an average member of his occupation, or that a woman is unwilling to have her husband be run-of-the-mill in his field. Individuality is the value category which most nearly incorporates the same theme as eminence, applied in a broader fashion. Of the six items classified under individuality, two (24, 25) are associated with eminence for both men and women, three (8, 14, 26) are associated for women only, and one (18) is not associated for either. However, the pattern of associations is so close to that for the mobility type of ambition that no clue to the distinctive character of eminence ambition is supplied. With one exception, the items show the same pattern of correlation with either occupational ambition or

Table 45. Values Associated with Eminence Ambition, for Males and Females

Value item[a]	$P \leq$[b]	
	Male	Female
8. Can do a few things perfectly vs. can do many things fairly well	--	.001
11. Believes in having it out vs. drops until tempers cool	--	.01
13. Real success in business vs. real family man (woman)	--	.001
14. Shows how to argue intelligently vs. smooths over disagreements	--	.01
16. Puts community ahead of friends vs. puts friends ahead	.02	--
17. Rather be his own boss vs. will take orders to get ahead	--	.05
20. Tries new ways of doing things vs. sticks with time-tested ways	.05	.01
22. Pride in doing things on his own vs. likes advice and help	.02	--
24. Does better than friends vs. does as well as friends	.01	.001
25. Tries to get things his way vs. quick to go along with group	.01	.001
26. Respected, hard to get along with vs. easy to get along with	--	.02
27. Always making new friends vs. sticks with tried-true friends	--	.01
29. Talks foreign policy and politics vs. talks popular music and sports	.01	--
31. Never lets an insult go by vs. laughs off any insult	--	.01
34. Risks what he has to get ahead vs. prefers secure position	.001	.001
37. Always looking for something better vs. satisfied with what he has	.001	.001

a/ The alternative associated with high eminence ambition has been listed first in each instance.

b/ Significance is based on chi-square, with three degrees of freedom. Items that showed curvilinear relationships have not been reported.

the ambition index (Table 15). The exception is the preference for
(14) showing people how to argue intelligently rather than smoothing over disagreements. This is one of the items most clearly associated with occupational, material, and educational ambition in the
case of men, but is only associated with eminence ambition for women.
The general value of individuality, then, affords no clue to the distinctive character of eminence ambition.

The group of items concerned with secular success does offer some
clue to the connotations of eminence. If we disregard item (9) which
was unrelated to general ambition and item (17) which was negatively
related, there are five items which were probably related to mobility
ambition both for men and women. Of these five, only two are related
to eminence ambition for both men and women. These are the preference for (34) risk rather than security and (37) looking for something
better rather than being satisfied with what one has. These are the
two items which do not oppose secular values to the alternative of
the tender values. Secular success is valued in its own right, both by
the students with mobility ambition and with eminence ambition.
Two items are unrelated to eminence ambition for either sex. These
are the preference for (21) being a smooth operator rather than too
kind to take unfair advantage, and (36) getting ahead by breaks and
pull rather than mere hard work. The items which sharply oppose
secular success to the value of kindness and progress based on one's
own worth distinguish those students with mobility ambition, but
not those students with eminence ambition. The remaining item, the
preference for (13) business success rather than being a family man or
woman, is associated with eminence ambition for women, but not
for men.

Thus, more support is lent to the interpretation that men whose
ambitions are for mobility are distinguished from men who want
eminence without mobility, not by their endorsement of secular success per se, but in their willingness to sacrifice the tender values for
its attainment. That the distinction does not appear so sharply for
women probably results from the fact that the women are speaking
of eminence for their husbands rather than for themselves. A certain
discounting of the value of being just a good family person is probably inevitable in the girl who is prepared to say that her husband
should not relax until he is a "big man" in his field.

Other items associated with eminence ambition for the men are
the preference for (16) putting community welfare ahead of friends,
for (22) pride in doing things on one's own rather than getting advice and help, for (29) serious talk rather than popular talk, and pos-

sibly for (20) trying new ways rather than time-tested ways. Two of these items (22, 29) are associated with mobility ambition for both men and women. The preference for community welfare has been associated with no other measures, except for a reverse correlation with material ambition. This is an item which we stressed in the initial statement of a conception of youth culture, since it counterposes the primary- and secondary-group systems of loyalty. The suggestion of a secondary-group perspective fits with the borderline preference for innovation. The latter item would hardly warrant notice except for the presence of a more convincing association among women. Not only do the women with high eminence scores prefer to try new ways; they also prefer to (27) meet new people rather than stick to old friends.

For women, the two items suggest that a high eminence score carries with it a receptiveness to change and repudiation of tradition which is not associated with any other type of ambition or with background. The suggestion is more tenuous in the case of men. However, receptiveness to change, like the preference for community rather than primary-group loyalty, is a secondary-group attitude. On the basis of the present data it is little more than a hunch that concern with mobility may be distinguished from concern with eminence by more conservative primary-group values. In a society like ours, the effort to climb the stratification ladder is fully consistent with conservative and primary-group values, while the effort to excel in any particular area may be less so.

Three items correlate with eminence ambition for women but not for men. Women with high eminence ambition scores prefer (11) to have it out rather than wait until tempers cool, (17) to be their own boss rather than get ahead by taking orders, and (31) never to let an insult to their own or their family's honor go by. The first and third of these items are not associated with mobility ambition, and have in common a sort of aggressive self-assertion, or perhaps a sort of self-righteous determination to set things right. These are two of the three items originally classified as "punitive justice," the omitted item having to do with justice turned inward rather than toward others. Whether these associations indicate the character of women with high eminence scores or whether they are a by-product of the fact that women were asked to set standards for their husbands rather than themselves can hardly be determined from these data.

A comprehensive look at some of the items which are not correlated with eminence ambition among the men reveals three out of the four items which we have called manipulative individualism. Unlike the men with high mobility ambition, the men with high eminence ambition do not prefer (14) to show people how to argue intelligently, (17) to be their own bosses rather than take orders to get ahead, or (23) to be good at making decisions for others rather than to try never to influence them. Both groups, however, prefer to get the group to do things their way rather than to fit in. A continuum is suggested here with manipulative individualism most characteristic of the boys from high backgrounds, least characteristic of those with exclusively high eminence ambition, and of intermediate strength in the case of men with high mobility-type ambition. The importance of a manipulative-individualism complex as an adjunct of high socioeconomic standing is emphasized by this systematic kind of differentiation. Since three of the four items are related to eminence ambition for the women, our observations about manipulative individualism apply only to men.

In summary, the men of high eminence ambition are not distinguished, as are the men with high mobility ambition, by a willingness to sacrifice tender values for secular success, nor by a value of manipulative individualism. They may, on the other hand, be somewhat more oriented toward the secondary values of change and community welfare, though this latter possibility cannot be asserted with any confidence. Women with high eminence ambition are similarly distinguished from women with high mobility ambition by the sacrifice of tender values for success, and are more clearly distinguished than men with respect to the willingness to entertain change. They also seem to exhibit a sort of concern over righting wrongs against them aggressively which is not characteristic of women with high mobility ambition.

We conclude our discussion of eminence ambition by noting that a ninefold correlation analysis employing Tschuprow's T shows no relationship between this kind of ambition and *friend rating*. It is ambition to attain a high station in society rather than to excel in one's special field that carries with it the heightened desirability among one's peers.

SUMMARY

Mobility refers to a comprehensive change in the individual's position. To the extent that people emphasize different aspects of this change there is reason to suppose that the effects of the mobility experience will differ. Our principal interest is in distinguishing between those whose ambitions involve disproportionate stress on material gain and those who stress educational achievement. We have also attempted to measure the degree to which ambition for eminence—high standing within an occupational level—supplies an alternative to mobility ambition. Finally, we have considered the men to whom independent rather than employee status is an aspect of ambition.

Of the various measures of ambition, including occupation, education is most strongly related to background, both for men and women. There is a negative relationship between material-educational polarization of ambition and background, which remains significant after I.Q. has been partialed out. Students from high backgrounds place greater emphasis on education, while students from low backgrounds expect to go further with less education. It also appears that they choose occupations according to the education demanded, men from low backgrounds particularly favoring the semiprofessions which offer high standing by other routes than formal education. Unlike the general level of ambition, the type of emphasis is less importantly affected by neighborhood than by family background.

The level of eminence ambition is high. Because relationships with occupational ambition and the ambition index are low, eminence affords an alternative to mobility for men with high ambitions. When occupational ambition is held constant, eminence ambition for men is positively related to educational ambition but not to material ambition. Eminence ambition is practically unrelated to level of family background or neighborhood.

Ownership ambition is generally unrelated to other indicators of ambition and background, with two related exceptions. Ownership and eminence striving are correlated for men who aspire to skilled labor, suggesting that this traditional entrepreneurial combination remains effective only in the occupations which embody most fully the traditional value of individual skill. Ownership ambition is likewise unrelated to background level, except that men from small-business backgrounds are much more likely than others to aspire to independence. There is no clear value complex related to ownership ambition.

There appears to be a fairly clear pattern of difference among neighborhoods in the relation between emphases and background for men. High background is related to a strong emphasis on education and even negatively related to material ambition in the low neighborhoods but not in the high, and eminence ambition is related to background in low neighborhoods only. Perhaps it is only in the low neighborhoods that a rather extensive segmentation of ambition is possible, and where only the students from higher backgrounds have a comprehensive concept of ambition.

A comparison of students with high material and educational ambitions brings to light no differences in degree of anticipatory socialization, but points to different value constellations. For both men and women, educational emphasis is related to a favorable evaluation of "genteel culture," while material emphasis is related to heightened evaluation of secular success. There is some indication of deferred gratification associated with educational ambition for both men and women, and a clear stress on self-reliance for men. Material ambition is associated with a sort of antinormative and antiorganizational-control value for men, and a heightened emphasis on individuality for women. The traditional middle-class value complex appears to be most highly represented in students with high educational ambition, although formal schooling is one of the newer avenues to mobility. There may be a slight social preference for students who emphasize education rather than material ambition. Cleavage according to emphasis is marked in low neighborhoods, but lacking in high neighborhoods. Just as evidence from previous chapters suggested that the peer organization in lower neighborhoods may commit a boy earlier in life to a course of high or low ambition, groups are also formed on the basis of the kind of emphasis dominating ambition.

Eminence ambition is unrelated to social acceptability, but exhibits an associated value complex which sheds light on the nature of mobility ambition. Like the students with high mobility ambition, those with high eminence ambition endorse secular success values, but only so long as they are not opposed by tender values. Unlike the mobility oriented, the high eminence men show no special value of manipulative individualism. Eminence ambition is distinctively related to values suggesting a cosmopolitan rather than a provincial outlook and a receptiveness to change. The kind of ambition which does not stress abandoning one stratum for another seems to incorporate the more humane and open-minded values which are not associated with mobility.

The data of the chapter do not carry us far enough to reach confident conclusions regarding predispositions to marginality. However, we note that no difference in degree of anticipatory socialization between the high material and high education aspirants is indicated. On the other hand, the slight preference for high education aspirants may indicate that their transition in social ties is facilitated. In the low neighborhoods, the association of educational emphasis with high background and the cleavage by emphasis may mean that it is the high education emphasizers rather than the high material aspirants who have already begun the necessary social transition.

Finally, the type of values endorsed by education aspirants resembles the traditional middle-class complex more closely than the type endorsed by high material aspirants. If we discount high-background students as the standard on the grounds that anticipatory socialization has already eroded some of the middle-class complex among those who are nonmobile, anticipatory socialization may in fact be more extensive among students who emphasize educational ambition than among those who emphasize material ambition. Completer anticipatory socialization and social transitions should both lessen the likelihood of marginality. Accordingly, students who emphasize material ambition will be more predisposed to marginality than those who stress educational ambition.

CHAPTER EIGHT

Conclusions and Implications

BECAUSE FINDINGS and conclusions have been discussed as each chapter progressed and in chapter summaries, there is no need to reproduce in detail and with full qualification the many observations to which we have been led. Instead, we shall highlight the evidence regarding mobility as a marginality-inducing experience, and point out the implications of the investigation for larger issues in the sociology of stratification and socialization.

MOBILITY AND THE MARGINAL MAN

The marginal-man hypothesis asserts a causal linkage between situation, experience, and personality. The situation is extensive involvement in two societies or subsocieties whose relationship is such that loyal membership in one means disloyalty to the other and acceptance of the values of one constitutes violation of the values of the other. The experience is the inability to choose between groups, with involvements in the area of personal loyalties impeding choice in the realm of values, and vice versa. The personality consequences are less clearly specified, but consist generally of personal conflict and lack of self-confidence and of heightened objectivity, relativity, and often creativity.

For the upwardly mobile experience to be that of marginality, social strata must be characterized by severe cleavage in friendship and interpersonal loyalty and by incompatible subcultures. The contrasting possible relationships between social strata are class consciousness and value contradiction, or prestige identification and value discrepancy. Within the schools, the presence of mechanisms to facilitate the transition in class identity and the operation of a youth culture obscuring differences in background would mitigate the tendencies toward marginality brought on by value contradiction and class consciousness.

Our evidence deals only with the youth group and cannot tell us about the characteristics of the adult society in which the students live. But among the youth, prestige identification appears to exceed class consciousness, and value discrepancy is more characteristic than value contradiction. The problems of moving between strata should consequently be less intense than those envisaged by the theory of the marginal man. It was not possible to show that youth culture played a special part, though it may do so in middle-level neighborhoods. But anticipatory socialization and social cleavage by ambition suggest that there are mechanisms facilitating the transition for the mobile person.

We found no evidence either that the mobile person was more relativistic or uncertain in his choice of values, or that he took the values of the stratum of his destination more seriously than did persons born in the stratum. In other respects the symptoms and experiences of marginality were not explored.

The mobile person may be marginal, but the attitudes of his high-school peers will neither insure nor prevent his marginality. While the impact of family background is not erased, class differences are not sharp and transitions in values are frequently made at this stage in life. Whether transitions in actual social affiliations are being made with great frequency we do not know, but we do know that they are with respect to friendship desirability. On the whole, it appears that the high-school peer situation is one in which the discontinuities which normally lead to marginality are moderated.

The Nature of Ambition

In speaking of marginality we have treated ambition as all of one kind. Sociologists, by their stress on rates of mobility as the measure of democracy, often seem to adopt a view that there is only one kind of success—movement up the socioeconomic ladder. But it is clear that people are ambitious for very different accomplishments. In this investigation we have attempted to take some simple differentiations of ambition into account.

Social strata are broad groupings of people who are only relatively more homogeneous than the entire population. By almost any desideratum, the strata overlap greatly. Likewise, there is a wide range within each stratum. Consequently, a person who is ambitious to improve himself has the option of doing so within his occupational bracket or by entering a different type of occupation. In societies in which the range of value attainable within any given stratum is large, the measure of interclass mobility is only a very partial measure of the individual's success in improving himself.

To allow for ambition which does not find expression in interclass mobility, we employed a question dealing with eminence. We found eminence ambition to be almost unrelated to mobility ambition, and to be prevalent at all levels. In values we found that the boy with high eminence ambition showed the same commitment to secular success as the boy with mobility ambitions, except when success was opposed to the tender values of family and kindness. There was also a bare suggestion that he might have a more "enlightened" or secondary-group attitude toward his social responsibilities.

These suggestive findings raise anew the question of what values the individual must sacrifice for the sake of interclass mobility. They also raise the question as to what values in an "acquisitive society" sociologists are implicitly endorsing and perhaps reinforcing by their use of interstratum ascent as the sole measure of success.

In an unreported small-scale study of university men students we also found little relationship between objective mobility and (a) willingness to sacrifice personal convenience to attain success and (b) the degree to which students set improvement over parental achievement as their standard of success. Clearly, there is need to recognize another dimension of ambition and to measure more adequately what was only approximately indicated by our measure of eminence ambition. There is need for an entire body of theory dealing with the choice of this kind of ambition and with the social experience and personality consequence of pursuing it.

Among those whose ambition directs them toward interstratum mobility there are again differences. We explored only one of these differences, but found distinctions in value constellations and even a possible social cleavage. We employed educational and material ambition as the very approximate indexes respectively of types of ambitions stressing the improvement in material goods and comforts that everyone wants, and the achievement of a genteel or cultured style of life which many would not want. No greater degree of anticipatory socialization characterized either type. But a somewhat stronger development of some of the traditional middle-class values (or entrepreneurial values) characterized the latter, and a strong theme of institutional repudiation marked the former.

The mobility experiences of persons with these divergent emphases in ambition will probably be different, and what they expect to encounter in completing their mobility prepares them differently for the movement between social strata. If the students who emphasize education are most likely to achieve mobility under the present trends on our society, the coming generation of the "successful" may bring back some of the entrepreneurial values. It would be foolhardy to make a firm prophecy. But it should be worth watching to see what happens to men who emphasize the new middle-class route to success by way of education, while adopting more of the entrepreneurial middle-class value system than either their ambitious peers who emphasize education less or their peers from high-status family backgrounds.

A key task in the development of theory and research regarding mobility is the delineation of alternate channels of mobility, alternate emphases in ambition, and segmental and complete forms of mobility. Theories such as marginality can then be examined for their applicability to each such type separately.

IMPLICATIONS FOR LARGER ISSUES: STRATIFICATION

In order to interpret the data at hand, it has frequently been necessary to suggest approaches and propositions dealing with the realm of stratification on a much wider scale than the specific problems of the investigation. Three of these areas deserve special mention.

Stratification of Destination

The basic model of "class man" in stratification research is the established adult male. He has a station in society which is both based upon and contributive to his occupation and his position in the economic system on a broader scale. When women and persons too young to have earned comprehensive stations of their own are studied, it is customary to identify their class positions by their family connection. Thus the wife is known by her husband's position, and the child by his father's. From two standpoints this treatment of the child is theoretically justified. It is justified insofar as the impact of life situation is felt through the family. The mutuality of the family means that resources, opportunities, and obstacles are shared by family members. It is also justified as the process of socialization takes place through the family. Children learn the values and perspectives of their parents and consequently acquire a class outlook to the extent that their own parents have such a set of attitudes.

But to the extent that they share in life situations other than their families' and experience socialization which does not come through the family, some of the effects of family background may be lessened. Reciprocally, as people react to them less according to their family and family-linked characteristics, the social consequences of background are lessened. It is customary then to think of a progressive neutralization of the impact of class position. Accordingly, class factors and nonclass factors are sometimes weighed against one another in this context.

However, stratification of origin is already a small departure from the prototype class man. It is only appropriate to speak of the class position of an eighteen-year-old boy as that of his father on the basis of the assumed continuities with the past that we have just mentioned. But if it is proper to speak of a person's class position by reference to something in his past rather than in his present, may it not be equally justifiable to speak of his class position by reference to his future? Indeed, which reference for stratification is more appropriate must depend upon the time orientation which a person himself holds and which dominates the society or subsociety in which he interacts. It may be argued that the past refers to actual experience and the future to hopes which in many cases will not be realized. But social position is not merely an attribute or possession of the individual which he acquires and holds; it is, as W. Lloyd Warner and others have noted, a datum and product of interaction. Insofar as individuals interact in a society or subsociety governed by an orientation to the future, people will identify themselves and be identified according to the future as they conceive it.

Richard Centers performed a service in pointing out that one's conception of his class identity adds something to the objective determinants of social position. W. Lloyd Warner contributes the other variable in the social equation, the manner in which others conceive the individual's position in their interaction with him. The suggestion made here is that both of these forms of social definition are related to the objective or ecological foundations of stratification on a time dimension. Underlying the fact of stratification is the folk assumption that objective, subjective, and social placement should coincide.[1] The coincidence may be contemporary, and this is the time perspective within which we normally view the middle-aged adult. The time-perspective may be to the past, as it is in traditional societies. But whenever current activity is viewed as preparation for a future which is more significant than the moment, it is the anticipated objective standing which determines social placement and self-conception.

In two important respects this treatment of stratification is different from an emphasis on subjective stratification. First, it acknowledges the pragmatist's insistence that conception and action cannot

[1] Cf. Ralph H. Turner, "The Normative Coherence of Folk Concepts," *Research Studies of the State College of Washington*, 25 (June, 1957), pp. 127–136.

be separated, that it is the fact that activity is oriented about a future goal rather than the mere fact of imagining oneself to be of a given status which is significant for social participation and the constellation of values which is adopted. Second, it is the interaction of self and others rather than the mere fact of imagined self-placement which must be stressed. Stratification of destination is a fact because the society or subsociety is oriented toward the future and each member is dealt with on the basis of his apparent orientation toward the future. Within the group, the socializing and life situation impact upon the individual is geared to this future.

Future-oriented components in stratification are not uncommon throughout society. The occupation "with a future" conveys more prestige than an occupation without a future, even though the objective facts at the moment do not justify the difference in standing. In all probability, societies and regions differ in the extent to which stratification of destination is a component of the total stratification. Probably youth is the period of life in which stratification of destination is most salient. The weaning from the home and the concentration of attention upon future-determining decisions maximize the orientation.

Defining stratification exclusively according to origin or contemporary objective characteristics runs the danger of underestimating the importance and prospects of stratification in a future-oriented society such as high-school youth. Some of the classic "middle-class" values were uncorrelated with stratification of origin, but were correlated with stratification of destination. Social cleavage with respect to desired friendships was absent when related to stratification of origin, but appeared when related to stratification of destination. There is good reason to suppose that the cleavage and value differentiation are portents of the nature of the adult stratification into which the students are moving. The stratification of destination may provide a better clue to stratification in the larger society than the stratification of origin.

In spite of our emphasis upon destination, we hasten to recall that the lines of origin are not eradicated. Effective stratification is not a unidimensional phenomenon, but a somewhat heterogeneous product of the simultaneous operation of several stratification principles. By separating the *wheel* from the *brain,* we acknowledged two different principles of stratification operating within the school environment. In their discussion of *situs,* Richard T. Morris and Raymond

J. Murphy point to important parallel stratification systems.[2] In dwelling upon time-orientation, we have sought to identify another respect in which the empirical fact of ordered inequality among men may be the product of the simultaneous operation of several principles of stratification.

Values and Social Stratification

Values are inferences we make from behavior, and when we characterize the behavior of a class of people, we usually do so on the basis of conspicuous representatives of the class. On both counts, there are problems for the theory of "social-class values." The most conspicuous members of higher strata are the eminently successful, and the most conspicuous members of lower strata are the unsuccessful and the deviant and delinquent. The behavioral contrasts between strata are likely to approach caricatures unless corrections can be made for conspicuousness and ease of class identification. Inferring values from behavior encounters the further problems of deciding how directly or indirectly the value has been applied in the situation, the extent to which the effective value is a specific choice or a general value in a hierarchy, and how effectively compartmentalized the values are. Only with trepidation can assertions be made about "social-class values."

The first impression from our data is that the relationships between stratification and values are remarkably small. There is a temptation, then, to suppose that the items did not pinpoint the appropriate value issues, to ascribe the results entirely to selective drop-out of students, or to wonder whether Los Angeles is notably more amorphous than other cities that have been studied. But two lines of further observation mitigate the impression of unusual findings. First, a careful re-examination of some of the prior studies of class differences in values shows that relationships found by others have often been quite modest. Frequently, only significance measures are reported so that the low degree of relationship is not called to the attention of the reader. Often indexes composed of several items conceal the fact that some of the items are not themselves related to stratification. Second, recent studies of childrearing patterns have revealed much less impressive class differences than were heretofore supposed to exist, and Miller and Swanson have supplied a rationale

[2] "The Situs Dimension in Occupational Structure," *American Sociological Review,* 24 (April, 1959), pp. 231–239.

for the lessening of class-value differences through the emergence of a new middle class.[3] Perhaps the conviction of sharp value differences is unwarranted by the evidence available. The emergence of serious stratification study during the Depression years and in communities in which lower-class and recent peasant origin were inseparable may have instituted biases which now need to be re-examined.

One principle, though inadequately tested in these data, may supply an important key in the understanding of class-value differences. It is proposed that groups differ not only in the values they endorse, but also in the relevance they see in situations. In particular, there is a difference between accepting a value and translating it into a goal in one's own behavior. One may believe sincerely in the value of artistic beauty, but hesitate to attempt to paint for oneself. Hence, we hypothesized that strata would differ more in the values they accepted as goals for their own behavior than in the values which they would endorse in less personal contexts. With data of limited adequacy, there was fairly impressive support for this view in case of stratification of origin among males.

The issue of class values is the extent to which people in different social strata have a common frame of reference within which to judge the worth of themselves and others. If social strata differ less in frame of reference than in behavior, the condition is one which facilitates fluidity within the class system and discourages nonaccommodative class consciousness. The members of each stratum will have considerable capacity to understand the motives of the members of other strata.

Before the implications of the principle of value relevancy can be fully clear, it will be essential to understand why it applied only to stratification of origin and not to stratification of destination, and why only to men. We shall disregard the sex difference for the moment. But the difference in relation to time-perspective is consistent with the explanation already offered for the value-relevancy hypothesis. It was initially proposed that there are fewer restraints imposed by the situation upon the application of values in judging others, particularly people outside of the immediate circle of interaction, than there are upon the translation of values into goals for one's self. The practical limitations of opportunity and example at the lower levels and the dependence of the entire life constellation upon secular success among the middle class are among the situational restraints which account for discrepancies between values accepted in an im-

---

3 *The Changing American Parent* (New York: Wiley, 1958).

personal situation and personal goals. The specific cause of the value-relevancy phenomenon is contact with a situation which blocks the direct pursuit of one's values.

It is the nature of stratification of destination that the ultimate situation in which the values are to be expressed has not yet been experienced intimately. Hence, the situational pressures cannot operate in the way that they can in the stratification of origin or of the contemporary situation. What seems to happen instead is that boys bring their values into line with their goals. The very future-orientation which accounts for the stratification of destination seems also to make personal goals the pivotal point in the formation of more impersonal values. Orientations to the past, and perhaps also to the present, are less active stances. As such they can tolerate the discrepancies between values and personal goals. But the highly active stance of future-orientation leads to adjustment of values in the abstract to greater correspondence with the goals being sought.[4]

The implication of the foregoing highly speculative line of reasoning is that the value-relevancy principle may re-emerge as the stratification of destination gives way to a stratification based upon the contemporaneous situation during the life cycle of the individual. No such view can be asserted as a conclusion from the present investigation; it is offered entirely as an extension of a line of thought only begun here.

Women in Stratification

Stratification studies often treat the family as a unit, accepting the husband or wife indiscriminately as an informant regarding class values and styles of life. In explorations of ambition women are often treated in the same fashion as men, as if educational and occupational ambition meant the same thing to them as to men. While we have placed major emphasis on men students, we have also attempted to explore when possible the unique features of the woman's relationship to stratification. Our limited efforts have been productive enough to warrant the judgment that stratification should be more extensively studied from the standpoint of the woman.

The observation of most general interest in this connection is that most of the same values which differentiate strata also differentiate men from women. For the most part the masculine values are the high-strata values, and the relationships are perhaps even clearer for

4 This hypothesis might well have been stated in the language of cognitive dissonance theory. Cf. Leon Festinger, *A Theory of Cognitive Dissonance* (Evanston, Illinois: Row, Peterson, 1957).

sex than for stratification. The association may be an artifact of our choice of values, concentrated disproportionately in the realms of individualism and secular success. But even if the relationship does not apply to other areas of values, the finding suggests that each family unit incorporates some heterogeneity in class values through its division into male and female roles. The assumption that socialization to class attitudes takes place in a value-homogeneous family microcosm comes under questioning. A more complex process of transmission must be in operation, if the family does transmit class values.

The further observation that some of the values adopted by ambitious girls, but not associated with high background among girls, are values linked to high background among the boys is related. Somehow the ambitious girl acquires in certain respects a less feminine constellation of values than other girls. Possibly in some respects she identifies with boys from high backgrounds and takes over some of their values.

There is apparently a complex interplay between class values and masculine-feminine values in relation to class position and ambition. The boy is exposed to some heterogeneity within the home, but through role identification he is able to acquire a set of values which fit his sex, even though his mother carries a set of values which are appropriate for a male of lower standing. Perhaps because ambition is so characteristically masculine, ambitious girls take on some values from across the sex line.

While ambitious women do adopt some masculine values, they also exhibit a special set of values which fits the peculiarities of their sex role. The values of deferred gratification in the ambitious male and individuality in the ambitious female appear to express the peculiarities of their roles. Deferred gratification in some sense epitomizes the active posture, the planning, controlling attitude toward events. If the male is to control later and more important events, he must accumulate his resources now. By contrast, individuality, when divorced from other aspects of individualism, epitomizes the passive posture in self-advancement. The ambitious female makes herself conspicuous, so that she will have a wide rather than narrow range of choice in the marriage market.

This function of individuality is underlined by the difference between women who stress material ambition disproportionately and those who stress educational ambition. The latter apparently take a more active orientation toward ambition, expecting to advance to some extent by their own accomplishment, while the former probably include more of the girls who expect to advance by being chosen. It is the girls who have high material ambitions without proportionately high educational ambitions who stand out most clearly for their endorsement of individuality values. Individuality values are also related to high background among girls, but not so comprehensively as they are to ambition.

A further consequence of the feminine role is the apparently different emphasis in ambition upon the scale of living and the specific occupation of the husband. Our data are not sharply enough directed toward this problem to force a specific interpretation upon us. But examination of the comparative intensity of ambition in various directions renders one interpretation plausible. The male investment is likely to be in a specific occupation; it may be called a career-orientation. Investment of the self in career reaches the point that he does not readily turn from one occupation to another for the sake of tangible advantage. The woman's orientation is toward the *products* of occupational activity, rather than toward the husband's career itself. The product is not merely material, though many girls who are willing to set very low occupational standards nevertheless set their material standards considerably higher. The girls include a severe standard of eminence striving in the ambitions they set for their future husbands. There are probably elements of dignity and pride in effort and accomplishment which they expect along with material reward, without, however, being equally restrictive about the occupation itself.

Ambition is both formed and realized within the family. Somehow or other, these divergent views of success and the divergent values attached to ambition in male and female must come into a working relationship within the family of procreation. Our data indicate that very few girls plan to escape these problems through avoiding entirely the homemaker role. As the distinctive perspectives are brought into the family, their interplay in turn must constitute an element in the socialization experience of the next generation.

A final hypothesis regarding male and female roles in social stratification may be constructed from the findings regarding values and sociometric choice. Women appear to be less weaned from their strata of origin than men are at this stage in life. They are oriented toward the future, and they do reveal anticipatory socialization. But they appear in certain respects to have gone less far than boys in giving up the anchorage to their strata of origin. One scrap of suggestive evidence is their failure to conform to the value-relevancy hypothesis. Men differ less according to background in the values that determine whom they admire than in the values that determine their personal goals. They have gone further in erasing the traces of background in the set of values they employ impersonally than the constraints of their life situations will allow them to do with respect to their personal goals. The girls, however, continue to accept in more impersonal contexts the class-of-origin-linked values which shape their personal goals. Stated another way, the girls continue to believe in the values which their backgrounds have forced on them while the men do not.

We attempted to use the reputation of a student in his schoolwork as a device to separate the impact of the official school social system from the indigenous peer system in accounting for the structure of social preference. Among the boys, the association between socioeconomic background and student leadership *may* have been principally a consequence of the correlation between scholastic reputation and background. Both boys and girls from higher backgrounds were likely to be reputed as *wheels*. The peer system accommodates itself to the official school system to the extent of according some preference to the outstanding student. Among boys this accommodation to the official school system might be enough to account for the slight preponderance of high background among *wheels*. Among girls, however, student leadership is related to background apart from the impact of the scholastic system. Stratification of origin is a significant variable in the indigenous peer social system for girls, but not for boys.

The foregoing observation refers to the choices received as *wheels* rather than to the choices given. It is not that the girls are more class-of-origin-conscious in their selection of *wheels*; it is rather that a girl's peer status as a *wheel* is more likely to be a function of her background independently of scholastic reputation. The data, then, say something about the determinants of the girl's role in the high-school social system. If the high-school girl clings more seriously to the values of her stratum of orientation than the high-school boy, it may be because the peer system is more likely to take her origin into account in the status it accords her. The connection is, of course, wholly speculative in relation to present data. But it represents one more aspect of stratification in which sex differentiation might be profitably examined.

IMPLICATIONS FOR LARGER ISSUES:
SOCIALIZATION

We have already touched unavoidably upon the problem of socialization to the prevailing system of stratification, and each of the following areas has been adumbrated. But special mention should be made of reference-group theory, youth culture, and the social function of the school.

Reference-Group Theory

A constant guide to interpretation of the data from this investigation has been reference-group theory.[5] The theory was not built into the design of the study as were the notions of anticipatory socialization and value relevancy, but was employed because it supplied a framework for bringing diverse observations into plausible relationship. Hence, there is nothing compelling about the interpretations. But the application of any theory to data is always a two-way process: not only is something learned about the data; suggested amplifications or modifications of the theory necessarily emerge.

In its most general form, reference-group theory asserts that from two facts there proceeds a third. First, integral to the course of some act-in-process, the individual has strong feelings toward some group. The simplest form of this relationship is that in which the individual seeks to be accepted as a member of the group. The most general feeling is the assignment of prestige toward the group, though it may also be the favorable or unfavorable comparison arising out of the principle of distributive justice.[6] The act-in-process is a requirement of the theory, since the postulated effect on the individual's behavior does not follow from the assignment of prestige in a passive context. Second, the individual perceives aspects of the group's behavior which are relevant to the act-in-process. The perceptions may come from direct contact with members or indirect exposure, and the degree of accuracy may vary widely. From the first and the second conditions comes the third, that the individual will employ the perceived behavior of the reference group as some kind of criterion for his own behavior. Again, the simplest relationship is that in which the perceived behavior serves as a model for the individual's behavior.

We have found use for two applications of reference-group theory in the present study. First, in accounting for the relatively low ambitions of students from schools in low neighborhoods in spite of the peer preference for the ambitious, we invoked reference-group theory. Striving for success becomes the act-in-process. People in the neighborhood are perceived as a group, in conjunction with an attitude

---

5 For a comprehensive discussion of reference-group theory, see Robert K. Merton, *Social Theory and Social Structure* (Glencoe, Illinois: Free Press, 1957), pp. 225–386.

6 Cf. George C. Homans, *Social Behavior: Its Elementary Forms* (New York: Harcourt, Brace and Co., 1961), pp. 75 ff.

which views them as a somewhat normal universe. The range of success in the neighborhood is the behavior which the act-in-process directs the individual to perceive. As a consequence, the individual sets his own success goals relative to the standard supplied by the reference group.

Second, we attempted to account for variations in anticipatory socialization. We assumed that students were striving to elevate themselves socially. Assigning prestige to the group of students who had come from high socioeconomic backgrounds, they sought to join them. Consequently, they adopted many of the values which they perceived in the students from high backgrounds.

However, in the second situation we noted that anticipatory socialization did not take place in the low-neighborhood schools. Although students from top backgrounds were lacking, still there was a range of background and some students stood out as coming from relatively high backgrounds. Furthermore, the high-background students did not themselves exhibit the full range of values held by such students in other neighborhoods. But with respect to the values they did hold, no anticipatory socialization seemed to have occurred. The theory tells us to look for the failure of anticipatory socialization in (a) absence of a relevant act-in-process, (b) failure of the individuals to assign prestige to the group in question, or (c) failure to perceive the relevant behavior of the group. The act-in-process appears to be comparable in the various neighborhoods. Cleavage by background, which might have been an obstacle to perception of behavior, was not present at any level. The narrower range of values associated with high background in the lower neighborhoods might have lessened the visibility of a distinctive complex of values.

But another observation seems to bear directly upon the second condition. In high- and middle-level neighborhoods, where anticipatory socialization is in evidence, there is a generalized preference for students from high backgrounds. But no such preference exists in the lower neighborhoods. It is possible that stratification of origin is honored to the extent of according prestige to the highborn in the middle and higher neighborhood, but that stratification of origin is denied legitimacy entirely in the low neighborhoods. Mobile students are likely to name as desired friends persons of higher backgrounds than their own, even in the low neighborhoods. But it is further possible that the attitude of the community, or the peer community, determines whether the ambitious students adopt the values of students from high backgrounds. Where the peer community assigns them prestige, students with the appropriate act-in-process (upward mobility striving) adopt students from high backgrounds as a reference group. Without such community indication, they may still prefer them, but fail to learn their values.

One of the important aspects of reference-group theory which requires amplification is the basis for adopting the values of a reference group. The act-in-process supplies a portion of the answer in each instance. But there must also be something to point the individual's attention to the group in question. Here we have suggested that it is the attitude of the peer community. Because prestige was generally accorded the high socioeconomic group, the ambitious person adopted it as reference group. The attitude which is general in the community need not be crucial, however; whether it is crucial may depend upon the attitude of the community to the act-in-process. When the community supports the act-in-process, the community and the actor are in harmony and the actor is led to adopt their indications in selecting his reference group. Since ambitious students were consistently favored by their peers throughout our data, the condition of harmony exists. It would require a situation in which such support was lacking while other conditions were present to determine whether, in fact, this limitation is appropriate.

We do not, of course, know what other reference groups the ambitious students may have adopted. They may have taken successful adults as their models. But here the problem of perceiving behavior enters the situation. Their contact with adults is probably not intimate enough to disclose the character of the values in which they believe; only in relations with peers is there close enough contact to allow this kind of perception to occur.

Reference-group theory does not yet supply a complete interpretation of our findings, however. So long as there are values which distinguish the ambitious student and which do not characterize students from high backgrounds, the latter cannot serve as a sufficient reference group. Explanation for such values must attribute them either to the situation itself or to the impact of some other reference group or socializing agent. A value such as deferred gratification might arise out of the very experience of mobility striving itself, rather than as a product of subcultural transmission. But it is also possible that the special impact of the mother or of schoolteachers may transmit these values.

A clue to interpretation is supplied by noting the kinds of values that are associated with ambition and background. Values related to ambition but not to background seem to be more appropriate to the entrepreneurial than the bureaucratic middle class,[7] to the old than to the new middle class.[8] A fuller and more specifically selected range of values would be required to determine whether this distinction holds as a general observation. But if we assume that it does, we find it harder to account for these distinctive values on the basis of the situation of mobility itself and easier to attribute them to some group or agent which is somewhat insulated against contemporary changes in middle-class values. If the new middle-class values derive from the bureaucratic way of life, the breadwinner should feel their impact soonest and most pervasively. We might well expect his wife, if she is primarily a homemaker, to be somewhat more wedded to the older middle-class values. When the ambitious students come from families in which the mother has more education than the father, the mother seems a likely source of influence in transmitting old middle-class values to the child. Teachers, as a group who are self-conscious transmitters of respectable values, are also likely to be slower in accepting the new values.

Youth Culture

Youth culture was included in the design of this study because it seems impossible to examine ambition, mobility, or the system of social stratification among adolescents without allowing for its impact. Youth culture has generally been regarded as an impediment to high ambition and a neutralizer of class background. In the terminology of the present investigation, it tends to dull the discriminations of both stratification of origin and stratification of destination. In their place, it erects a stratification of the present, limiting the temporal base by adopting as criteria of position specifically those attributes which are most ephemeral, such as athletic prowess, glamour, and popularity.

Outside of its implications for sexual behavior, youth culture has been the subject of impressionistic observation rather than controlled investigation. As a result, a number of fundamental questions have remained unanswered. First, there appears to be sufficient similarity between descriptions of youth culture and lower-class culture that the relationship between these two sets of values must be clarified. Second, we are still dependent upon impressions to identify the content of youth culture. We need criteria to delimit the relevant youth society and test each of the hypothesized elements to determine just what is the content of youth culture and what kind of hierarchy exists among

---

[7] Miller and Swanson, *op. cit.*
[8] C. Wright Mills, *White Collar* (New York: Oxford University Press, 1953).

its values. Third, we need to understand better the relation of youth culture to the private views of youth and to other segments of their lives. Not all roles that are conscientiously enacted are equally deeply felt or equally lasting in their impact on the actor.

Because of earlier evidence that high ambition is the rule and that the ambitious are generally favored by their peers, we were led in the design of this study to seek a reconciliation with the classic descriptions of youth culture by attributing to it a somewhat ritualistic character. In general, we found a higher degree of conformity to youth-culture values in response to a question asking for the kind of person one preferred to have as a friend than in response to questions asking for personal goals or admiration. Here, we felt, was some support for the ritual hypothesis of youth culture. In addition, we failed to discover any general relationship between endorsement of youth-culture items and either ambition or background. Because of the failure of most of the value indexes employed in the investigation, we were unwilling to draw any conclusions from such negative findings, until the division into neighborhoods revealed that there might be a negative correlation between youth culture and ambition in middle-level schools. Also in middle-level schools there was a possible cleavage between the high and low endorsers of youth culture. The greater class heterogeneity of these modally lower-middle-class and upper-working-class neighborhoods and the greater status insecurity of such middle positions may provide the environment in which youth culture becomes more than a ritual performance, entering more deeply into the private ambitions and preferences of students.

Youth culture is a complicating fact in the conventional view of stratification, but one which cannot continue to be overlooked. We are inclined to hazard the guess that within the time sense of contemporary American culture, socializing experiences geared to the fleeting present may be the most intense but least indelible, experiences geared to the past may be felt but denied legitimacy, and experiences geared to the future may be the most vital in their impact upon private convictions. Socialization, then, must take account of the time perspective of each experience. Youth culture may play its distinctive part in socialization by bridging the gap between past and future orientations.

The Social Function of Formal Education

It has often been remarked in sociological studies that the school falls far short of its formally stated objective to facilitate mobility. A disproportionate number of persons from high backgrounds secure

a high degree of education, and educational attainment is highly related to income and occupational level. Observations such as these
have led Bernard Barber to assert that "education is primarily a
mechanism, so far as social stratification is concerned, whereby social
class positions are stabilized across the generations; only secondarily
is it an important mechanism providing for social mobility." [9]

A statement such as the foregoing is much more than either the assertion that the majority of people who pass through the schools do
not change their position by doing so or that the schools are only able
partially to counteract the forces for continuity of social position over
generations. It says that in a social order in which there is both fluidity
and stability between generations the school system strengthens the
latter at the expense of the former. If there were historical evidence
that intergenerational mobility declined as formal schooling increased,
it would support such a generalization. Or if it could be demonstrated
that the level of educational attainment was the specific cause of occupational level in most instances of observed relationship, the generalization would have important reinforcement. But since no such
historical evidence is available, and since it is highly plausible to suppose that many of the same qualities which determine occupational
success determine school success, any such appraisal of the social function of the school at this juncture is largely intuitive.

From the present investigation there emerges no contribution to
any general assessment of the mobility function of formal schooling.
But there are a number of suggestions about the manner in which the
school facilitates or limits mobility in specific ways. It is clear that the
school does serve as a training ground for the class system of the future,
because the students stratify and divide themselves according to destination. This is not a contribution to intergenerational continuity; it is
rather a rehearsal of the stratification of destination. Within the school,
social class is inculcated to the extent of allowing social cleavages to
develop between the future highs and lows.

How this apprenticeship in stratification is appraised depends upon
whether the school is seen as operating in a vacuum or as one force in
a field of forces, and whether one employs as a standard the classless
society or the stratified society with a maximum of mobility. Clearly,
there is no contribution to the unstratified society here, though other
phenomena such as the working of youth culture may make such a contribution. The problem here is that if the school is functioning in a
stratified society in which there are strong tendencies toward inter-

9 Bernard Barber, *Social Stratification* (New York: Harcourt, Brace and Co., 1957),
p. 395.

generational continuity of class position, the most effective device to facilitate mobility may be the institution and rehearsal of a system of stratification oriented toward the future. The anomaly is that sensitization to stratification and establishment of a counterstratification may be the most effective devices to neutralize the stratification of origin. That such neutralization is incomplete is revealed by a number of correlations involving background. But that the stratification of destination should be clearer than that of origin, both with respect to values and sociometric choice, indicates that considerable neutralization has been achieved.

The school plays a part in relation to the residential segregation of the community. By bringing students together in groups that are somewhat more homogeneous in background than the total community, schools reinforce the existing advantages and disadvantages, as our evidence reveals. However, two qualifications are necessary. First, the schools are larger and more heterogeneous universes than the immediate neighborhood of each individual. By expanding each youth's effective neighborhood, the school is probably lessening the degree of reinforcement between family and neighborhood which would otherwise prevail. Second, given the many extrascholastic sources of intergenerational continuity, there is a question as to whether more actual mobility will be achieved when everyone strives for maximum mobility, or when mobility aspirations compromise with the ladder model. Segregation by neighborhoods is a factor tending toward the ladder model for mobility. Anticipatory socialization is probably more successful when only a few steps intervene between origin and destination; very likely the same principle applies to gaining social acceptance up the ladder. When the transitions in values and social acceptance are not made, we suspect that the prognostication for successful completion of mobility is impaired.

The foregoing discussion reveals how little of the necessary information we have for accurately assessing the impact of education in facilitating or retarding mobility. The twelfth grade may already be a unique year in schooling because of the selection which has gone before and the maximization of future-orientation in preparation for leaving high school. Los Angeles may be a more amorphous, more mobility-oriented community than many of the more settled metropolises in the United States. But within this special environment, the establishment of large, moderately heterogeneous school communities in which there is a strongly destination-directed stratification of values and social preference would appear to facilitate more than impede mobility.

The Questionnaire

THE QUESTIONNAIRE reproduced in detail on the following pages is the basic form, designated in the text as Form A. In addition, there were two alternate forms which differed only in the introductory statement and the specific query which preceded each of the thirty-one items in Part II. The unique wordings employed in Form B and Form C are reproduced below.

[Form B]

PART II—SOME QUESTIONS ABOUT YOUR PERSONAL PREFERENCES

All of us have some ideas about the kind of person we admire most. In each of the following questions we want you to tell us which kind of person you admire most, the kind labelled "a" or the kind labelled "b."

Maybe you don't really admire either, or you admire both—but we want you to make a choice every time, no matter how hard it is to choose.

Please put a check mark in front of either "a" or "b" for each question.

8. Which kind of person do *you admire* most?

[Form C]

PART II—SOME QUESTIONS ABOUT YOUR PERSONAL PREFERENCES

All of us have some ideas about the kind of person we want to have as a friend. In each of the following questions we want you to tell us which kind of person you would rather have· as a friend, the kind labelled "a" or the kind labelled "b."

Maybe you don't really want either kind as a friend, or you want both —but we want you to make a choice every time, no matter how hard it is to choose.

Please put a check mark in front of either "a" or "b" for each question.

8. Which kind of person would *you* rather have as a friend?

61._____
62._____
63._____
64._____
65._____
66._____
67._____
68._____
69._____
70._____
71._____
72._____
73._____
74._____
75._____
76._____
'7-80._____

SURVEY

OF

STUDENT PLANS

AND

PREFERENCES

Ralph H. Turner
Assistant Professor

University of California
Los Angeles

==

PART I -- SOME GENERAL INFORMATION ABOUT YOURSELF

Please check the <u>one</u> correct answer.

1. How old were you at your last birthday?

☐ 15   ☐ 16   ☐ 17   ☐ 18   ☐ 19   ☐ 20   ☐ 21   ☐ Over 21
(1)   (2)   (3)   (4)   (5)   (6)   (7)   (8)

2. What is your sex?

☐ (1) male   ☐ (2) female

1

3. Where were you born?

☐ (1) United States
(2) Other (Please name the country.)_____

4. Where was your father born?

☐ (1) United States
(2) Other (Please name the country.)_____

5. Where was your mother born?

☐ (1) United States
(2) Other (Please name the country.)_____

6. What course of study are you taking in high school? (check **one**)

☐ (1) Academic
☐ (2) Business Education
☐ (3) Fine Arts
☐ (4) General
☐ (5) Homemaking
☐ (6) Industrial Arts
☐ (7) Vocational

7. Eventually, how much more schooling do you expect to get after you finish high school? (check **one**)

☐ (1) no schooling beyond high school.
☐ (2) Junior College or 1 to 3 years of college.
☐ (3) 1 to 3 years of business school, trade school, or technical school.
☐ (4) graduate from university or four-year college.
☐ (5) one or more years of post graduate college work or professional school **after** graduating from university or four-year college.
☐ (6) other (please explain)_____

_____
_____

PART II -- SOME QUESTIONS ABOUT YOUR PERSONAL PREFERENCES

All of us have some ideas about the kind of person we would really like to be. In each of the following questions we want you to tell us which kind of person you would rather be, the kind labelled "a" or the kind labelled "b."

Maybe you would rather not be either kind really--but we want you to make a choice every time, no matter how hard it is to choose.

Please put a check mark in front of either "a" or "b" for each question.

8. Which kind of person would <u>you</u> rather be?

   ☐ (a) Someone who can do many things fairly well but nothing perfectly;

       or

   ☐ (b) Someone who can do a few things perfectly but can't do many things fairly well.

How strongly do you feel about the choice you just made?

   ☐ I feel strongly about it--I am quite sure of my choice;

   ☐ I don't feel strongly--I am not too sure of my choice.

9. Which kind of person would <u>you</u> rather be?

   ☐ (a) Someone who enjoys art and music and likes to read books, but just barely makes enough money to live on;

       or

   ☐ (b) Someone who makes a very good living but doesn't enjoy art or music or reading books at all.

How strongly do you feel about the choice you just made?

   ☐ I feel strongly about it--I am quite sure of my choice;

   ☐ I don't feel strongly--I am not too sure of my choice.

10. Which kind of person would <u>you</u> rather be?

   ☐ (a) Someone who likes to see things work out naturally without much organization whenever a group of people get together;

       or

   ☐ (b) Someone who likes to have things quite organized whenever a group of people get together.

How strongly do you feel about the choice you just made?

   ☐ I feel strongly about it--I am quite sure of my choice;

   ☐ I don't feel strongly--I am not too sure of my choice.

3

11. Which kind of person would <u>you</u> rather be?

    ☐ (a) Someone who usually believes in "having it out" right
           now when he gets into an argument with anyone else;
           <u>or</u>
    ☐ (b) Someone who believes in always dropping the subject
           until people's tempers have had a chance to cool
           whenever he gets into an argument with anyone.

How strongly do you feel about the choice you just made?

    ☐ I feel strongly about it--I am quite sure of my choice;
    ☐ I don't feel strongly--I am not too sure of my choice.

12. Which kind of person would <u>you</u> rather be?

    ☐ (a) Someone who spends most of his extra money on his
           friends;
           <u>or</u>
    ☐ (b) Someone who saves all of his extra money for the future.

How strongly do you feel about the choice you just made?

    ☐ I feel strongly about it--I am quite sure of my choice;
    ☐ I don't feel strongly--I am not too sure of my choice.

13. Which kind of person would <u>you</u> rather be?

    ☐ (a) Someone who is a real success in business, but isn't
           much of a family man (or woman);
           <u>or</u>
    ☐ (b) A real "family man" (or woman) who isn't very successful
           in business.

How strongly do you feel about the choice you just made?

    ☐ I feel strongly about it--I am quite sure of my choice;
    ☐ I don't feel strongly--I am not too sure of my choice.

14. Which kind of person would <u>you</u> rather be?

    ☐ (a) Someone who is good at smoothing over disagreements
           between people by getting them to talk about other
           things;
           <u>or</u>
    ☐ (b) Someone who is good at pointing out the real issues
           in any disagreement so that people can argue more
           intelligently.

How strongly do you feel about the choice you just made?

    ☐ I feel strongly about it--I am quite sure of my choice;
    ☐ I don't feel strongly--I am not too sure of my choice.

15. Which kind of person would <u>you</u> rather be?

☐ (a) Someone who can be counted on to tell a small lie to help a friend out of serious trouble;

or

☐ (b) Someone who can be counted on to stick by the truth, even when a small lie would get a friend out of serious trouble.

How strongly do you feel about the choice you just made?

☐ I feel strongly about it--I am quite sure of my choice;

I don't feel strongly--I am not too sure of my choice.

16. Which kind of person would <u>you</u> rather be?

☐ (a) Someone who works so strongly for the welfare of the community that he frequently neglects his friends;

or

☐ (b) Someone who puts his friends ahead of his interests in community welfare.

How strongly do you feel about the choice you just made?

☐ I feel strongly about it--I am quite sure of my choice;

I don't feel strongly--I am not too sure of my choice.

17. Which kind of person would <u>you</u> rather be?

☐ (a) Someone who doesn't mind taking orders from somebody else if he can get ahead that way;

or

☐ (b) Someone who would rather be his own boss than get ahead by taking orders from anyone else.

How strongly do you feel about the choice you just made?

☐ I feel strongly about it--I am quite sure of my choice;

I don't feel strongly--I am not too sure of my choice.

18. Which kind of person would <u>you</u> rather be?

☐ (a) Someone who has the reputation of being conceited, but is also respected for his real abilities;

or

☐ (b) Someone who has the reputation of being quite modest and not at all conceited, but whose acquaintances don't know his (or her) abilities.

How strongly do you feel about the choice you just made?

☐ I feel strongly about it--I am quite sure of my choice;

I don't feel strongly--I am not too sure of my choice.

5

19. Which kind of person would <u>you</u> rather be?

☐ (a) Someone who believes in taking the word of the best
authority on any subject;
or
☐ (b) Someone who will defend his own opinion against any
authority that he disagrees with, even when he knows
much less than the authority.

How strongly do you feel about the choice you just made?

☐ I feel strongly about it--I am quite sure of my choice;
I don't feel strongly--I am not too sure of my choice.

20. Which kind of person would <u>you</u> rather be?

☐ (a) Someone who usually sticks with the time-tested ways of
doing things;
or
☐ (b) Someone who usually tries some new way of doing things,
even when there is already a better way that has been
used for a long time.

How strongly do you feel about the choice you just made?

☐ I feel strongly about it--I am quite sure of my choice;
I don't feel strongly--I am not too sure of my choice.

21. Which kind of person would <u>you</u> rather be?

☐ (a) A "smooth operator" who comes out on top of every deal;
or
☐ (b) Someone who often loses out because he is too kind to
take advantage of anybody who isn't as smart as he is.

How strongly do you feel about the choice you just made?

☐ I feel strongly about it--I am quite sure of my choice;
I don't feel strongly--I am not too sure of my choice.

22. Which kind of person would you rather be?

☐ (a) Someone who prides himself on doing things on his own,
without asking anyone else for advice or help;
or
☐ (b) Someone who likes to have help and advice from other
people on anything he does and seldom does anything
entirely on his own.

How strongly do you feel about the choice you just made?

☐ I feel strongly about it--I am quite sure of my choice;
I don't feel strongly--I am not too sure of my choice.

6

23. Which kind of person would <u>you</u> rather be?

☐ (a) Someone who is good at making decisions for other people;

☐ (b) or Someone who thinks people should make their desicions by themselves and tries never to influence others.

How strongly do you feel about the choice you just made?

☐ I feel strongly about it--I am quite sure of my choice;

☐ I don't feel strongly--I am not too sure of my choice.

24. Which kind of person would <u>you</u> rather be?

☐ (a) Someone who does better than his close friends in many things;

☐ (b) or Someone who does most things just about as well as his close friends--no better and no worse.

How strongly do you feel about the choice you just made?

☐ I feel strongly about it--I am quite sure of my choice;

☐ I don't feel strongly--I am not too sure of my choice;

25. Which kind of person would <u>you</u> rather be?

☐ (a) Someone who is quick to go along with anything the group wants to do and never tries to get people to do things his way;

☐ (b) or Someone who has lots of ideas about things he wants the group to do and is always trying to get the group to do things his way.

How strongly do you feel about the choice you just made?

☐ I feel strongly about it--I am quite sure of my choice;

☐ I don't feel strongly--I am not too sure of my choice.

26. Which kind of person would <u>you</u> rather be?

☐ (a) Someone who has everyone's respect but is very hard to get along with;

☐ (b) or Someone who is very easy to get along with, but who is not respected very much.

How strongly do you feel about the choice you just made?

☐ I feel strongly about it--I am quite sure of my choice;

☐ I don't feel strongly--I am not too sure of my choice.

7

27. Which kind of person would <u>you</u> rather be?

☐ (a) Someone who would rather stick with a few tried and true friends than be always meeting new people;

    or

☐ (b) Someone who always wants to be meeting new people and making new friends rather than being especially close to a few old friends.

How strongly do you feel about the choice you just made?

☐ I feel strongly about it--I am quite sure of my choice;

   I don't feel strongly--I am not too sure of my choice.

28. Which kind of person would <u>you</u> rather be?

☐ (a) Someone who follows the old saying, "neither a borrower nor a lender be;"

    or

☐ (b) Someone who often borrows from his friends and is always lending things to his friends.

How strongly do you feel about the choice you just made?

☐ I feel strongly about it--I am quite sure of my choice;

   I don't feel strongly--I am not too sure of my choice.

29. Which kind of person would <u>you</u> rather be?

☐ (a) Someone who always has something interesting to say about popular music and sports, but doesn't know anything about foreign policy and political trends;

    or

☐ (b) Someone who always has something interesting to say about foreign policy and political trends, but doesn't know anything about popular music and sports.

How strongly do you feel about the choice you just made?

☐ I feel strongly about it--I am quite sure of my choice;

   I don't feel strongly--I am not too sure of my choice.

30. Which kind of person would <u>you</u> rather be?

☐ (a) Someone who always takes the full blame for his own failures and mistakes;

    or

☐ (b) Someone who can laugh off his failures and mistakes and go on as if nothing had happened.

How strongly do you feel about the choice you just made?

☐ I feel strongly about it--I am quite sure of my choice;

   I don't feel strongly--I am not too sure of my choice.

8

31. Which kind of person would <u>you</u> rather be?

☐ (a) Someone who never lets an insult to his honor or his family's honor go by.
or
☐ (b) Someone who tries to overlook or laugh off any insult to his honor or his family's honor.

How strongly do you feel about the choice you just made?

☐ I feel strongly about it--I am quite sure of my choice;

☐ I don't feel strongly--I am not too sure of my choice.

32. Which kind of person would <u>you</u> rather be?

☐ (a) Someone who won't stop trying even when he is beaten;
or
☐ (b) Someone who admits when he is beaten and tries something else instead.

How strongly do you feel about the choice you just made?

☐ I feel strongly about it--I am quite sure of my choice;

☐ I don't feel strongly--I am not too sure of my choice.

33. Which kind of person would <u>you</u> rather be?

☐ (a) A "man of action" (or "woman of action") who goes right at a job and gets it done without spending much time in thinking about it;
or
☐ (b) A "man of judgment" (or "woman of judgment") who spends a good deal of time thinking things through quite carefully without always getting them done on time.

How strongly do you feel about the choice you just made?

☐ I feel strongly about it--I am quite sure of my choice;

☐ I don't feel strongly--I am not too sure of my choice.

34. Which kind of person would <u>you</u> rather be?

☐ (a) Someone who takes advantage of any good opportunity to get ahead, even when he has to take the chance of losing what he has;
or
☐ (b) Someone who would rather have a small but secure position than take a chance on losing what he has to get ahead.

How strongly do you feel about the choice you just made?

☐ I feel strongly about it--I am quite sure of my choice;

☐ I don't feel strongly--I am not too sure of my choice.

9

35. Which kind of person would you rather be?

☐ (a) Someone who doesn't let his plans for the future keep him from enjoying the present;

or

☐ (b) Someone who doesn't mind giving up all of his pleasure now so that he can be sure of the future.

How strongly do you feel about the choice you just made?

☐ I feel strongly about it--I am quite sure of my choice;

I don't feel strongly--I am not too sure of my choice.

36. Which kind of person would you rather be?

☐ (a) Someone who watches for "breaks" and for contacts which will give him "pull" while he is working to get ahead;

or

☐ (b) Someone who works hard and carefully, and refuses to use luck or pull to help get ahead.

How strongly do you feel about the choice you just made?

☐ I feel strongly about it--I am quite sure of my choice;

I don't feel strongly--I am not too sure of my choice.

37. Which kind of person would you rather be?

☐ (a) Someone who tries always to be satisfied with what he has and never to want more;

or

☐ (b) Someone who is always looking for something better than he has.

How strongly do you feel about the choice you just made?

☐ I feel strongly about it--I am quite sure of my choice;

I don't feel strongly--I am not too sure of my choice.

38. Which kind of person would you rather be?

☐ (a) Someone who won't say what he really thinks of anybody if he might hurt their feelings by saying it;

or

☐ (b) Someone who always tries to be completely honest in letting other people know how he really feels about them.

How strongly do you feel about the choice you just made?

☐ I feel strongly about it--I am quite sure of my choice;

I don't feel strongly--I am not too sure of my choice.

10

FOR MEN ONLY--women skip to page <u>13</u>

PART III-MEN -- SOME QUESTIONS ABOUT YOUR FUTURE PLANS

39. What occupation do you think you will make your <u>life work</u>?
--what do you expect to be doing <u>ten</u> and <u>twenty</u> years from now?
(If you can't name one occupation, then write down the <u>kind</u> of
job you expect to be in)

_____

40. In a few words, please tell us the kind of work you expect to
be doing in your chosen occupation (The occupation you have just
named.)

_____

_____

41. Are you sure that you really want to spend your life in this
occupation or one very much like it?

☐ (1) just about positive

☐ (2) fairly sure

☐ (3) not sure--hardly more than guessing

42. When you are working at your chosen occupation, twenty years
from now, do you think you will own your own business or be
employed by someone?

☐ (1) Own your own business or practice.
<u>or</u>

☐ (2) Be employed by someone

43. Please tell us anything you have done to prepare yourself for
the occupation you have named in question 39.

_____

_____

☐ Have done nothing to prepare.

44. What else does it take to get started in the occupation that
you have named in question 39?

_____

☐ Nothing-just apply for the job.

45. Please write down any <u>other</u> occupations that you are seriously considering for your life work. List any occupation you might go into if you can't get into your first choice or any that you sometimes prefer to the one named in question 39.

_____

_____

46. What do you expect to be doing the year after you graduate from high school? (check <u>one</u>.)

☐ (1) working at the occupation which will be your life work.
☐ (2) working, but not at the occupation you plan to make your life work.
☐ (3) attending college or junior college.
☐ (4) attending business school, trade school, or some other technical school.
☐ (5) other (please explain.)_____

47. After you are in the occupation which will be your life work, when will you consider yourself successful enough that you can relax and stop trying so hard to get ahead? (Check the <u>one</u> statement which fits best.)

☐ (1) When I am doing well enough to stay in the occupation.
☐ (2) When I am doing as well as the average person in my occupation.
☐ (3) When doing a little better than the average in my occupation.
☐ (4) When doing much better than the average in my occupation.
☐ (5) When recognized as one of the top persons in my occupation.
☐ (6) When doing better than everyone else in my occupation.
☐ (7) Never

48. Will you be a little disappointed if you never have much money? Check either "yes" or "no" for <u>every</u> item below.

Will you feel a little disappointed if--in your whole life-- the best you can ever afford to have is---

Yes No

☐☐ (1) A one-room house and a fifteen-year old car?

☐☐ (2) A 3-room house & a used low-priced car?

☐☐ (3) A 5-room house & a used middle-priced car?

☐☐ (4) A 7-room house & new middle-priced car?

☐☐ (5) A 9-room house & new top-priced car?

☐☐ (6) A 12-room house & two new top-priced cars?

☐☐ (7) Two large houses & several new top-priced cars?

☐☐ (8) Several large houses & several new top-priced cars?

12

FOR WOMEN ONLY--men skip to page <u>15</u>

PART III-WOMEN -- SOME QUESTIONS ABOUT YOUR FUTURE PLANS

39. Do you expect to

☐ (1) Have a life-time career?

☐ (2) Be a homemaker?

☐ (3) Both a life-time career and be a homemaker?

40-41. <u>If you plan on a life-time career</u>, what occupation do you think you will make your life work?

_____

42. Would you feel a little disappointed if your future husband spent his whole life in <u>any</u> of the following occupations? Check either "yes" or "no" for <u>every</u> item.

Would you feel a little disappointed to have your husband spend his life as a ---

<u>Yes No</u>

☐☐ (a) Ordinary laborer

☐☐ (b) Machine operator

☐☐ (c) Skilled craftsman (like carpenter and electrician)

☐☐ (d) Clerk, bookkeeper, or store sales person.

☐☐ (e) Building contractor

☐☐ (f) Salesman (like car or television salesman)

☐☐ (g) Small business owner or manager

☐☐ (h) Sales representative (for real estate, insurance, etc.)

☐☐ (i) Large business executive

☐☐ (j) Professional (like doctor and lawyer)

43-44. What kind of occupation would you <u>like</u> your future <u>husband</u> to have?

_____

13

45. After your husband is in the occupation which will be his life work, when will you consider him successful enough that he should relax and stop trying so hard to get ahead? (Check <u>only one</u> statement).

 ☐ (1) When he is doing well enough to stay in the occupation.
 ☐ (2) When he is doing as well as the average person in his occupation.
 ☐ (3) When doing a little better than the average in his occupation.
 ☐ (4) When doing much better than the average in his occupation.
 ☐ (5) When recognized as one of the top persons in his occupation.
 ☐ (6) When doing better than everyone else in his occupation.
 ☐ (7) Never.

46. Would you be a little <u>disappointed</u> if your future husband didn't have a certain amount of education? Check either "yes" or "no" for <u>every</u> item.
Would you be a little disappointed if your husband---
Yes No
 ☐☐ (1) had no schooling at all?
 ☐☐ (2) had no schooling beyond grade school?
 ☐☐ (3) did not finish high school?
 ☐☐ (4) had no schooling beyond high school?
 ☐☐ (5) attended business school, trade school, or technical school but didn't go to college or junior college?
 ☐☐ (6) had no schooling beyond junior college?
 ☐☐ (7) graduated from university or four-year college but did not take post-graduate work or attend professional school?

47. Will you be a little disappointed if you never have much money? Check either "yes" or "no" for <u>every</u> item below.
Will you feel a little disappointed if--in your whole life-- the best you can ever afford to have is---
Yes No
 ☐☐ (1) A one-room house and a fifteen-year old car?
 ☐☐ (2) A 3-room house & a used low-priced car?
 ☐☐ (3) A 5-room house & a used middle-priced car?
 ☐☐ (4) A 7-room house & new middle-priced car?
 ☐☐ (5) A 9-room house & new top-priced car?
 ☐☐ (6) A 12-room house & two new top-priced cars?
 ☐☐ (7) Two large houses & several new top-priced cars?
 ☐☐ (8) Several large houses & several new top-priced cars?

PART IV--SOME QUESTIONS ABOUT YOUR FAMILY

49. How many older brothers (and step-brothers) do you have?

☐1 ☐2 ☐3 ☐4 ☐5 ☐6 or more ☐None

50. How many older sisters (and step-sisters) do you have?

☐1 ☐2 ☐3 ☐4 ☐5 ☐6 or more ☐None

51. How many younger brothers (and step-brothers) do you have?

☐1 ☐2 ☐3 ☐4 ☐5 ☐6 or more ☐None

52. How many younger sisters (and step-sisters) do you have?

☐1 ☐2 ☐3 ☐4 ☐5 ☐6 or more ☐None

53. Have you lived with your father (or step-father) most of your life?

☐(1) Yes   ☐(2) No

54. Have you lived with your mother (or step-mother) most of your life?

☐(1) Yes   ☐(2) No

55. In your family, who has earned <u>most</u> of the money to pay most of the bills during your lifetime?

☐(1) Your father or step-father

☐(2) Your mother or step-mother

☐(3) Both mother (or step-mother) and father (or step-father) nearly equally.

☐(4) Someone else (Please tell us who.)_____

56. What has been the occupation of the person you checked in question # 55 during most of your life? (If you checked "both," please answer for your father or step-father)

_____

57. In a few words, tell us the kind of work this person has done in his (or her) occupation during most of your life.

_____

58. Has this person worked for himself or has he (or she) been employed by somebody during most of your life?

☐(1) Worked for himself (or herself) or owns own business.

☐(2) Employed by somebody else.

☐(3) Sometimes worked for himself and sometimes employed by somebody else.

15

59. How far did this person go in school? (check <u>one</u>)

☐ (1) did not attend school at all.

☐ (2) attended grade school.

☐ (3) attended high school.

☐ (4) attended business school, trade school, or technical school.

☐ (5) attended college or junior college.

☐ (6) graduated from university or four-year college.

☐ (7) attended professional school or did graduate work after completing college or university.

☐ (8) other (please explain)_____

60. How far did your mother, or the person who took the place of a mother for you, go in school?

☐ (1) did not attend school at all.

☐ (2) attended grade school.

☐ (3) attended high school.

☐ (4) attended business school, trade school, or technical school.

☐ (5) attended college or junior college.

☐ (6) graduated from university or four-year college.

☐ (7) attended professional school or did graduate work after completing college or university.

☐ (8) other (please explain)_____

PART V -- SOME QUESTIONS ABOUT STUDENTS IN THIS CLASS

61. Suppose you wanted to pick some people to be your <u>close friends</u> -people you would enjoy doing things with and would like to have as close friends for a <u>long time</u>--. What <u>three</u> people who are <u>in this classroom right now</u> would you pick?

1._____

2._____

3._____

62. In every school some people get to be known as the "<u>big wheels</u>" around campus. Please pick out the <u>two</u> people who are <u>in this classroom right now</u> who are the "biggest wheels" and write their names below.

1._____

2._____

63. In your class there must be some people who learn their school-work better than the others. Please pick out the <u>two</u> people who are <u>in this classroom right now</u> who you think are the best at learning their schoolwork.

1._____

2._____

A Prestige-Subcultural Classification of Occupations

THE DECISION to employ a special occupational classification to suit the purposes of this investigation was made after a careful examination and some experience in using several of the major extant schemes. Although there have been many useful systems of classification, four have emerged as "standard" in American sociology. The oldest of these is the Alba Edwards' socioeconomic grouping, designed for the treatment of occupations as recorded in the United States census.[1] The scheme with the most adequate empirical support is probably the North-Hatt prestige ratings of a set of occupations, based upon evaluations made by a national sample of adults.[2] The scheme which developed out of the most intimate exploration of social standing within an American community is that of Warner, Meeker, and Eels.[3] The most recent scheme is that of August Hollingshead.[4]

Several considerations guided evaluation of the usefulness of these schemes and subsequent development of our own. (1) The classification should supply a prestige ranking, so that it would be possible to speak of upward and downward mobility. (2) The classification should group occupations according to similarity of subculture. Since one of the major ideas in the theory of marginality is the movement between subcultures, this criterion was more crucial in the present investigation than in many others. (3) Because prior studies lead us to expect con-

[1] Alba Edwards, *A Social-economic Grouping of the Gainful Workers of the United States, 1930* (Washington: United States Government Printing Office, 1938).

[2] National Opinion Research Center, "Jobs and Occupations: A Popular Evaluation," *Opinion News,* 9 (September 1, 1947), pp. 3–13.

[3] W. Lloyd Warner, Marchia Meeker, and Kenneth Eels, *Social Class in America* (Chicago: Science Research Associates, 1949).

[4] August B. Hollingshead and Frederick C. Redlich, *Social Class and Mental Illness* (New York: Wiley, 1958), pp. 387–397. The still more recent Duncan classification was not available at the time that the present work was being done. Cf. Albert J. Reiss, Jr., *Occupations and Social Status* (New York: Free Press of Glencoe, 1961), pp. 263–275.

siderable high ambition, discrimination at the upper end of the continuum is more important in a study of this sort than in an investigation concerned only with current social standing. (4) The classification should not depend upon information which twelfth-graders are unlikely to have about their parents' occupations, such as business income, supervisory hierarchy, etc. (5) The classification must be suited to the normal vagueness of ambition regarding details of the job situation. (6) The classification should be based on information which could be secured by questionnaire alone, without benefit of interview probing techniques.

With these criteria in mind, the Edwards' scale was discarded as failing to differentiate fully enough among occupations in the upper half of the scale. The North-Hatt classification was felt to rest too exclusively on the single criterion of prestige, and the operational definition of prestige itself bears a somewhat uncertain relationship with theoretical conceptions. The Warner scheme had much in its favor, but it is difficult to apply without an interviewer probing for special information, and sometimes demands information which only the person in question and his spouse could supply and which would not be envisaged in normal formulations of ambition. Partly for the same reasons and partly for its failure to keep business and professional occupations separate, the Hollingshead system was also not used.

Because of the importance of subculture, it seemed indispensable to introduce two kinds of separation into the classification of higher-level occupations. The true professions, marked by the requirement of college graduation and usually postgraduate work, should be distinguished from the profession-like occupations which depend more upon personal skills than formal training. Second, the existence of a new and old middle class with somewhat different subcultures should be acknowledged. C. Wright Mills was among many who pointed out this distinction,[5] and subsequent to the preparation of our own scheme, Miller and Swanson have published a more intensive discussion of the difference.[6] For our purposes this new middle class (apart from professionals) includes two kinds of employees of large-business concerns, the sales agent or wholesale representative and manager or department head.

The nine major headings, in order of standing, are as follows:

(1) Unskilled laborers and service workers

[5] C. Wright Mills, *White Collar* (New York: Oxford University Press, 1951).
[6] Daniel R. Miller and Guy E. Swanson, *The Changing American Parent* (New York: Wiley, 1958), pp. 30–60.

(2) Semiskilled laborers
(3) Skilled laborers and foremen
(4) Clerical workers and salesclerks
(5) Small-business owners and managers and retail salesmen
(6) Semiprofessionals
(7) Business agents and managers
(8) Professionals
(9) Large-business owners and officials

It will be noted that the first three categories are the standard divisions among manual laborers and menial-service workers. The fourth category isolates low-level white-collar workers, including the behind-the-counter salesclerk. This, we believe, is the group which was once the bottom of the upper half of the occupational scale, but which has now been effectively cut off by the requirement of higher education from entry into most of the higher brackets. The fifth category is the repository of the old small-entrepreneur group. Included here is only the business small enough for the owner to keep an active hand in all its operations. Semiprofessionals include entertainers, writers, professional athletes, etc., and many of the would-be professionals, such as "doctors" without M.D. degrees. The business agents and managers have been mentioned as a new upper-middle class. Large-business owners and officials have been ranked above professionals on the grounds that, at least in Los Angeles where the impact of traditional criteria of prestige is weakened, their scale of living and effective recognition in the community require it. Internal evidence from our data further justify this ordering except with respect to amount of education.

Independent classification of 300 cases by two coders employing this system, after appropriate briefing, produced an initial agreement of 87 percent. Consultation over instances of disagreement led to considerably higher agreement.

THE CLASSIFICATION

The following listing presents the nine major occupational groups in approximately ascending order of socioeconomic standing. There is no significance to the ordering of occupational subcategories. The listing of specific occupational titles after each subcategory title is purely illustrative, rather than exhaustive, and is based upon actual occupational titles which appeared in our data.

1. Unskilled Laborer
   1–0 *No other classification,* "Laborer"

1-1 *Service:* Custodian, dishwasher, elevator operator, janitor, maintenance man, porter, kitchen attendant, watchman, maid

1-2 *Factory:* Checker, chipper, hammer driver, machine helper, loader, oiler, metal sorter, steel loader, warehouseman

1-3 *Construction:* Asphalt raker, cement mixer, house mover, sand mixer

1-4 *Agriculture:* Farmer (employed), field irrigator, fruit picker

1-5 *Gardener* (urban)

1-6 *Other:* Freight carrier, deep-sea diver, longshoreman, lumberjack, coal miner, grip, stevedore

2. Semiskilled Laborer

2-0 *No other classification,* "good job"

2-1 *Delivery:* Railroad brakeman, bus driver, parcel post driver, truck driver, taxi driver, milkman

2-2 *Operator:* Assembler, auto attendant, belt-maker, blueprinter, buttermaker, chemical operator, chrome plater, coil winder, coremaker, creamery man, die caster, draw-bench operator, drill-maker, distiller, film developer, film technician, flour miller, processor (rubber), punch press operator, quality-control tester, RR carman, sand blaster, seamstress, finisher, foundry worker, furnace operator, galvanizer, gear cutter, hydraulic operator in construction, hydraulic-press operator, lathe operator, lather in construction, lift-truck operator, machine maintenance, machine operator (by education), metal cutter, metal polisher, millman, molder, oil driller, sheet-metal worker (by education), shirt-maker, steel pourer, stickerman, RR switchman, tire builder, vending-machine operator, garment cutter, soap-maker, presser, chemical operator, color matcher

2-3 *Laundry:* Laundry worker

2-4 *Food:* Butcher, food checker, meat packer, meat weigher, renderer, waiter, fruit, vegetable, and nut sorter

2-5 *Other:* Attendant, exterminator, foster mother, labeler, model, pottery checker, mineral prospector

3. Skilled Laborer

3-0 *No other classification,* "craftsman"

3-1 *Foreman:* Foreman, caddymaster, floor lady, supervisor, freight conductor, inspector, government meat inspector, RR engineer, quality-control supervisor

3-2 *Protective:* Air Force ground crew, airline hostess, Army, Navy, Marines, Coast Guard, Air Force, detective, fireman, lifeguard, policeman

3-3 *Draftsman:* Draftsman, surveyor, design checker

3-4 *Electrical:* Electrician, electronics technician, telephone installer, telephone lineman, radio repairman, telephone switchman, electrical lead man

3-5 *Metal and mechanical:* Boiler "engineer", boilermaker, crane operator, diesel mechanic, steel finisher, flight engineer, grinder, structural iron worker, jig-maker, machine-maintenance man, machine operator (by education), machinist, mechanic, millwright, mold-maker, painter, photo-engraver, pipe fitter, plumber, riveter, pattern maker, tool- and die-maker, welder, neon sign-maker, blacksmith, hand engraver on precious metals, scaleman, sheet-metal worker (by education), ship fitter, template maker

3–6 *Construction and related:* Brick mason, cabinetmaker, carpenter, carpet layer, cement finisher, glazer, paint mixer, painter, plasterer, propman in movies, roofer, upholsterer, weather stripper, tile setter, cooper, linoleum layer, form setter

3–7 *Printing:* Lithographer, printer, compositor

3–8 *Food and personal service:* Baker, barber, bartender, beauty operator, brewer, chef, cook

3–9 *Other:* Movie projectionist, horse trainer, diamond setter, jeweler, milliner, tailor, shoe repairman, furrier, watchmaker

4. Lesser White-collar Worker

4–0 *No other classification,* "white-collar"

4–1 *Clerical:* Bank teller, bookkeeper, cashier, clerk, dispatcher, IBM operator, key punch operator, mail carrier, mailer, meter reader, order clerk, receiving clerk, secretary, shipping clerk, tabulator, typist, dental assistant, estimator, traffic man, freight adjuster, personnel interviewer, claims investigator, office or desk job, receptionist, title searcher

4–2 *Salesclerk:* Cashier, display man, florist, interior decorator, produce clerk, salesclerk, window trimmer

4–3 *Other:* TV cameraman, movie cameraman, photographer, magazine photographer, telephone operator

5. Small-business Owner, Manager, and Salesman

5–0 *No other classification,* "small-business"

5–1 *Contractor, construction and other:* Contractor

5–2 *Retail owner:* Florist, gas-station owner, interior decorator, mortician, motel owner (small), photographer, restaurant owner (size), pawn broker, dry cleaner, grocer, haberdasher, laundry owner, trailer-park owner

5–3 *Manager:* Service-station manager, manager of small business, share-cropper

5–4 *Agriculture:* Farmer, nursery owner, rancher, landscaper

5–5 *Nonretail:* Junk dealer, upholsterer, trucking business, plastering business, printing business, rubbish collector, logger

5–6 *Commission sales:* Car, TV, appliances

6. Semiprofessional and Public Administrator

6–0 *No other classification*

6–1 *Art:* Artist, cartoonist, art designer, interior designer, makeup artist, fashion illustrator, architect, dress designer, fashion consultant, fashion designer, ceramicist

6–2 *Music and general entertainment:* Actor, TV or radio announcer, coach, professional athlete, choreographer, movie or stage director, singer, musician, sound editor, film editor, "private" music teacher, sound technician, professional race-track driver, physical culturist

6–3 *Literature:* Writer, journalist, reporter, translator, advertising copy writer

6–4 *Scientific and medical service:* Statistician, dietician, nurse, nutritionist, embalmer, funeral director, lab assistant, lab technician, mortician, physical therapist, x-ray technician, dental hygienist, actuary, medical librarian, home economist, weatherman, tree surgeon, recreational therapist

6–5 *Government administration:* Postmaster, post-office inspector, tax collector, substation head, chief of police, foreign service (consulate), public official, forest ranger, forester, game warden, state interviewer, military officer, tax assessor, politician, secret-service agent

6–6 *Miscellaneous semiprofessional:* Airplane pilot, investment counselor, labor-relations counselor, librarian, public-relations man, securities analyst, "practical" nurse, agricultural consultant, industrial-relations counselor

7. Business Agent and Manager

7–0 *No other classification*

7–1 *Management:* Advertising manager, art director, personnel manager, plant superintendent, department head, real-estate manager, business manager, credit manager, production manager, sales manager, escrow officer, construction superintendent, field superintendent

7–2 *Insurance:* Insurance collector, insurance sales, insurance underwriter, claim investigator

7–3 *Real Estate:* Broker

7–4 *Accounting:* Accountant

7–5 *Sales representative:* Advertiser, agent, auctioneer, buyer, distributor, foreign trade for big company, retail-furniture dealer, marketer, meat jobber, stockbroker, wholesaler, labor-union business agent, loan-company agent, manufacturer's representative, advertising space seller, metal trader

8. Professional

8–0 *Unspecified*

8–1 *Medical:* Doctor, physician, dentist, psychiatrist, osteopath, psychoanalyst

8–2 *Legal:* Auditor, CPA, lawyer, criminologist, judge, judge advocate in army

8–3 *College educator and scientist:* Educational administrator, psychologist, chemist, archeologist, astronomer, bacteriologist, geologist, geophysicist, horticulturist, hydrographer, mathematician, meteorologist, oceanographer, physicist, researcher, sociologist

8-4 *Educator:* Primary and secondary levels, church school teacher

8-5 *Engineer:* Electronics researcher, civil engineer

8-6 *Certificated social service and related:* Certificated speech therapist, school psychologist, occupational therapist, recreation director, psychotherapist, social worker

8-7 *Religious:* Minister, missionary, nun

8-8 *Lesser medical:* Veterinarian, pharmacist, optometrist, chiropodist, chiropractor

9. Large-business Owner and Official

9-0 *No other classification*

9-1 *Owner:* Advertiser, auctioneer, bookmaker, cottonbroker, financier, importer, large-business owner, manufacturer, motel owner, producer, rancher, real-estate owner, restaurant owner, stock owner, import-export broker, grain broker, department-store owner, hotel owner, property owner (large)

9-2 *Official:* Bank president, banker, business executive, producer, hotel manager, area representative

APPENDIX C

Responses to Value Items on Questionnaire Form A[a]

THE RESPONSES are tabulated on the four pages that follow.

[a] In this, as in other tabulations, all questionnaires which were incomplete or un-codable with respect to occupational background or ambition were eliminated. Among the Form A questionnaires, 72 males and 23 females were omitted from the tabulation for this reason.

APPENDIX C

Table 46. Responses to Value Items on Questionnaire Form A[a]

Value item	Male: n=993					Female: n=1143				
	a Strong	a Weak	b Weak	b Strong	NR	a Strong	a Weak	b Weak	b Strong	NR
8.a. Can do many things fairly well b. can do a few things perfectly	261	320	221	191	0	347	408	233	153	2
9.a. Enjoys art, music, books b. makes very good living	235	120	239	398	1	418	186	266	270	3
10.a. Likes things to work out b. likes groups quite organized	145	80	82	686	0	258	97	93	695	0
11.a. Believes in having it out now b. drops until tempers cool	160	68	129	635	1	233	75	114	721	0
12.a. Spends extra money on friends b. saves extra money for future	107	76	198	610	2	84	77	213	769	0
13.a. Real success in business b. real family man	116	200	293	382	2	70	102	308	663	0
14.a. Smooths over disagreements b. shows how to argue intelligently	372	121	130	368	2	587	147	109	300	0
15.a. Will tell lie to help friend b. sticks to the truth	292	218	152	330	1	246	248	195	454	0

16.a. Puts community ahead of friends	114	158	278	442	1	161	188	327	466	1
b. puts friends ahead	573	126	57	236	1	765	123	58	197	0
17.a. Will take orders to get ahead										
b. rather be own boss	177	146	250	419	1	213	177	277	476	0
18.a. Conceited, abilities respected										
b. has reputation for modesty	592	117	94	189	1	616	170	120	235	2
19.a. Takes word of best authority										
b. defends own opinion	235	116	172	469	1	319	116	215	491	2
20.a. Sticks with time-tested ways										
b. tries new ways of doing things	278	159	153	401	2	173	155	185	626	4
21.a. Smooth operator, comes out on top										
b. too kind to take advantage	650	156	83	101	3	717	174	109	141	2
22.a. Pride in doing things on his own										
b. like advice and help	197	137	180	478	1	151	106	229	655	2
23.a. Good at decisions for others										
b. tries never to influence	285	109	133	465	1	195	99	145	702	2
24.a. Does better than friends										
b. does as well as friends	350	206	185	250	2	501	257	214	169	2
25.a. Quick to go along with group										
b. tries to get things his way	352	331	198	109	3	398	448	220	73	4
26.a. Respected, hard to get along with										
b. easy to get along with	238	146	224	384	1	286	165	232	460	0
27.a. Sticks with tried-true friends										
b. always making new friends	260	108	180	444	1	329	143	240	431	0
28.a. Neither a borrower nor lender										
b. often borrows-lends										

continued.

Table 46 (continued)

Value item	Male: n=993					Female: n=1143				
	a		b		NR	a		b		NR
	Strong	Weak	Weak	Strong		Strong	Weak	Weak	Strong	
29.a. Talks popular music and sports	476	270	136	109	2	550	338	170	84	1
b. talks foreign policy, politics										
30.a. Takes full blame for failures	404	112	122	353	3	465	116	179	383	0
b. laughs off failures, mistakes										
31.a. Never lets an insult go by	482	121	192	194	4	509	144	211	279	0
b. laughs off any insult										
32.a. Won't stop trying when beaten	359	97	155	377	5	256	88	192	606	1
b. tries something else										
33.a. Man of action	365	177	171	278	2	486	210	184	263	0
b. man of judgment										
34.a. Risks what he has to get ahead	342	207	158	284	2	266	174	194	509	0
b. prefers secure position										
35.a. Enjoys the present	473	188	107	224	1	609	173	103	256	2
b. gives up pleasure for future										
36.a. Uses breaks, pull to get ahead	436	161	116	278	2	395	213	141	393	1
b. refuses breaks, pull										

190	95	177	530	1	413	196	191	341	2
434	175	102	281	1	565	161	112	303	2

37.a. Tries to be satisfied
  b. always looks for better
38.a. Won't hurt feelings
  b. honest about attitudes

a/ In this, as in other tabulations, all questionnaires which were incomplete or uncodable with respect to occupational background or ambition were eliminated. Among the Form "A" question- naires, 72 males and 23 females were omitted from the tabulation for this reason.

Index